happy
foods

happy foods

OVER 100 MOOD-BOOSTING RECIPES

BY KAREN WANG DIGGS

V!va
EDITIONS

Published in the United States by Viva Editions, an imprint of Start Midnight, LLC, 101 Hudson Street, Thirty-seventh Floor, Suite 3705, Jersey City, New Jersey 07302.

Printed in the United States.
Cover design: Scott Idleman/Blink
Cover photo: iStock
Illustrations: Hovin Wang (www hovinwang com)
Text design: Frank Wiedemann

First Edition.
10 9 8 7 6 5 4 3 2 1

Trade paper ISBN: 978-1-63228-008-4
E-book ISBN: 978-1-63228-014-5

Library of Congress Cataloging-in-Publication Data is available on file.

Contents

Recipes in This Book

Main (Lunch or Dinner)

Sides

Soups

Salads

Beverages

Sweet Treats

Dressings & Miscellaneous

 # Foreword

IT WAS ONE OF THOSE COLD AND RAIN-DRENCHED DAYS WHEN IT felt as if the whole world were trapped in a veil of endless gray. I longed for a ray of sunshine, but it was nowhere to be found. Sitting alone in my kitchen, I felt the blahs creeping in, and wanted desperately to escape.

As my eyes roamed toward the door, my gaze took a detour when it was distracted by the vibrant, yellow-orange beckoning of a winter squash, lounging on my kitchen counter. The bright warm colors cheered me immediately, and I wanted that glow to permeate my being. Instantly, I knew that making a soup with that wonderful vegetable would be my solace.

As I sipped and savored the color and flavors of my golden soup, it dispelled my melancholy. This happened not only because it tasted good, but also because my body and brain recognized as true nourishment many nutrients from the squash, along with other ingredients I added, such as ginger, nutmeg, and cardamom.

The truth is, no matter how young or old, we all quest for happiness, every single day. Some days are more sunny then others, some are just plain dreary. Sometimes, those dreary days can turn into weeks, months, even years.

According to the World Health Organization, by 2030, depression will be the second most common disease after heart attacks. We are a world of sad people, popping Prozac and putting on false smiles to keep it all together, barely.

Is the solution to keep popping pills, or is there a more organic way to deal with being down in the dumps? Here's a morsel to chew over: Parallel to the global increase of depression is the rise of processed fast foods around the world.

Could there be a correlation between what we eat and how we feel? Thanks to recent studies by concerned scientists, we don't need to guess. The results of one study[1] with over 12,000 participants, published in *Public Health Nutrition* journal, reveal that consumers of fast food, compared to those who eat little or none, are fifty-one percent more likely to develop depression. This clearly shows that there *is* a link! In fact, it is dose-dependent. Meaning that the more junk food you eat, the more likely you run the risk of falling into that dark pit of despair.

Even without scientific validation, don't we all know deep inside that our most immediate and profound connection with nature is through food? We cannot survive without food, but more importantly, we cannot be healthy and happy without the right foods.

I can personally attest to the power of wholesome organic food vs. fragmented junk food in the arena of depression. Before I became a nutritionist, I was a workaholic chef, cooking for five-star hotels and opening up restaurants. The tremendous stress and long hours, plus a bad breakup with my ex of seven years, caused me to binge on an endless array of fat-laden, starch-filled, sugar-saturated junk food as a means of self-medication.

Lamenting the demise of my relationship, suffering physical and mental fatigue from my stressful job, and lacking the energy to exercise, I literally ate my way into a hapless depression. Coming home from work, I would collapse into a corner and gorge on ice cream, cookies, and cup-a-noodles. Yes, in that particular order. And I would repeat the multicourse junk-a-thon again until I fell into torpor. Eventually, I would pass out from the sugar overload, subconsciously hoping that when I awoke I would be somewhere else and be someone else.

I totally hit rock bottom and had to take a leave of absence from my work. Fortunately, during this hiatus, I came to realize that though I was a chef, I knew nothing about eating well! I had no clue about the nutritional value of ingredients I encountered every day in my kitchen. I had no idea that a candy bar was causing me to suffer hypoglycemia, that a milkshake contributed to my brain fog, or that donuts were the culprit of my constant bloat. It was that moment of lucidity that prompted me to return to school to study nutrition.

Once I learned that white sugar leached minerals from my body, that

---

1   Almudena Sánchez-Villegas, Estefania Toledo, Jokin de Irala, Miguel Ruiz-Canela, Jorge Pla-Vidal, Miguel A Martínez-González, "Fast-food and commercial baked goods consumption and the risk of depression," *Public Health Nutrition*, 2011; 15 (03).

factory-farmed chicken caused hormonal imbalances leading to PMS, and that using processed vegetable oils caused inflammation, I was saved from the downward spiral of bad food and sad moods. Knowing what to enjoy and what to avoid changed my world—and without feeling deprived or hungry, my depression lifted, my energy increased, and I had the desire to participate in life again.

So, can a bowl of frilly lettuces dressed with vinaigrette really liberate one from the chains of woe? Can a piece of grilled salmon topped with pesto part the dark clouds in your head? Is it possible to feel energized and cheerful by having scrambled eggs for breakfast instead of a sugar-coated Danish? Well, if the empirical evidence shows that eating junk food leads to depression, then it's likely true that refraining from junk food leads to improved mood. Of course, there are myriad biochemical and psychological factors that contribute to sad moods, but certainly, what we put into our bodies does affect how we feel.

The journey to happiness begins with a single healthy bite. So, let's cook!

Introduction:
Why You Sing the Blues

SOAR AND SLUMP: BLOOD SUGAR BALANCE

Why Going Up and Down Is Bad

Come, let's take a ride. A thrill ride! An extreme, stratosphere-reaching, adrenalin-pumping roller-coaster ride like those in popular amusement parks. Let's call our ride: The Mammoth Mega Rush.

Ready? Sit tight and strap yourself in real good. Take a deep breath and prepare to be catapulted two hundred feet above the ground. Hover precipitously at the dizzying summit, and then plunge down, down, down—back to the bottom, accompanied by your own hair-raising scream, Ahhhhhhh! And then get ready to do a few more loops of the same.

Exhilarating though it may be, would you take this ride several times a day? Day after day? Even if you were a fearless thrill seeker, could you ride the Mammoth Mega Rush on a regular basis? Probably not.

Yet, we do the metabolic equivalent every time we eat a sugar-drenched snack or gulp down a syrupy beverage. The glucose sends our energy soaring, but it also takes a heavy toll on our pancreas to produce enough insulin to deal with the excess sugar. This useful little organ gets worn out after prolonged demands on it, and if it could scream as we crash downward on the Mammoth Mega Rush, it would be screeching, "Too much sugar, too much sugar! Please, stop!"

The sad irony is that when we're dealing with the blahs, merely the anticipation of eating something sweet, such as ice cream or cake, momentarily parts the dark clouds, creating a false sense of comfort. However, the reward is always short-lived, and soon after the treat is finished, disappointment sets in. Worse, you start to crave more of the same, causing a battle with your will-power.

Then guilt looms, followed by remorse, and maybe even a tummy ache. "Oh, I shouldn't have eaten the whole thing! I'm supposed to be on a diet. I already had a milkshake today. I feel like a blob." You name it, it's all bad, and sad.

So what's causing all the grief? Here's a step-by-step explanation of what happens physiologically when you ingest, say, a candy bar:

Anticipation: You start to salivate.

You rip open the wrapper, take a big bite, and chew.

The masticated candy goes down the esophagus and enters your gut, where digestion begins.

The sugar and other carbohydrates from the candy bar turn into glucose and enter your bloodstream.

Your blood sugar rises, giving you a boost of energy.

At the same time, insulin responds to the upsurge of glucose.

There's too much glucose in the bloodstream, so insulin sweeps the excess away to be stored as fat in your cells. And now your energy starts to wane, and you crave more sweets.

As this scenario is repeated again and again—candy bar, latté with hazelnut syrup, chocolate-glazed cupcake at 3:00 p.m., a cocktail after work—it will wear out your pancreas and your body's ability to produce insulin, or make your cells become insulin resistant.

High blood sugar becomes the norm, and you are now on the endless roller-coaster ride of energy highs and lows, mood swings, and endless cravings.

• •

INSULIN RESISTANCE

Too much insulin in the bloodstream triggers the body to retain salt and water, leading to high blood pressure and heart disease. When insulin is high, it also activates the stress hormone adrenalin. A little adrenalin is good, but constant release will wear out your adrenals. High insulin also affects production of neurotransmitters such as dopamine and serotonin. It negatively affects sleep patterns, and can also damage the kidneys, eyes, nerves, and skin.

• •

Unfortunately, many people are trapped in a cycle of craving for sugar or carbohydrates, causing the repeated demand for insulin, and then the plunge. It's normal for the stock market to fluctuate up and down, but not your blood sugar.

In other words, the internal roller coaster will wreak havoc on your pancreas and also stress out your adrenals, which produce important hormones. When this happens, you could become an overweight human carnival ride, facing premature aging, fatigue, and even cardiovascular disease. Sounds depressing, doesn't it?

But there's a way out!

More Than One Kind of Fuel

Believing that carbohydrates or sweet foods are the optimal way to fuel our brains and bodies is a misconception that has done us tremendous harm. Since energy is such a precious resource, doesn't it make sense that humans would strategize a biological plan to ensure an endless supply from different means?

Glucose does fuel the brain, but carbohydrates are not the only raw material. Protein and fat can also be converted to glucose. There's a nifty service that our livers perform called *gluconeogenesis*: a long word that simply means "production of new glucose." So, when carb intake is too low to convert to glucose, the liver utilizes stored amino acids from protein to give us fuel. What's even better is that we can also burn fat for fuel. Glycerol, a by-product of fat metabolism, can also be turned into glucose, either through fats we eat or from adipose (body) fat. And that's good news, especially if you want to shed some pudge.

Just a Teaspoon

Simply put, we need less—a lot less—carbohydrates than you think. In fact, we only need the equivalent of about one teaspoon of sugar in our bloodstream at any given time to function properly. Normal blood sugar is around 99 mg/dl, which translates to an intake of about five grams of sugar, or one teaspoon.

One of the most popular breakfast foods is the bagel, which packs a lot of carbs! A medium bagel, with a diameter of 3½ inches, has about sixty grams of carbohydrates. Sixty grams of carbs converts to sixty grams of sugar, which means that by eating a bagel in the morning, you get off to a really bad start, sending your pancreas into a tizzy to provide enough insulin to deal with that bagel. If you do the math, sixty grams of sugar is equivalent to twelve teaspoons!

Too much sugar or carbohydrates in a meal can actually deprive your brain of glucose, deplete its energy supply, and mess up your ability to concentrate, remember, and learn.

Glycemic Index vs. Glycemic Load

The word glycemic means "causing glucose in the blood." When it comes to keeping blood sugar in a healthy range, the Glycemic Index (GI) and Glycemic Load (GL) can be very useful.

GI measures how quickly foods become sugar in your bloodstream, while GL measures the amount of carbohydrates in each serving of food.

GI: Low=1-55 Mid=56-69 High=70-100
GL: Low=1-10 Mid=11-19 High=20 or more

Glycemic Index/Glycemic Load of Selected Foods

Food	Glycemic Index (Glucose=100)	Serving Size (grams)	Glycemic Load/Serving
Whole wheat bread	71	30	9
Corn tortilla	52	50	12
Oatmeal	55	250	13
Quinoa	53	150	9
White rice	89	150	43
Brown rice	50	150	16
Sweet corn on cob	60	150	20
Apple	39	120	6
Banana	62	120	16
Peach	42	120	5
Pear	38	120	4
Raisins	64	60	28
Black beans	30	150	7
Chickpeas	10	150	9
Lentils	29	150	5
Green peas	51	80	4
Carrots	35	80	2

Parsnips	52	80	4
Baked russet potato	111	150	33
Sweet potato	70	150	22

From Harvard Health Publications
http://www.health.harvard.edu/healthy-eating/glycemic_index_and_glycemic_load_for_100_foods

Summary

Being on the Mammoth Mega Rush may be fun for a while, but you'll pay heavily with energy crashes and mood swings.

To fuel your brain and body, cut down on sugar and carbohydrate-centric foods. Instead, eat protein- and fat-based snacks and meals.

When your blood sugar is constantly fluctuating, your body will try to compensate by secreting stress hormones. This signals your body to hold on to calories, causing your metabolism to slow down. This usually translates to weight gain, feeling tired, and getting the blues.

Stabilize your blood sugar and you have seized the day!

To revive your sluggish brain and fight sleepiness around the 3:00 p.m. slump, try these superbly energizing options:

1 tablespoon tahini with one fresh medjool date

½ cup full-fat, organic cow or goat yogurt with 1 teaspoon maple syrup and 1 tablespoon toasted sunflower seeds

½ avocado with a sprinkling of sea salt and dash of lemon juice

Instead of drinking coffee, have a bottle of rosemary essential oil handy in your desk drawer. Place three drops in the palm of your hands and rub them together for a few seconds, then inhale deeply three times.

CARPE DIEM BREAKFAST

YIELD: 1 serving

It takes just five minutes to cook this breakfast, yet it will give you hours of steady energy without the blood sugar spike. The coconut oil helps to rev up your metabolism while nourishing your thyroid, and the eggs provide vitamins A and D along with omega-3 fatty acids.

1 tablespoon coconut oil
1 small zucchini, thinly sliced
2 eggs from pasture-raised hens
sea salt, to taste
freshly ground pepper, to taste

Heat a medium sauté pan over medium heat with the coconut oil.

Toss in the zucchini slices along with a little salt and cook for a couple of minutes until the slices are tender.

Break the eggs over the zucchini, and stir to make a scramble.

Add more sea salt and freshly ground pepper to taste. Serve immediately.

FRAZZLED: STRESS AND ADRENAL HORMONES

Stress, Hormones, and Food

Is there anything worse than being stuck in gridlocked traffic, or suffering a gut-wrenching breakup, or working for a bad boss? Yes. A poor diet.

We discussed the negative effects of too much sugar, which causes constant insulin surges and creates a relentless demand on your body. I hope I've made it clear that excess sugar is a major form of stress. Nutritional stresses can be more damaging than the external assaults of life's outrageous misfortunes. And if you have to deal with both, then your adrenals and your thyroid will have to work very hard to provide the necessary hormones to maintain balance. As cortisol rises in response to stress, other hormones such as DHEA and sex hormones dwindle. It becomes a cycle of depletion. You get fat and depressed, while not being able to maintain growth and repair.

. . . .

CORTISOL

Cortisol, perhaps the most infamous stress hormone, actually provides many necessary functions: enhancing your brain's use of glucose to heighten cognitive function; controlling inflammation; and helping you wake up in the morning. However, when it is constantly high due to stress (diet, environment, emotions), your digestion and immune system suffer, and eventually your cortisol will plummet. When that happens, weight gain, fatigue, and depression follow.

. . . .

If you are still not totally convinced about the negative effects of nutritional stress, let's look at these examples of poor food choices, and the consequences that follow:

- Eat a Twinkie-like snack. The enormous amount of sugar and carbs depletes your B vitamins. When B vitamins become depleted, many enzymatic functions are compromised, which can cause low energy and low mood.

- Eat a bag of corn chips. The sodium and MSG will cause you to become dehydrated and irritated. The GMO corn can cause indigestion, and even an allergic reaction. You become bloated and grumpy.

- Eat a pizza slathered with gooey cheese and pepperoni. Oh, dear, this is a doozy of a combo: there's gluten, processed cheese, and nitrate-filled meat. The gluten will cause tummy upset and bloating, the cheese could cause an allergic reaction, and the nitrate will convert to nitrite when you eat it. Nitrite is a known carcinogen, and in high amounts, causes red blood cells to become inefficient at delivering oxygen. So, after a slice or two, you'll feel like a fat whale with brain fog.

The point I am trying to make is that all stresses affect your adrenals.

What Are the Adrenals and Where Are They?

The adrenals, also known as "the glands of stress," are located on top of your kidneys. Although each weighs less than a grape and is no bigger than a walnut, these mighty little glands significantly affect the functioning of your body, along with the way you think and feel. The adrenal glands produce hormones that you can't live without, such as epinephrine (adrenalin), norepinephrine (noradrenalin), cortisol, sex hormones, DHEA, and aldosterone, which regulates fluid retention. In turn, adrenal hormones affect your neurotransmitters, which directly affect your cognitive, emotional, and even spiritual well-being.

When you have adrenal exhaustion, good moods are endangered: it can cause fear, anxiety, and depression, not to mention poor memory and lack of ability to concentrate on a task.

Easy Ways to De-stress

These are simple, short techniques that you can do any time, anywhere:

1. Facing the early morning or afternoon sun (between 2:00 and 5:00 p.m.), close your eyes and swing your head very slowly from side to side. Do this for about five to ten minutes. Why? Because sunlight is nourishing and relaxing. Doing this will also give your eyes a rest from the strain of working in front of the computer.

2. Sit with back straight, eyes closed, and breathe deeply for two to three minutes, counting your breaths. Try to slow down to six breaths per minute. Why? Because breathing slowly is one of the best ways to bring oxygen to your brain, while also lowering your heart rate.

3. Inhale essential oils such as bergamot or lavender. Why? The olfactory sense is directly linked to the brain. Breathing in soothing oils is one of the quickest ways to relax and heighten your parasympathetic pathway.

4. Massage your ears from tip to lobe, rubbing up and down, for one minute. Why? Because your ears have acupuncture points that connect to all parts of your body. By massaging your ears, you will stimulate energy and open any blockages in your organs.

5. Take a vitamin C supplement, food sourced, 500 mg in divided doses, up to 2,000 mg or more. Why? Although this book is about food and not

supplements, this is one exception. Since our adrenal glands rely heavily on vitamin C to function, and since we cannot make vitamin C on our own, we need to get it from a food source or from a high-quality, food-based supplement.

Summary

- There's a connection between insulin and stress response.
- Both lifestyle and dietary stress can hurt your adrenals.
- Adrenal exhaustion leads to negative moods.
- Dial down dietary stress by cutting carbs and sugar. Enjoy lots of vegetables, high-quality protein, and healthy fats.
- In addition to a nourishing diet, explore different ways to de-stress.

SPARKLING BLUSH REFRESHER
YIELD: 1 serving

Instead of drinking sodas that contain high fructose corn syrup or fake sugars, try this refreshing effervescent rose-tinted beverage.

8–10 ounces chilled sparkling mineral water
1 tablespoon fresh lemon or lime juice
¼ teaspoon vanilla extract
½ teaspoon pomegranate molasses
lime slices, for garnish

Pour ingredients into a tall glass and stir well. Garnish with lime slices.

ADRENAL-LOVING MINERAL BROTH

YIELD: approximately 6 cups

This simple mineral broth contains potassium, magnesium, and other alkalinizing nutrients that will nourish your adrenals, while keeping you hydrated. Take it in a thermos to your office and sip on it throughout the day in lieu of coffee or soft drinks.

1 small potato, skin on, cut into large chunks
1 zucchini, cut into large chunks
¼ red cabbage, cut into large chunks
2–3 shiitake mushrooms
½ onion, sliced
½ inch fresh ginger root, sliced
sea salt, to taste

Place all the ingredients in a medium pot and cover with water.

Bring to a simmer and simmer for 35 minutes.

Strain the broth, reserving the vegetables. (They are delicious with just a drizzle of extra virgin olive oil, sea salt, and freshly ground pepper.)

Sip 2 cups of mineral broth a day.

Use Celtic Sea Salt* or other high-quality sea salts instead of table salt. Table salt is stripped of minerals, and can cause acidity, while sea salts are good sources of alkalinizing minerals. Your dishes will also taste a lot better when seasoned with sea salt.

Brew a cup of valerian-root or passionflower tea in the evening to unwind.

Potassium is a mineral that helps buffer stress. Although eating a banana provides a lot of potassium, its high starch and sugar content can trigger an insulin spike. Instead, enjoy two raw celery sticks with one tablespoon of tahini. (Tahini, or sesame butter, contains calcium, which also helps to buffer stress.)

Instead of coffee, which contributes to adrenal exhaustion, try a coffee substitute such as Dandy Blend (see the Shopping Guide at the end of chapter 8 for where to get it) and add coconut milk. This combo is naturally sweet and creamy, without the sugar, dairy, or caffeine.

Instead of potato or corn chips, peel and cut jicama into thin slices and enjoy with salsa or guacamole, or try it with the Mood-Lifting Dip (recipe, page xxx). Jicama gives a satisfying crunch without the carbs.

BONE BROTH
YIELD: approx. 4 quarts

Ingredients:

3-4 lbs. bony parts of pasture-raised chickens, such as backs, necks and feet (You can also save the carcass from a roasted chicken and add it to the pot)

4 quarts filtered water

¼ cup fresh lemon juice or apple cider vinegar

1 Tbsp. sea salt

2 bay leaves

1" x 3" strip of Kombu (optional)

2 tsp. black pepper corns, whole

2 carrots, rough chopped

1 onion, rough chopped

3-4 ribs celery, chopped

Place chicken (bones/carcass) into a large pot and fill with cold water to cover. Add in lemon juice or vinegar and leave for 30 minutes. Place pot on stove and bring to a gentle boil. Skim well, add in bay leaves, pepper, and sea salt. Reduce heat until broth is on a very gentle simmer; skim more if needed. Simmer for around 8–12 hours (uncovered), adding in more water as necessary. Add in the vegetables during the last 45 minutes.

When done, allow broth to cool, then strain through a cheesecloth. Place broth in glass jars and store in refrigerator. You can also place in the freezer. (To minimize the possibility of the glass jars cracking in the freezer, make sure that you use freezer-safe glassware.)

I enjoy the simmered vegetables with a drizzle of olive oil and sprinkling of sea salt.

You can also follow this basic recipe using beef bones, knuckles, tendons, etc. (with a total weight of about 3 – 4 lbs.)

It is also possible to use a crock pot, but your broth will be cloudy due to the need to have the cover on while simmering

Nutritional Value of Bone Broth:
Glycine
Proline
Phosporous
Hyaluronic acid
Chondrontin sulfate
Magnesium, potas-
    sium sulfate,
fluoride

Use broth to cook:
Soups
Grains, rice
Add in ¼ cup when
    sautéing vegetables
Drink as a clear broth
Add texture and flavor to
    any sauce

BRAIN DRAIN: DEPLETED NEUROTRANSMITTERS

Finally, the paradigm is shifting, and we are realizing that our brain is actually connected to our body! So, when we suffer nutritional deficiencies due to poor food choices, it not only depletes us from the neck down, but can drain our brains too.

As Dr. Candace Pert, neuroscientist and author, poetically phrases it, neurotransmitters are "molecules of emotion":

> The body is not an appendage dangling from the almighty brain that rules over all systems. Instead, the brain itself is one of the many nodal or entry points into a dynamic network of communication that unites all systems—nervous, endocrine, immune, respiratory, and more. This is called the psychosomatic network, and the linking elements to keep it all together are the informational substances—peptides, hormones and neurotransmitters— known as the molecules of emotion.[1]

Neurotransmitters are made of protein, and they help us function by acting as bridges between neurons that act to direct cell-to-cell communication. They are the spark plugs that define our moods. While there are hundreds of neurotransmitters, here are a few well-studied ones that affect our behavior and mood:

Dopamine

What it does: Helps to control the brain's reward and pleasure centers. Dopamine also regulates movement and emotional responses, and it enables us not only to anticipate rewards, but to take the necessary steps to move toward them.

Signs of deficiency: Inability to concentrate, obesity, fatigue, low libido, depression (common in low-protein diets). Deficiency can trigger: Cravings for alcohol, caffeine, sugar, or chocolate. Foods that help boost level: Foods high in tyrosine, such as dairy, almonds, avocado, pumpkin seeds, sesame seeds, and animal protein.

Acetylcholine

What it does: Critical for memory, such as recollection of events, names, and numbers. It also affects our ability to learn and our processing speed.

Signs of deficiency: Forgetfulness (where you parked your car, placed your keys, phone numbers), paranoia, loss of creativity, wanting to be alone (common in low-fat diets). Deficiency can trigger: Craving for fatty foods such as ice cream, cheesecake, fried foods. Foods to help boost level: Healthy fats, choline-containing foods such as eggs, beef liver, cauliflower, and lacto-fermented vegetables.

Serotonin

What it does: Brings a sense of joy, social engagement, healthy self-esteem, and good digestion.

Signs of deficiency: Insomnia, waking frequently during the night, IBS, PMS, aches and pains, anxiety, sadness, depression. Deficiency triggers: Cravings for carbs, sugar, and salt, increased appetite in the late evening, especially for starchy foods. Foods to help boost level: Foods high in trypto-phan such as poultry, lamb, sardines, cashews, sweet potatoes.

GABA (gamma-aminobutyric acid)

What it does: Promotes sound sleep, helps with relaxation, tolerance of stress and pain, good digestion; a natural sedative.

Signs of deficiency: Insomnia, anxiety, low tolerance for pain, heartburn, headaches, IBS, emotional eating. Deficiency can trigger: overeating. Foods to help boost level: Glutamic acid-containing foods such as almonds, walnuts, halibut, lentils, broccoli.

. . . .

DOPAMINE AND SEROTONIN

To help boost dopamine by day and serotonin by night, only eat carbs in the evening: this will keep insulin low throughout the day. Eating carbs triggers a release of insulin, which helps to get serotonin to the brain. Serotonin is needed at night for sound sleep; with the help of darkness, it transforms into the powerful hormone melatonin, which is an antioxidant that prevents cancer and helps your body repair itself and remain youthful.

. . . .

THE BRAIN AND GUT CONNECTION

In your mother's womb, your brain and gut start off from the same embryonic tissue. After the first few weeks of pregnancy, this tissue divides. One piece grows to become your central nervous system (brain and spinal cord), and the other becomes your enteric nervous system (digestive function), also known as the "second brain" because of its incredible complexity and the number of neurons it contains. As you develop further in utero, your two "brains" grow apart, but remain connected by the vagus nerve.[2]

So there is a direct line of communication between our brain and our gut. Through the vagus nerve, messages are sent back and forth. Notice that when you receive bad news, your stomach can get upset; and you may feel jittery or experience brain fog after eating something to which you are allergic.

One of the most important neurotransmitters for governing mood, serotonin, is found mainly in the gut. Actually, ninety to ninety-five percent of it! No wonder there is a profound connection between what we eat and how we feel.[3]

Why Gluten Is Bad for Your Gut and Your Brain

Gluten is the elastic-like protein found in wheat, rye, barley, and cross-contaminated oats. Because gluten is hard to digest, many people have a difficult time breaking down this protein in their gut, and the undigested gluten particles cause fermentation (aka putrefaction) in the intestine, leading to that uncomfortable bloated feeling. Overtime, those undigested particles can cause damage to the lining of your intestine, leading to an unfortunate condition called leaky gut.[4]

When leaky gut occurs, absorption of nutrients is compromised. In turn, this diminishes the precursors necessary to make neurotransmitters and other important nourishment for the brain. The resulting malnutrition may cause negative mental symptoms to arise. (More on gluten in chapter 1.)

Summary

- When you suffer from unstable blood sugar (the roller-coaster ride) you will wear out your adrenals, so they can't produce the necessary hormones to support good health and good mood.
- When the adrenals are worn out, your entire internal system is compromised, including the production of neurotransmitters, or "molecules of emotion," which stimulate positive actions and outlook.
- The connection between body and brain is undeniable. Feed your body well, and your brain will be happy. Your mood will follow suit.
- Get off gluten to heal your gut and your brain.
- Eat foods that help boost production of your neurotransmitters.

MOOD-LIFTING DIP
YIELD: approx. 1 cup

½ avocado, peeled and diced
⅓ cup pumpkin seeds (best if
 soaked for 4 hours in water
 with ½ teaspoon lemon juice
 or a pinch of salt; see chapter
 3, p. 73)
2 tablespoons nutritional yeast
1 tablespoon apple cider vinegar
 or fresh lemon juice
⅓ cup extra virgin olive oil
sea salt and freshly ground
 pepper, to taste
⅓ cup cilantro, chopped

Place the avocado, pumpkin seeds, nutritional yeast, and vinegar or lemon juice in a food processor and pulse a few times to blend the ingredients.

With the processor on, slowly drizzle in the olive oil.

Add the salt and pepper, to taste.

Remove the mixture from the processor, and fold in the cilantro.

Goes really well with jicama slices and celery or carrot sticks, or toss with salad greens.

Eat four to five Brazil nuts a day. They contain the trace mineral selenium, which helps with the production of neurotransmitters.

Boost your brain power by eating protein-rich foods that are high in tyrosine, an amino acid that is the precursor to dopamine, epinephrine, and norepinephrine. Best sources: eggs, turkey, meat, cheese, nuts.

Try using spaghetti squash instead of wheat noodles for your next "pasta" dinner. When the squash is cooked, the inside flesh can be scooped out in strands, resembling angel hair pasta.

NO-PASTA PASTA WITH SPICY MEAT SAUCE

YIELD: 4 servings

1 spaghetti squash, about 2 pounds
3 tablespoons extra virgin olive oil
1 small onion, diced
2 garlic cloves, minced
¾ pound ground beef, grass-fed
12 ounces tomato sauce (organic, in a glass bottle)
1 tablespoon balsamic vinegar
sea salt, to taste
freshly ground pepper, to taste
crushed red pepper, to taste (optional)
handful of fresh basil leaves, chopped
Parmesan cheese or Nondairy Cheesy Sprinkle (recipe, page 86)

Preheat oven to 375°F. Line a baking sheet with unbleached parchment paper.

Cut the squash in half lengthwise, scoop out the seeds, and brush the interior with 1 tablespoon olive oil. Place cut sides down on the prepared baking sheet and bake for about 35 minutes, or until the strands come out easily with a fork.

Allow the squash to cool until easy to handle, then scoop out the spaghetti-like strands with a fork.

Drizzle 1 tablespoon of olive oil on the "spaghetti" and toss well. Add a little salt. Set aside in a bowl or pot with the cover on to keep warm.

Heat a pan on medium heat with the remaining olive oil, then add the onion, and garlic. Sauté until the onion is translucent, about 3 minutes.

Add the ground beef and stir to break up clumps. Cook for about 2 minutes.

Add tomato sauce and balsamic vinegar. Season with salt and pepper and crushed red pepper, if using.

Simmer for about 8–10 minutes on low heat.

Taste for seasoning and adjust as necessary. Remove from heat and add basil leaves.

Serve immediately over the cooked spaghetti squash. Top with grated parmesan cheese or Nondairy Cheesy Sprinkle (recipe page 86).

Notes for Introduction

1   Candace B. Pert PhD, "Body Is the Subconscious Mind," 12/3/2011, http://cassiopaea. org/forum/index.php/topic,25979.msg309766.html?PHPSESSID=c13a40e62c0a918dd b0b7b694469b0d0#msg309766
2   Michael D. Gershon MD, The Second Brain (New York: HarperCollins, 1998).
3   Ibid.
4   William Davis MD, Wheat Belly (New York: Rodale, 2011).

Chapter 1

You Feel What You Eat

One cannot think well, love well, sleep well,
if one has not dined well.
—VIRGINIA WOOLF

We've all heard the old adage "You are what you eat." But it's really more relevant to look at how foods make us *feel*. While it is well known that there is a connection between physical illness and eating junk food, few people are aware of the relationship between sad moods and a nutrient-poor diet.

In this chapter, we will look at the core principles and edible ingredients that build the foundation for vibrant health—because the path that leads to being healthy is really the same path that will lead you to feeling happy, physically and emotionally. Isn't it wonderful to know that while we strive to be energetic, vital, and contented, we can also take pleasure in cooking and eating delicious meals?

Simply put, if you want to feel good, eat well.

THE MIGHTY MACROS

Macronutrients, the sources of life, are composed of three types: protein, fat, and carbohydrates.

Without these macronutrients we could not exist. They provide us with energy in the form of calories. Macronutrients also work synergistically with micronutrients (vitamins and minerals), together making it possible for us to live our lives and thrive. Therefore, a basic understanding of what they are, where they are found, and how they nourish us will instill a deeper appreciation and heighten consciousness of what we put into our mouths.

Since macronutrients are sources of calories, it all comes down to a matter of balance. However, balancing does not mean that we need to consume protein, fats, and carbohydrates in equal parts. What you will discover about the trio is that you can enjoy more fat than you thought possible, require more protein than you normally eat, and need a lot less carbohydrates than you crave.

POWERFUL PROTEINS

After water, protein is the most abundant substance that makes us who we are. It composes twenty percent of our body. We are made of protein, and we need a continuous supply of it to support the structure of our vital organs such as the heart, brain, liver, and kidneys, as well as hair, skin, fingernails, muscles, ligaments, and tendons. In addition, hormones, enzymes, and neurotransmitters, along with our chromosomes, are all made from protein.

This macronutrient is composed of individual units called amino acids. When we eat a meal the process of digestion cleaves apart whatever protein we ingested into amino acids and then uses them to rebuild our body. You could say that amino acids are like organic Lego pieces that click together to create who we are.

There are two categories of amino acids: *essential* and *nonessential*. The *essential amino acids* are: leucine, isoleucine, lysine, methionine, phenylalanine, threonine, tryptophan, valine, and histidine. They are called essential because we cannot make these within our internal laboratory, and we must obtain them from foods.

The *nonessential amino acids* can be produced by our own metabolic processes, with the help of other amino acids. However, insufficient *nonessential amino acids* can result when digestion is faulty, or if the diet is depleting. And this can lead to lackluster health.

There is a difference between animal protein and protein that comes from plants. Animal sources provide the full gamut of essential amino acids, while plant-based sources need to be combined to create a meal that contains complete protein. For example, the essential amino acid *lysine*, which is involved in growth and energy, is found in low quantities in grains, but it is high in legumes such as lentils and chickpeas. *Methionine*, another important essential amino acid that contains sulfur, is abundant in grains. Therefore, combining lentils with rice is a nutritionally sound pairing.

• •

LYSINE: AN ESSENTIAL AMINO

Lysine deficiency can cause stunted growth in children and poor connective tissue growth in adults. Other symptoms include fatigue, agitation, irritabilty, poor concentration, anemia, and hair loss. Now, those symptoms are enough to make anyone quite miserable! What's more, both lysine and methionine are needed to make *carnitine*, another amino acid that is critical to metabolism, turning fatty acids into energy.[1]

• •

Combine to be complete! Vegetarian sources of protein are incomplete, which means that they do not contain all the essential amino acids. In order to get complete protein in a vegetarian meal, combining is the key.

Examples: brown rice and lentils, millet and cashew, or beans with corn.

QUINOA AND ADZUKI BEAN SALAD
YIELD: 2-3 servings

1 cup quinoa, preferably soaked overnight
2 cups filtered water
½ can cooked adzuki beans
1 cup cooked beets or cooked broccoli florets
1 green onion, finely chopped
4 cups organic salad mix
⅓ cup Yummy Tahini Dressing (recipe follows)
sea salt and freshly ground pepper, to taste

Drain the soaked quinoa and put in a pot with the water. Simmer gently for 20 minutes, covered.

Allow to cool, then mix in other ingredients, and serve on a bed of organic salad mix.

Drizzle Yummy Tahini Dressing over the salad.

YUMMY TAHINI DRESSING
YIELD: ¾ cup
Great on salads, baked chicken, or steamed veggies.

¼ cup raw apple cider vinegar
½ cup extra virgin olive oil
1 garlic clove
3 tablespoons tahini
1 tablespoon fresh lemon juice
sea salt and freshly ground pepper, to taste

Put all ingredients in a blender or food processor and process well.
Store extra dressing in a glass jar in the fridge.

How Much Protein?
Humans need thousands of different proteins to create and maintain physical structure and internal metabolism. Research shows that our paleo ancestors lived on more protein and fat, and less carbohydrates, than are present in our modern diet today.[2] Thanks to the advent of the agrarian age, we have come to rely on too many grains. And yet, on the evolutionary timeline, we have not evolved to process them as well as we should.

· ·

HOW TO CALCULATE YOUR PROTEIN NEEDS
The formula is quite easy, and you can adjust it according to your level of activity.
1. Weight in pounds divided by 2.2 = weight in kg
2. Weight in kg x 0.8–1.8 gm/kg = protein in gm.
Use a lower number if you are in good health and are sedentary (0.8). Use a higher number (between 1 and 1.8) if you are under stress, are pregnant, are recovering from an illness, or if you are involved in consistent and intense weight or endurance training.

Example:
135 lb female who likes to walk and cycles to work everyday
135 lbs / 2.2 = 61 kg
61 kg x 1.5 = 91.5 gm protein/day
(3 ounces of chicken = 20 grams of protein, 3 eggs = 20

grams of protein, ⅓ cup lentils = 20 grams protein. These are approximate measures.)

One of the best sources of protein is from nature's perfect package, the egg.

. . . .

. . . .

CONVENTIONAL VS. FREE-RANGE/PASTURE-RAISED EGGS

Chickens that are kept on factory farms are packed together in cages and never see the natural world. As a result of their extremely overcrowded conditions, they become stressed and will peck at each other, so they are debeaked. Since the beak is actually filled with nerve endings, the mutilation causes pain to the birds, leading to more stress. Disease among the hens is managed with antibiotics, and they are given cheap feed made from GMO soy, corn, or cottonseed meal. Then, in order to force the birds into another laying cycle, they are subjected to forced molting, whereby the chickens are starved for up to two weeks. It should be evident that such maltreatment, combined with substandard feed and heavy use of antibiotics, cannot produce eggs that are truly nourishing.

In vast contrast to conventionally raised chickens, their pasture-raised counterparts enjoy the natural cycles and conditions that honor what they need to thrive. Pasture-raised birds are allowed to roam in open spaces and to forage on green plants and insects. They are not debeaked and typically live longer and much more healthy lives. The eggs that come from such birds are far more nutritious, and, to egg aficionados, taste much better. In fact, according to a study done by *Mother Earth News*, pasture-raised eggs may contain:

- seven times more beta carotene
- three times more vitamin E
- two times more omega-3 fatty acids
- two-thirds more vitamin A
- a quarter less saturated fat
- a third less cholesterol

When it comes to a truly good egg, there is a difference between "free-range" and "pasture-raised." One of the most recognized entities that monitor the health and welfare of farm animals is HFAC (Humane Farm Animal Care). It has created very specific standards so that consumers can be educated on the various ways poultry is raised. According to the HFAC's website:

HFAC's Certified Humane® "Free Range" requirement is two sq. ft. per bird. The hens must be outdoors, weather permitting (in some areas of the country, seasonal), and when they are outdoors they must be outdoors for at least six hours per day. All other standards must be met.

HFAC's Certified Humane® "Pasture Raised" requirement is 1,000 birds per 2.5 acres (108 sq. ft. per bird) and the fields must be rotated. The hens must be outdoors year-round, with mobile or fixed housing where the hens can go inside at night to protect themselves from predators, or for up to two weeks out of the year due only to very inclement weather. All additional standards must be met.

http://certifiedhumane.org/free-range-and-pasture-raised-officially-defined-by-hfac-for-certified-humane-label/

• •

Perfect Boiled Eggs

When a boiled egg is overcooked, a greenish-gray ring appears around the yolk. Although not attractive, it is harmless. It is merely a chemical reaction of the iron in the yolk with the sulfur in the egg white. If you want perfect yellow yolks for your boiled eggs, simply place the uncooked eggs in their shells into a pot of cold water. When the water comes to a simmer, turn the heat off and cover the pot. Allow the eggs to cook in the hot water for ten minutes, then rinse under cold water.

FABULOUS FATS

This macronutrient is critical to our physical and mental survival and well-being. Of the three Mighty Macros, fat is perhaps the most misunderstood and maligned, due to a lot of bad information and bad press.

Many people shake their heads in silent censorship whenever the word *fat* is mentioned in conjunction with health. Somehow, we've suffered a collective brainwashing by the no-fat, low-fat diet zealots, and the mere mention of "fat" has been demonized.

For those of you who secretly harbor longings for full-fat butter, full-fat cream, and a full-fat milk latte instead of the watery caffeinated beverage with low-fat milk you chug down every morning, there's glorious news coming up as you read about the significance of having healthy fats in your diet.

We Are Fat Heads

We are all fat heads, whether you want to admit to that or not. Our brains are composed of sixty percent fat.[3] Our neurons, myelin sheath, and synapses need fat to coat, protect, and facilitate transmission of information.

Our thought processes work by way of cell-to-cell communication, and this is dependent on the integrity of the cellular membrane. The membrane is composed of different types of fat that come from our diet.

According to Dr. Michael Schmidt, author of *Brain-Building Nutrition*:

> Like a temple in which each stone is carefully chosen for its purpose, the brain requires specific fats of specific size, length, shape, and function in order to conduct its daily business. From the retina of your eye to the nerve centers that control movement of your arms, brain-fats are required. The nerves that allow you to run, jump, throw, play the piano, paint a picture, laugh at a joke, and fall in love all depend on specific fats. The regions of your brain that govern your mood, behavior, and emotional intelligence require fats. The regions that give rise to your memory and your ability to learn new things require these fats. In one respect, we are who we are because of fat: not a glamorous notion, but fair.

Types of Fats

So, what are the types of fats that we need?

Saturated

These fats are highly stable because, on the molecular level, all the carbon bonds are occupied by a hydrogen atom. Basically, it means that the molecules have a tight relationship, and are not easily pulled apart by other needy elements. When all the carbon-atom linkages of a fatty acid are bonded, it is *saturated*. Saturated fats tend not to go rancid when exposed to air or high-temperature cooking. In nature, saturated fatty acids are found in animal fats (butter, lard, duck fat) and tropical oils (coconut, palm). By the way, Crisco *does not* exist in nature and is *not* a healthy saturated fat!

Monounsaturated

This category of fats is not quite as stable as its saturated counterpart because monounsaturated fats have one double bond with two carbon atoms double-bonded to each other and so are lacking two hydrogen atoms. In more decipherable terms, it means that monounsaturated fats are subject to losing a few carbon atoms off its molecular chain. When this happens, oxidation starts.

Your body can make monounsaturated fatty acids from saturated fatty acids.

Oleic Acid (Omega-9)

This is a type of monounsaturated fatty acid found in olive oil, which is good for the heart. It is also found in almonds, peanuts, tea seeds, sesame seeds, and avocados. Since monounsaturated oils are not as stable as saturated fats, they should only be heated moderately when used in cooking.

Polyunsaturated

Of the three, this fat is the most unstable, because it has two or more pairs of double bonds. A polyunsaturated fatty acid lacks four or more hydrogen atoms and is therefore very prone to rancidity; polyunsaturated fats should not be heated or exposed to air for a long period of time.

Many plant-based oils (except olive oil) fall into this category.

• •

OMEGAS

Two well-known polyunsaturated oils, omega-3 and omega-6, are vital for calming inflammation, supporting brain function, and supporting a happy disposition. They are known as *essential fatty acids*, or EFAs, and must be obtained through edible sources.

• •

That's enough carbon-hydrogen bondage science for now. The important thing to remember is that all fats and oils are composed of a combination of saturated, monounsaturated, and polyunsaturated fatty acids. Butter, lard, and other animal fats contain between forty to sixty percent saturated fats and are therefore solid or semisolid at room temperature. Tropical oils also contain high percentages of saturated fatty acids, but are liquid in warm climates and very solid in cold climates. *(Coconut oil is ninety-two percent saturated).*

In terms of cooking, the more stable or saturated the fat, the more it can hold a high cooking temperature without going rancid. And there lies the fulcrum of good health! Ingesting rancid oils causes raging oxidative damage by introducing a lot of free radicals into your body. This requires a lot of antioxidants to squelch the upheaval.

Benefits of Fats
Here are other great things that fats do for us:
- Allow for absorption of minerals and the fat-soluble vitamins: A, D, E, and K
- Prevent wrinkles and premature aging
- Nourish our skin and hair, making them lustrous
- Provide more energy, pound for pound, than carbohydrates.[4] (One molecule of glucose makes 38 units ATP, while one molecule of fat makes 146 units ATP. Adenosine triphosphate (ATP) is a unit of measurement for energy.)
- Provide satiety. That means feeling content and well fed after eating.

Healthy Fats to Include in Your Diet
Coconut oil, ghee (clarified butter), organic butter, sesame oil, red palm oil, extra virgin olive oil, flax oil (not for cooking), omega-3 and 6, cod liver oil.

See Best Oils for Cooking in chapter 8 for the recommended temperatures for cooking different oils, plus other interesting factoids on fats.

The Paradox Is Not Only French
Countless articles have been written about the "French Paradox": how those Frenchies get away with eating rich pâtés, butter, cream, lardons, etc., and yet are skinnier, better lovers, and suffer fewer heart attacks. Well, as it turns out, at least in regard to cardiovascular disease, several other countries such as Switzerland, Germany, Austria, Sweden, and the Netherlands also enjoy high fat intake and share the same statistics.[5] In other words,

higher saturated fat intake equates to lower heart disease.

Conclusion? Eat healthy saturated fats such as coconut oil, butter, and ghee.

It's better for your ticker *and* makes you happy!

SWEET POTATOES WITH SAGE AND CINNAMON BUTTER
YIELD: 1-2 servings

1 small sweet potato
2-3 tablespoons ghee or butter
6-8 fresh sage leaves
sea salt, coarse
¼ teaspoon ground cinnamon

Cook the sweet potato by boiling it in water (with skin) for about 15 minutes. The cooking time will vary depending on the size and quality of your sweet potato, so test for doneness with a paring knife.

Allow to cool by plunging the cooked sweet potato in cold water. Peel and cut into ¼-inch slices. Arrange in an attractive manner on a plate.

Heat the butter in a pan until it begins to bubble gently. Reduce heat and toss in the sage leaves. Allow leaves to swim in the hot butter until they start to curl slightly on the edges and the fragrance of the sage tickles your nose (about 40–50 seconds). Remove from heat.

Spoon the brown butter and sage leaves over the sweet potato slices and sprinkle with ground cinnamon and sea salt. Serve immediately.

Edible Oils for Beautiful Skin
Why spend a fortune on expensive moisturizers for your skin? Use extra virgin olive oil or coconut oil instead. They will make your skin smooth and supple. You shouldn't put anything on your skin that you can't eat, anyway.

Melt ½ cup coconut oil. Allow to cool slightly and blend in four to five drops of geranium or rose essential oil. Store in a small, clean glass jar. Use for hands and body.

Eat Less with Coconut Oil
To curb appetite and assist weight loss, melt one to three teaspoons coconut oil in warm water, and drink twenty minutes before a meal. Coconut oil speeds up metabolism, supports thyroid function, and provides a feeling of satiety so that you will eat less.[6]

CURB YOUR CARBOHYDRATES

Carbohydrates are produced through the process of photosynthesis. The sun's radiant energy shining on plants creates the natural chemical reactions with carbon dioxide and water that give us this third macronutrient.

Carbohydrates are a quick source of energy because they are easily converted to glucose, which fuels the cells in our body. Of the three Mighty Macros, carbs are probably the most popular and most overconsumed. Because carbohydrates quickly turn into glucose, an overindulgence can lead to blood sugar imbalance, weight gain, and an inadequate intake of the other two macronutrients.

As with protein and fat, carbohydrates are not just a one-dimensional, simple nutrient.

Traditionally, carbohydrates are divided into simple and complex. However, there's more to it than that, and a deeper understanding will help you make healthier carb choices.

Types of Carbohydrates in Foods

Simple
These are divided into:
Monosaccharides: glucose, fructose, galactose
Disaccharides: maltose, lactose, sucrose

Complex
These are divided into:
Oligosaccharides
This category includes fruto-oligosaccharides, which can serve

as food for our friendly bacteria, such as *bifidobacteria* and *lactobacilli*. (Food examples: artichokes, sunchokes, asparagus, garlic, chicory root, burdock.)

Polysaccharides
Long-chain, nonstarchy carbs, such as pectin, and gums.

Starches
Long-chain glucose polymers found in vegetables and whole grains.

Fiber
There are two different types of fiber: soluble and insoluble. Both are important for health, digestion, and prevention of diseases.
- *Soluble fiber* attracts water and turns to gel during digestion. This slows digestion. Soluble fiber is found in oat bran, barley, nuts, seeds, beans, lentils, peas, and some fruits and vegetables.
- *Insoluble fiber* is found in foods such as wheat bran, vegetables, and whole grains. It adds bulk to the stool and appears to help food pass more quickly through the stomach and intestines.

Healthy Sweeteners
White sugar is highly addictive, and even considered more so than some recreational drugs. Obviously, we want to avoid it. Here are a few healthy sweet substitutes:
- maple syrup
- raw honey
- stevia (in its most natural form, which is a green powder)
- blackstrap molasses
- palm sugar
- Sucanat
- turbinado sugar

Refrain from Refined
Our modern diets are inundated with refined carbohydrates, which are stripped of life-sustaining nutrients. Instead of nourishing us, refined carbs

deplete vitamins, minerals, and enzymes, which are needed for proper metabolism.

When refined carbohydrates such as processed white sugar, white flour, or high-fructose corn syrup are consumed, our bloodstream gets flooded with glucose, causing a sugar rush. Our pancreas goes into panic mode in an effort to deal with the sudden excess sugar, and pumps out insulin and other hormones in order to bring blood sugar back to normal levels. Repeated assaults of refined carbs day after day will eventually wear out the insulin response. From there, blood sugar imbalances (hyper- or hypoglycemia) will lead to diabetes along with its associated health detriments.

The solution to stop cravings for sugary snacks is to eat fat and protein instead.

Here are a few yummy suggestions:

- Put a slice of cooked ham or turkey and some avocado atop a piece of butter lettuce, and make a wrap.
- Enjoy a tablespoon of coconut butter with some nuts. (See the Shopping Guide at the end of chapter 8 for where to get coconut butter.)
- Spread two ounces liver pâté on gluten-free crackers.

Why Going Gluten Free Is So Good

It's all the buzz nowadays. Anybody who's into feeling good and looking good is seeking gluten-free foods. Even top personal trainers are coaching their clients to dump the wheat and other gluten-containing grains in order to optimize athletic performance. So, is the hot spotlight on going gluten free just another diet frenzy from Hollywood, or does it actually merit serious attention from those of us who are concerned about health and happiness?

When the digestive tract is irritated by gluten, absorption of nutrients is compromised. If left to continue, the irritation and inflammation can cause serious digestive issues, including leaky gut and celiac disease. In turn, this diminishes the precursors to neurotransmitters and other important nourishment for the brain. Negative mental symptoms may arise as a result of malnutrition, or by an allergic reaction to gluten.

Here are a few delicious gluten-free grains to try:
- amaranth
- buckwheat, also know as kasha
- millet
- quinoa
- teff
- wild rice

SENSATIONAL SEASONINGS—HERBS

Herbs are more than just decorative frilly things in a pot or sprigs of green to garnish a dish. These beautiful edibles are one of the most powerful mood-lifting allies that we have in the kitchen.

Just rubbing a sprig of rosemary between your fingers and inhaling the release of its volatile oils can help revive a sluggish brain, or brighten up the next few hours of doldrums in the office.

Basil

Basil stimulates the immune system, and it's also antiparasitic. It has long been considered the herb of love by the Italians. (When a woman puts a pot of basil on her windowsill, it means that she is ready to receive her lover.) In India, the indigenous basil *ocinum sanctum,* "holy basil," is associated with Vishnu and Krishna.

Bay Leaves

From the crowning of laureates to being an effective roach repellent, this versatile gift of the evergreen bay tree is also a culinary herb with a tale of love, desire, and hot pursuit gone wrong. According to Greek mythology, Apollo fell in love with a pretty wood nymph named Daphne. Becoming overstimulated by Daphne's beauty and grace, Apollo chased her and she ran. While desperately fleeing to protect her maidenhood, Daphne implored the gods to save her. The celestial beings came to her aid by turning her into a laurel tree. Apollo fell to his knees and clutched her with hopeless longing as her limbs transformed into the trunk and then the branches right before his eyes.

Bay leaves can also be added to a hot bath for relaxation.

Cilantro

This delicate-looking herb is a powerful chelator, meaning that it helps pull out toxic heavy metals, especially mercury. It is also antimicrobial and antibacterial, and has been used by the Greeks, Romans, and Chinese since ancient times to calm digestive issues. The seeds are known as *coriander*, which has aphrodisiac properties (see following spice section). Brew a cup of tea with the leaves to relieve stomach pains caused by junk food bingeing.

Dill

Both the leaves and seeds of the dill plant are used in cooking, and also used to preserve food. It helps digestion and fights infections. Got bad breath? No need to use those toxic mouthwashes, just chew on some dill!

Dill is from the old Norse word *dilla*, meaning to soothe or lull. The renowned seventeenth-century English herbalist Nicholas Culpeper called it "a gallant expeller of wind." So, if you ate too many beans, brew yourself a cup of dill tea for relief.

Parsley

Don't take parsley for granted. There's the curly, and then there's the Italian. Both are packed with superantioxidants and flavonoids. The *myristicin* oil contained in parsley wards off cancer. It also contains plenty of vitamin C.

For those of you who like to barbecue, parsley helps protect against the carcinogenic effects of charcoal smoke. So make a pesto with parsley for your next barbecue.

Oregano

This herb is much more than topping for pizzas. Oregano oil contains a strong antibacterial agent. The word *origans* means "joy of the mountain." And just in case you take hemlock and decide that you don't want to die yet, oregano is the antidote. The oil is used to treat parasites. It is also a folk remedy for baldness.

Rosemary

Known as the herb of remembrance, it was used to preserve meats before the days of refrigeration. When placed under a pillow, it will repel bad dreams. When placed around the house, it repels witches. It was used in hospitals, along with juniper berries as an antiseptic, as late as WWII.

Tarragon

This anise-flavored herb means "little dragon" in French because its root curls around like a dragon's tail. Known to numb the mouth, it is good for toothaches. Tarragon contains *rutin*, which helps strengthen capillary walls.

Sage

Known as an herb for the wise, and a cure-all because it aids digestion. Acts as a preservative, works as an antiperspirant, treats wounds, and is also believed to extend life. It was introduced to the Chinese by the Dutch; the Chinese so prized it that they traded three pounds of tea for one pound of sage. The herbalist John Gerard said of sage: "Singularly good for the head and brain. It quicketh the sense and memory, strengthens the sinews, restoreth health to those with palsy, and taketh away shaky trembling of the members."

Thyme

As with rosemary, thyme has been used since ancient times to preserve meat. It contains two powerful chemicals: *thymol* and *carvacol*, which are antiseptic. The mouthwash Listerine contains thymol. Thyme also helps loosen phlegm.

15-SECOND DRESSING WITH THREE HERBS
YIELD: approx. ¾ cup

½ cup extra virgin olive oil
2 tablespoons balsamic vinegar
1 teaspoon Dijon mustard
½ teaspoon honey or maple
    syrup
¼ teaspoon sea salt
freshly ground pepper, to taste
⅓ cup chopped fresh herbs: dill,
    parsley, and tarragon
1 tablespoon minced shallot
    (optional)

Put all the ingredients in a clean glass jar. (A recycled peanut butter or jam jar is perfect for this task.)

Screw on the lid securely and shake vigorously for 15 seconds. (*Okay, let me be clear here. You shake the jar up and down vigorously, not yourself.*)

Magically, you now have an emulsified dressing to enjoy with your crispy fresh salad. Add more salt and pepper, to taste.

Simply keep leftover dressing in the jar and store in the fridge. Allow to reach room temperature before using.

MIGHTY CILANTRO AND BASIL PESTO

1 small bunch basil, leaves only
1 bunch cilantro, bottom stems
    cut off
⅓ cup pine nuts
1–2 garlic cloves
½ cup extra virgin olive oil
2 tablespoons fresh lemon juice
sea salt and freshly ground
    pepper, to taste

Put the herbs, nuts, and garlic in a food processor or blender and pulse for a few seconds to puree the ingredients.

Slowly add the olive oil and lemon juice while continuing to puree. (You may need to add a little more olive oil if the mixture is too thick.)

Season with salt and pepper.

Pesto will keep for a week in an airtight container in the refrigerator. You can use it on grilled chicken or fish, spread it on sandwiches, toss with gluten-free pasta, or add to steamed vegetables.

You can also experiment with different fresh leafy herbs such as parsley, dill, and arugula.

HERB SALT

Making herb salt is a wonderful way to enjoy the flavors of herbs in cooking, and it is a great DIY (do-it-yourself) gift for friends and family during the holidays.

It is important that you dry the herbs with the salt in a low-temperature oven (200°F), because temperatures above 250°F will destroy the volatile essential oils and make the salt clump together.

Equipment:
mortar and pestle or a food processor
clean jar(s) to store the finished product
a large cookie sheet
a large bowl

1 cup mixed dried herbs: dill, rosemary, chives, tarragon, thyme, oregano, basil
2 large garlic cloves (optional)
1 cup sea salt

Mix the herbs, garlic (if using) and sea salt in a large bowl. Stir to combine ingredients.

If you are using a mortar and pestle, spoon a manageable amount of the mixture into the mortar and pound with pestle. Repeat till all of the mixture is well pounded. Alternatively, you can use a food processor.

Spread the blended ingredients evenly onto a cookie sheet lined with parchment.

Bake at 200°F for 40 to 50 minutes to dry the salt mixture. Stir frequently to break up any lumps.

Cool the herb salt completely before storing it in clean jars.

You can also follow the ratios below:

For fresh herbs:
1 part salt : 4–5 parts herbs
(by weight)

For dried herbs:
1 part salt : 1 part herbs
(by weight)

SENSATIONAL SEASONINGS—SPICES

Allspice

Originates from the tropical Americas, with the best coming from Jamaica. Also known as Jamaica pepper, pimento, or new spice. Living up to its name, allspice carries hints of pepper, cloves, cinnamon, nutmeg, and juniper. It contains *eugenol*, an oil with antiseptic properties, and is good for digestion and toothaches.

Allspice is also one of the secret ingredients in two famous liqueurs, Chartreuse and Benedictine.

Caraway

One of the most ancient spices, dating back to 3000 BC. In the West it is mostly associated with German, Eastern European, and Scandinavian cooking, though it is also used widely in the Middle East and India. The Egyptians buried their dead with caraway seeds, which were thought to ward off evil spirits. For the living, caraway helps with digestion.

Cardamom

One of the sexiest and most expensive spices on earth. Also known as the "grain of paradise." It is mentioned many times in *Arabian Nights* and the *Kama Sutra*. Cleopatra's favorite perfumed oil was made from cardamom.

Used to heal dyspepsia and can increase *acetylcholine*, a neurotransmitter that helps with memory.

Cinnamon

Not just for apple pies. This spice is often abused and overused in cheap Christmas candles and the like, but its culinary qualities can add deep, rich flavor to foods both savory and sweet. Studies conducted by the FDA show that cinnamon is great for balancing blood sugar; just ½ teaspoon per day provides benefits.

Sprinkle liberally on your hot chocolate or on toasted gluten-free bread for a delicious cinnamon toast.

Cumin

The second most popular spice after black pepper. The flavor of cumin can be found in dishes ranging from Nepal to Cuba. Don't confuse it with caraway seeds, which look like cumin, but are longer, with a different aroma and taste. Cumin helps improve digestion and contains antioxidants.

Cayenne

Hot, spicy, and warming, this exciting spice increases circulation and helps rev up metabolism. The main active ingredient, *capsaicin*, is well researched for its ability to reduce headaches and quell inflammation.

Coriander

Prized for centuries for its flavor and medicinal properties, this spice was favored by the Greeks and Romans. It is the seed which grows cilantro. Used for curry powders, pickling, sausages, and baking.

Nutmeg

This fragrant spice is not just for Christmas eggnogs. Nutmeg offers many health benefits, including aiding digestion and improving appetite. An active ingredient, *myristicin*, has been shown to inhibit an enzyme in the brain that contributes to Alzheimer's disease and is used to improve memory. In Arab countries, nutmeg is prized as an aphrodisiac.

Saffron

It's the most expensive spice in the world. But aren't you worth it?

Used in the Middle East and India to add a luxuriant rich color to foods. It also relieves stomachaches, eases the pain of kidney stones, and may be useful in treating depression by increasing serotonin. Some studies suggest that saffron may also have anticancer and memory-enhancing properties.

Turmeric

The cheapest spice available, but don't let its humble cost fool you. It is a potent spice that is well documented for having powerful anti-inflammatory effects and anticancer properties by cutting off circulation that feeds cancer cells.

An indispensable component of curry powder mix.

SIX-SPICE CHICKEN WITH COCONUT RICE

YIELD: 3–4 servings

3 tablespoons coconut oil or ghee
½ teaspoon ground cardamom
½ teaspoon ground coriander
½ teaspoon ground cumin
½ teaspoon ground cinnamon
¼ nutmeg, freshly grated from
    the whole nut
1-inch piece fresh ginger root,
    peeled and shredded
1 medium onion, sliced
2 chicken thighs, boned and cut
    into large pieces
2 chicken breasts, boned and cut
    into large pieces
2 cups chicken or vegetable stock
4–5 garlic cloves, peeled
1 medium carrot, peeled and
    diced
½ cup coconut milk
1 bunch chard or kale, cut into
    strips

Heat a large braising pot over a medium flame. Add the coconut oil or ghee along with the dried spices. Sauté for about 3 to 4 minutes, until you hear the spices begin to sing gently and smell their enticing aroma.

Add the ginger and onions and continue to sauté for another 3 minutes or so.

Add the chicken and season well with salt and pepper. Allow the meat to brown slightly on both sides, and then add the stock and garlic cloves.

Bring to a simmer and cook for about 15 minutes. Add the carrot and simmer until chicken and vegetables are cooked but still firm, about 15–20 minutes.

Add the coconut milk along with the chard or kale. Cook until greens are tender.

Adjust flavor with sea salt and pepper as needed.

Serve immediately over cooked coconut rice (recipe follows).

COCONUT RICE

YIELD: 3-4 servings

1 cup brown jasmine rice, soaked
    overnight in water and pinch
    of sea salt
1 cup filtered water
¾ cup coconut milk
pinch of sea salt

Drain the rice after soaking. Put in a pot with the water and bring to a simmer. Lower heat and add the coconut milk along with the salt.

Cover and cook over very low heat for about 20 minutes. Turn heat off and allow the rice to sit in the pot, covered, for another 10 minutes.

Fluff with a fork and serve with Six-Spice Chicken.

SPICY CHAI WITH STAR ANISE

YIELD: 1 serving

2 teaspoons loose Darjeeling or
    other black tea leaves
1 cup filtered water
2 slices fresh ginger
⅛ teaspoon black peppercorns,
    lightly crushed
1 cinnamon stick
1 star anise
⅓-½ cup organic milk or
    nondairy substitute, such as
    hemp or almond milk
1 teaspoon raw honey or Sucanat

Put the tea, water, ginger, and spices in a small pot and bring to a gentle simmer for about 8-10 minutes.

Add the milk, heat for another minute, then strain into a cup.

Sweeten with honey or Sucanat to serve.

SUNSHINE TAPIOCA PUDDING
YIELD: 3-4 servings

½ cup "seed" or "pearl" tapioca
(Do not buy Minute tapioca,
which is highly refined)
3 cups filtered water
⅛ teaspoon sea salt
¼ teaspoon saffron strands
soaked in 2 tablespoons
water
1 can coconut milk
maple syrup to serve
toasted shredded coconut
(optional)

Cover the tapioca with 1 cup water for 15-20 minutes, or until granules expand slightly. Pour off excess water.

Put tapioca, salt, and 2 cups water in a pot over high heat. Bring to a boil. Reduce heat and simmer for 15-20 minutes. Stir occasionally, adding a little more water if necessary to prevent tapioca from bubbling and sticking to the bottom of the pan.

When tapioca turns soft and a little gooey, switch off heat and stir in the saffron strands, then cover tightly. Let tapioca rest in the pan for at least 10 minutes.

Spoon into 3-4 small bowls or ramekins and cover them. Put in the fridge.

To serve: Pour on coconut milk and maple syrup, and top with toasted coconut if desired.

NUTRIENTS FROM NATURE—VITAMINS
The word *vitamin* is a combination of two Latin words: *vita* for life, and *amine*, because vitamins were thought to contain amino acids. The "e" was dropped when researchers realized that vitamins do not contain amino acids.

Fat-Soluble Vitamins
Let's start with the fat-soluble vitamins: A, D, E, and K. In order to absorb these four, we need to have adequate fat in the diet. Healthy fats are also sources of some of these vitamins.

A—needed for good vision and skin
Follicular hyperkeratosis, a skin condition characterized by buildup of cellular debris in hair follicles, gives the skin a permanent goose-bump appearance and is a common sign of deficiency, as are night blindness and increased infections.

Carotenes are precursors to vitamin A.

Food sources: cod liver oil, liver, raw butter, eggs, dairy

Carotenes: dark leafy greens, yams, sweet potatoes, squashes, carrots

D—both a vitamin and a hormone

Also known as the "sunshine" vitamin, because we can make this vitamin by being in the sun. However, if sunscreen is used, our skin cannot absorb the UVB rays necessary to make this vitamin.

Vitamin D is needed for healthy bones and feeling happy. Recent studies show that adding adequate D supplementation helps with clinical depression. It is also cancer preventive.

Food sources: cod liver oil, liver, eggs, mushrooms

E—known as the antisterility vitamin

Indeed, the Greeks knew of the importance of this vitamin, calling it *tokos*, which means "offspring," and *phero*, which means "to bear."

Vitamin E helps protect the cell membrane and acts as an antioxidant that helps prevent heart disease. It also increases blood circulation to the brain, thus improving memory.

A high intake of polyunsaturated oils (vegetable oils) requires a lot of vitamin E to balance the omega-6 fatty acid.

Food sources: nuts, seeds, oils, whole grains, wheat germ, avocado, sunflower seeds

K—known as the clotting vitamin

So known because it allows normal clotting of blood. It helps prevent hemorrhagic disease in newborns and also excessive menstrual bleeding.

In addition, vitamin K plays a role in bone health and deters calcification of arteries.

Our gut bacteria can make it, but our digestion needs to be healthy.

Food sources: dark leafy greens such as kale, collard greens, Swiss chard, spinach; green tea; broccoli; fermented food such as sauerkraut

Water-Soluble Vitamins

C—common, but oh so important!

Greatly underused in spite of its fame. We need to take more C. Scurvy is the most famous sign of deficiency.

This vitamin is critical for the formation of collagen (connective tissues, cartilage, tendons). It prevents easy bruising. Highest concentration is found in the brain and then the adrenals, which is the home of our stress hormones.

Vitamin C also supports immune function and buffers stress, both physically and psychologically.

Food sources: rose hips, acerola berries, peppers, collard greens, fermented foods such as sauerkraut

B_1 (thiamine)—the first B vitamin discovered

The most famous disease related to B_1 deficiency is "beriberi," which often occurred in populations that consumed polished or dehusked rice and other grains. Concentrations of B vitamins are found in the outer husk, which is stripped away when they are refined.

Food sources: brown rice, sunflower seeds, peanuts, nutritional yeast

(Note that this vitamin is extremely sensitive to tannins which are found in tea and coffee, alcohol, and sulfites. So these compounds should not be combined with foods containing B_1 if you want to boost it in your diet.)

B_2 (riboflavin)—the vitamin that gives your urine that yellow fluorescent glow

Unlike its cousins, riboflavin is not destroyed by cooking, but by light.

Deficiency signs include cracks on lips and corner of the mouth, and problems with vision.

Food sources: liver, almonds, mushrooms, whole grains, dark leafy vegetables.

B_3 (niacin)—can be made in the body from the amino acid tryptophan

Niacin plays an essential role in energy production and regulation of blood sugar, as well as maintaining healthy cholesterol levels. It is also an important cofactor in hormonal and adrenal health.

Food sources: eggs, fish, peanuts, nutritional yeast, brown rice

B_5 (pantothenic acid)—known as the "antistress" vitamin, central to adrenal function and cellular metabolism

This B-vitamin is needed for the manufacturing of red blood cells and synthesis of cholesterol, and to maintain a good balance of LDL to HDL. Food sources: liver and organ meats, milk, fish, poultry, nutritional yeast, sweet potatoes

B_6 (pyridoxine)—one of the most important B-vitamins, when it comes to overall health

Deficiency can lead to depression, convulsions, glucose impairment, anemia, nerve problems, and eczema. It is also a cofactor for transforming tryptophan into serotonin.

Food sources: whole grains, legumes, seeds and nuts, Brussels sprouts, cauliflower

Biotin—needed in the utilization of fats and amino acids

It is manufactured by our gut bacteria and can also be obtained from food.

Food sources: nutritional yeast, liver, eggs, mushrooms, nuts

Folic acid—also known as folate or folacin, works with B_{12}

It is one of the most commonly deficient vitamins worldwide. Deficiency affects fast-dividing cells of the digestive and genital tracts, so can result in abnormal pap smears. Low folic acid may also cause depression, insomnia, forgetfulness, and shortness of breath.

Folic acid got its name from the Latin word *folium*, which means "foliage," since high concentrations are found in edible leafy plants such as kale, spinach, and chard.

Food sources: nutritional yeast, dark leafy greens

B_{12} (cobalamin)—one of the most important B vitamins

It works along with folic acid in many pathways. A severe deficiency leads to a deadly condition known as *pernicious anemia*. B_{12} is only found in animal foods, so strict vegetarians need to use its supplemental form.

Deficiency in this vitamin can lead to nerve damage, depression, dementia-like symptoms, and anemia.

Food sources: liver, eggs, cheese, meat, fish

NUTRIENTS FROM NATURE—MINERALS

Dr. Linus Pauling, winner of two Nobel Prizes, said, "You can trace every sickness, every disease, every ailment, ultimately to a mineral deficiency."

Calcium—most abundant mineral in the body

Maintains alkalinity and affects release of neurotransmitters. It is involved with heart and bone health.

Deficiency can cause depression, anxiety, and insomnia.

Food sources: dairy, sea vegetables, dark leafy greens, sesame seeds, bone broth

Phosphorus—involved in forming bones and teeth, energy production, and cell repair
Food sources: meat, dairy, eggs, legumes, nuts

Potassium—we lose a lot of this mineral through sweat
It is an electrolyte that works with chloride and sodium.
Deficiency can lead to mental and emotional apathy, thirst, insomnia, fatigue, racing pulse, and nausea.
Food sources: apples, avocados, squashes, bananas

Sulfur—needed by our joints and connective tissues, and for healing wounds
Food sources: eggs, meat, fish, poultry, kale, cabbage, broccoli, legumes, garlic, onions

Sodium—helps regulate body fluids and boosts nerve and muscle function
Food source: sea salt

Chloride—maintains the body's fluid balance and digestive juices
Food sources: most chloride is consumed with sodium, since chloride is a component of table salt, though table salt is extremely unhealthy. (More information on table salt in chapter 8.) Use sea salt instead.

Magnesium—calms the nervous system and works in tandem with calcium to maintain heart and bone health
About sixty percent of the magnesium in our bodies is actually found in the bones. Like calcium, magnesium maintains alkalinity. Other organs that need magnesium are the heart, kidneys, brain, and liver.
Deficiency leads to agitation, irritability, sleep disturbances, mental confusion, muscle cramps, and predisposition to stress.
Food sources: sea vegetables, cashews, almonds, dark leafy greens, mineral broth (recipe, page xxv).

Zinc—needed by every cell in the body
Without zinc, our thyroid would not function and we wouldn't be able to produce sex hormones or insulin. Vision, taste, and smell are also affected by zinc.

Low zinc leads to smell and taste problems, as well as skin-related issues such as eczema, psoriasis, and acne.

Zinc is highly concentrated in red and white blood cells. It is deficient in those with Alzheimer's.

Food sources: oysters, shellfish, grass-fed meats such as beef and lamb, pumpkin seeds

Boron—a trace mineral linked with calcium and magnesium metabolism

Food sources: fruits and vegetables

Chromium—extremely important in blood sugar regulation

Chromium helps insulin work properly and helps with weight loss. Especially important for people with diabetes.

Food sources: meats and whole grains; found in high amounts in nutritional yeast

Copper—third-most-abundant trace mineral after zinc and iron

The highest amounts are found in the brain and liver. Copper works with iron and zinc and controls tissue repair, elastin growth, and red blood cell formation.

Food sources: oysters, shellfish, legumes, Brazil nuts

Iodine—needed for thyroid function

Deficiency leads to goiters. Thyroid malfunction leads to depression and other mood issues.

Food sources: seafood, seaweed, sea salt

Iron—absolutely imperative to our existence

Iron is at the center of the molecular structure of our red blood cells, facilitating oxygen delivery to our lungs and tissues and CO_2 transportation from tissues to the lungs.

Iron deficiency is the most common deficiency in the U.S., especially among women. Deficiency can lead to anemia, fatigue, and restless leg syndrome.

Food sources: liver, beef, kelp, nutritional yeast, blackstrap molasses

Manganese—helps with sprains and inflammation

Manganese also helps regulate sugar metabolism.

Deficiency leads to disruption of normal growth and metabolism, skin rashes, hair loss, low HDL, and infertility.

Food sources: pecans, Brazil nuts, cacao powder, sesame seeds, oysters and shellfish, brown rice, garbanzo beans

Molybdenum—involved in uric acid and sulfur metabolism, and alcohol detoxification

Deficiency may manifest as having allergies to sulfur-containing foods.

Food sources: legumes, whole grains, nuts

Selenium—works with vitamin E and a powerful antioxidant enzyme, *glutathione peroxidase*, to prevent cellular damage

Selenium enhances the immune system, stimulates white cell growth, and helps with thymus function.

Selenium is important to soil quality. Studies show that cancer rates are higher in regions where the soil is depleted of this element.

Food sources: Brazil nuts (very high), fish, pork, bacon, oysters, liver

Silicon—second-most-abundant element, after oxygen

Silicon is critical for skin, ligaments, tendons, and bones. It helps with thickening of skin and hair growth.

Food sources: whole grains, oatmeal, root vegetables

Vanadium—named after the Norse goddess of beauty (Vanadïs, or Freya)

Helps with blood sugar balance by acting like insulin.

Food sources: black pepper, dill seeds, scallops, cod

Case Study

Christine held a great job as an account executive and used to be an avid long-distance runner, until she started to suffer joint pains. While it is not unusual to experience inflammation of the joints now and then, Christine was particularly worried because both her mother and older sister were diagnosed with rheumatoid arthritis in their mid-thirties. Results from her blood test showed that she had *megaloblastic anemia,* an iron deficiency due to low B_{12} and/or folic acid. She also had borderline hypothyroidism. With all these health issues troubling her, she started to feel depleted and depressed.

Because she didn't want to go on prescription drugs, she decided to consult with me and see if a change in diet could help her.

Although she thought she ate well, when I examined her current food choices, I realized that she was not getting enough protein for her level of activity and stress. She had also been on several rounds of antibiotics in the past two years due to repeated urinary infections.

Our first step was to help repopulate her gut with healthy bacteria, which were depleted by the use of antibiotics. So I asked her to include yogurt and fermented vegetables, such as raw sauerkraut, as part of her diet, along with probiotic supplements. Then I created a protocol that would boost her intake of nutrients, especially the B vitamins, folic acid, and iron.

To address her concern about developing rheumatoid arthritis, we concentrated on an anti-inflammatory diet, which meant removing gluten, processed sugar, and coffee.

I also encouraged her to use anti-inflammatory herbs and spices, especially turmeric and ginger, when she cooked at home. Adding small amounts of seaweed, along with an improvement in digestion and diet, helped with her thyroid health.

Since Christine really wanted to get rid of her joint pains and prevent the rheumatoid arthritis that plagued her family, she was diligent in following my suggestions. When I checked in with her about two months into her protocol, she was feeling really positive and was happy that she was well again. A follow-up blood test by her doctor showed that she was no longer anemic, and there was also improvement in her thyroid results.

Notes for Chapter 1
1 Michael Murray ND, *Encyclopedia of Nutritional Supplements* (New York: Three Rivers Press, 1996), 283.
2 Janette Brand Miller et al., "Paleolithic Nutrition: What Did Our Ancestors Eat?" 35th Professor Harry Messel International Science School: Genes to Galaxies, Lecture, July 13, 2009, http://www.scienceschool.usyd.edu.au/history/2009/media/lectures/4-brand-miller-chapter.pdf
3 Michael A. Schmidt, *Brain-Building Nutrition: How Dietary Fats and Oils Affect Mental, Physical, and Emotional Intelligence* (Berkeley: Frog Books), 8.
4 Joseph Mercola MD, "Fat, Not Glucose, is the Preferred Fuel for Your Body," August 10, 2012, http://fitness.mercola.com/sites/fitness/archive/2012/08/10/fat-not-glucose.aspx
5 John Briffa MD, "The French Paradox Is Not a Paradox," October 2, 2012, http://www.drbriffa.com/2012/10/02/the-french-paradox-is-not-a-paradox/
6 Mary Enig and Sally Fallon, *Eat Fat, Lose Fat* (New York: Hudson Street Press, 2005), 159.

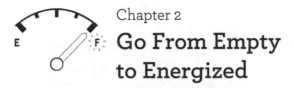

Chapter 2

Go From Empty to Energized

We are indeed much more than what we eat, but what we eat can nevertheless help us to become much more than what we are.
—ADELE DAVIS

CAUSES OF FATIGUE

Do you start the day struggling to wake up after tumbling out of bed? Are you a zombie until you get that first jolt of coffee into your veins, then need another brew before midmorning in order to make it until noon? Do you feel like you're in a murky slow-motion movie by 3:00 p.m., and find it nearly impossible to concentrate? Do you cancel evening engagements because you are just plain worn out after work?

What's causing you to move like molasses when you used to flow like a babbling brook? You could blame it on a heavy workload, bad relationships, or perhaps even a sting by the tsetse fly, but the simple truth may be that you've lost your oomph due to poor diet, stress, and energy-depleting habits.

In this chapter, we will look at the causes that zap us of vitality, and turn the spotlight on nutrient-dense foods and lifestyle changes that will end fatigue and bring the spark back to your life.

What is energy? Well, as humans, we derive most of our fuel through eating. Just as plants transform sunlight into energy by the process of photosynthesis, we transform edibles into fuel through metabolism. When we eat or drink something, our incredible digestive system breaks down long chains of molecules into smaller components, which are then utilized by our cells for energy.

Before we explore the rich cornucopia of delectable foods and excellent actions that we can take to infuse our days with exuberance, let's take a look at two very important endocrine glands: the thyroid and the adrenals. They are the wellsprings that drive metabolism, and thus affect our ability to generate energy.

. . . .

WHAT AND WHERE ARE YOUR ENDOCRINE GLANDS?

Your endocrine glands are part of a system that produces hormones to regulate your body's growth, metabolism, sexual development, and function. Hormones are released from these glands and then transported to tissues and organs throughout your body. The endocrine gland system includes: hypothalamus, pineal, pituitary, thyroid, heart, thymus, adrenals, kidneys, pancreas, ovaries, and testes.

. . . .

THE THYROID: FRAGILE YET POWERFUL

Picture an iridescent, beautiful fluttering butterfly at the center of your throat.

The thyroid gland, located at the base of your neck just below your Adam's apple, is often compared to a butterfly because it is shaped like one. It has two wings, or lobes, which lie on either side of the windpipe. Just as butterflies are an indication of the state of our environment and ecosystem, the health of your thyroid is a reflection of the ecology of you! Therefore, you should nourish and protect your thyroid as you would an endangered species of butterfly. Like them, we can experience serious damage to our well-being and existence by polluting factors such as pesticides, toxic water, exposure to radiation, and lack of proper sustenance.

. . . .

THE FALSE PROMISE OF FLUORIDE

Touted as being good for our teeth, fluoride is one of the most damaging chemicals for your thyroid. Added to many municipal water systems, fluoride causes depletion of iodine, which is needed for production of *thyroxine*, a thyroid hormone.[1]

32

What's more, when iodine is depleted, it depletes our immunity. Blood circulates through the thyroid every seventeen minutes, and the presence of iodine, a powerful germ killer, will weaken any invading pathogens, thus supporting our immune system to rid the body of dangerous invaders.

Fluoride also causes damage to the pineal gland, which is the source of two mood-enhancing and health-supporting hormones: melatonin and serotonin.[2]

To make matters worse, fluoride does not protect our pearly whites. Rather, constant exposure to fluoride (through water and toothpaste) can lead to *fluorosis,* a defect of tooth enamel caused by fluoride's interference with tooth-forming cells. The condition shows as cloudy spots, streaks, brown stains, and even tooth erosion.[3]

• •

In order to fully appreciate what the thyroid does, let's take a closer look at several key functions performed by our internal "butterfly":

The thyroid moves, stores, and releases thyroid hormones T3 and T4 into your bloodstream. These thyroid hormones affect every cell of your body, and thus your metabolism.

If you have too much T3 and T4 circulating, your body could be in hyper mode, causing hyperthyroidism. If you have too little, your metabolism will slow down, leading to hypothyroidism.

Thyroid-Supportive Ingredients

- Coconut oil: helps nourish the thyroid and rev up metabolism.
- Seaweed: contains iodine, which is needed to produce thyroid hormones. (Eating too much seaweed can have a negative effect on the thyroid, so moderation is key. See sidebar for more information.)
- Mushrooms: contain the trace mineral selenium, which helps in conversion of T4 to T3. T3 is the form used by your cells for energy production.
- Nutritional yeast: Contains B vitamins, which are cofactors in the production of adrenal hormones, and help buffer stress. This in turn, affects the thyroid.
- High tyrosine-containing foods: grass-fed chicken, beef, or

lamb, plus eggs, nuts, and avocados. Tyrosine is an amino acid, which is a precursor for thyroid hormones.

- Lacto-fermented foods such as sauerkraut, kimchi, and yogurt. A healthy balance of gut flora helps in the conversion of thyroid hormones, so foods containing good bacteria are a vital contribution.[4] Probiotics such as lactobacilli strains support the immune system, and strengthen digestion.

• •

SEAWEED IS SUPER IN SMALL DOSES

While sea vegetables are rich in bioavailable minerals, eating more is not better. Like other superfoods, seaweed provides many health benefits when we eat it on a regular basis, but in small amounts. In addition to minerals and vitamins, iodine is what helps maintain good thyroid function. Too much can have the opposite effect of slowing down the thyroid, so enjoy seaweed, but in measured amounts.

Here are four of my favorites:

Nori: This is perhaps the most familiar sea vegetable to many people, since it is used in wrapping sushi. It comes in pressed sheets and is readily available in most supermarkets.

Please steer clear of brands that add sugar or MSG, plus other "natural" flavors.

Recommended amount: one half to one sheet per day.

Kombu: This variety is also known as kelp, and can be found as long dried strips. It is added to make the traditional Japanese broth, *dashi*. Dried kombu needs to be soaked in water before using. It can be added to grains in cooking and to soups or stews and even legumes for a boost of minerals.

Recommended amount: one square inch (dried measurement) daily.

Dulse: This is a beautiful red-purple seaweed found in Ireland and Canada. Dulse has a delicate flavor and is really easy to prepare; soaking is not necessary.

Recommended amount: one tablespoon daily.

Hijiki: Although this variety is known to have the highest calcium content of all seaweeds, it has been linked with arsenic contamination. For this reason, I recommend that hijiki be consumed only sparingly, and make certain that it is organic.

• •

Foods That Suppress Thyroid

- Raw cruciferous vegetables: cauliflower, cabbage, broccoli, kale, and other vegetables in the *Brassica* family contain sulfur compounds, which confer many health benefits. However, they are also *goitrogenic*, meaning that overconsumption can cause hypothyroidism. This issue is greatly mitigated when these vegetables are cooked or fermented, as in raw sauerkraut. So enjoy them cooked or fermented, and minimize eating coleslaw or juicing with these greens.
- Soy: Also known as a goitrogen, because, like raw cruciferous vegetables, it depletes iodine reserves and can upset hormonal balance. In addition, many soy products are made from GMO soybeans.
- Wheat and other gluten grains: Refer to chapter 1 on gluten, page 13.
- Refined sugar
- Coffee

• •

IRON UP

Anemia affects some 3.5 million Americans, and is one of the primary causes of fatigue. Your red blood cells are responsible for carrying oxygen throughout your body, and they need iron to do their job and to make new red blood cells.

According to Dr. Datis Kharrazian, an expert on thyroid health, anemia needs to be treated before true healing begins.[5] Here are a few things to consider:

- Do a blood test to see if you are anemic.
- Eat vitamin B_{12} and iron-rich foods regularly. (Iron from animal products is more bioavailable to us than iron from plants.)

- Take a digestive enzyme, use herbal digestive bitters before a meal, or eat raw sauerkraut and other fermented foods to help with digestion and assimilation of iron-containing foods.
- Soak grains overnight or for at least six hours before cooking to minimize the presence of *phytates*, compounds found in seeds that inhibit mineral absorption. (See recipe for Perfect Brown Rice, page 97.)

• •

TREAT YOUR THYROID STEW
YIELD: 4 servings

2 tablespoons coconut oil
½ medium onion, sliced
1 garlic clove, minced
8 to 10 fresh shiitake mushrooms, stems removed and sliced
1 strip kombu,* about 2 inches by 1 inch, soaked for 10 minutes in water, then sliced into thin strips
1 small sweet potato, diced (about 2 cups)
1 small zucchini, cubed
½ chicken broth or filtered water
½ cup coconut milk
½ teaspoon turmeric
¼ teaspoon cayenne
½ teaspoon sea salt, or more as needed
freshly ground pepper, to taste
handful of cilantro leaves, for garnish

*Kombu is a type of seaweed. It can easily be found in most health food stores or Asian markets.

Heat a medium pot on high heat, and add the coconut oil to melt.

Toss in the onion and garlic and sauté for about one minute, or until onion is translucent.

Add all the rest of the ingredients except cilantro and allow to simmer with cover on until the sweet potatoes are tender, about 20 minutes.

Check seasoning, and add more salt or cayenne as needed.

Garnish with cilantro.

Delicious over cooked brown basmati rice or quinoa.

ADRENALS: TINY POWERHOUSES

A symbiotic relationship exists between the thyroid gland and the adrenals. Much like two riders on a bicycle built for two, these two endocrine glands need to work in tandem in order for us to be in balance.

In the Introduction, we learned that the adrenals are known as the "glands of stress." These tiny little organs sit on top of our kidneys, one on each side. Like our thyroid, they are small and lightweight, but have powerful effects on our health and how we feel.

Here's a list of hormones produced by the adrenals and what they do:

Epinephrine (adrenalin)

Both a stress hormone and a neurotransmitter. When we encounter danger or stress, epinephrine sharpens our focus, increases oxygen, blood flow, and muscle strength to prepare the body for the fight-or-flight response. Excess epinephrine can bring on anxiety and hyperactivity.

Norepinephrine (noradrenalin)

A counterbalance to epinephrine, helping the body to return to homeostasis after release of adrenalin. Norepinephrine also helps elevate mood, motivation, sexual arousal, and memory.

DHEA

A growth hormone that keeps us youthful. It is suppressed by high cortisol.

Pregnenolone

Known as the master hormone because all other hormones start their life cycle as pregnenolone. When stress is high, a lot of pregnenolone will be needed to make cortisol, which means that other hormones will become depleted.

Progesterone

A critical hormone in females for healthy pregnancy and balancing actions of estrogen. It is also needed by males to relax muscles of the bronchi and for bone health. Progesterone helps reduce anxiety for both sexes.

Estrogens

Although estrogens are primary produced in the ovaries, the adrenal glands, liver, and breasts can also make them. These secondary sources become important for women going through menopause. Men also produce estrogens, but in far smaller amounts than women.

Testosterone

Although associated with men and maleness, testosterone is also necessary for women to maintain a lean physique, muscle mass, libido, and good mood.

Androstenedione

Converts to estrogen and testosterone in both men and women.

Cortisol

A hormone released in times of stress. It signals insulin to rise and triggers the body to store fat. However, cortisol also helps quell inflammation, regulates blood pressure, and heightens cognitive function when we are stressed.

Aldosterone

Helps maintain the balance of sodium to potassium, therefore regulating fluid retention and affecting kidney health.

Suboptimal adrenal function is caused by poor eating habits and chronic stress. For example, if you are stuck on that Mammoth Mega Rush rollercoaster ride (as explained in the Introduction), your adrenals are driven relentlessly to pump out cortisol and will eventually be exhausted, leading to what is commonly called *adrenal fatigue*. Once they fizzle out, from either too many junky meals or emotional upheavals, the body will go into a state of catabolism. Sounds bad? It is.

You see, when cortisol output is constantly high, your little adrenal glands will be pushed to their limits. As a result, the body will try to compensate by breaking down collagen and protein to generate energy.

In those bygone days when life was gentler and slower, we had time to relax, smell the roses, and allow our adrenals to recover. However, in today's cyber-hyper world, filled with traffic jams, financial worries, and addiction to wired devices, we never get a chance to relax deeply. And if you are constantly chomping down fast foods and sodas, the catabolic state will continue unabated. When proteins (collagen, muscles) are broken down and not adequately replaced, signs of premature aging start to show: wrinkles and lackluster skin on the outside, organs becoming clogged and worn-out on the inside, while joint and muscle pains may develop after physical activity.

So, in an attempt to deal with this degradation, your body will push the brakes on production of thyroid hormones, and overall metabolism slows down. As a result, energy wanes, and weight starts to pile on. And since the thyroid and adrenals help produce neurotransmitters, they will also be affected, which can result in a plummet in cognitive health and good mood. The feel-good neurotransmitters, such as serotonin, GABA, and dopamine, will drop, leading to anxiety, deep dark blues, fatigue, and more stress as you worry over why you are so stressed and depressed! It becomes a relentless cycle until you take the necessary steps to exit the endless loop, by starting with a healthy diet.

Adrenal-Supporting Ingredients:
- Organic protein from free-range animals (poultry, eggs, beef, lamb)
- Adaptogenic herbs such as ginseng, ginger, and gingko
- Maca, a powder made from a Peruvian radish. It can be easily added to a drink, smoothie, or healthy sweet treats (Maca Mocktail recipe, page 48)
- Alkalinizing foods such as dark leafy greens, squashes, and mineral broth (recipe, page xxv)

Adrenal-Depleting Ingredients:
The same list as those that deplete your thyroid (page 35), plus:
- Table salt: Common processed salt is stripped of minerals and nutrients, and can cause excess sodium retention, which strains your kidneys, as well as your adrenals. Always use a good-quality sea salt. See the Shopping Guide at the end of chapter 8 for recommendations.
- Caffeine and other adrenal stimulants, such as energy drinks
- Skin care or household products with toxic man-made chemicals
- Exposure to plastic compounds such as *phalates*, which are found in plastic water bottles and canned foods.

ADORE YOUR ADRENALS SOUP

YIELD: 4 servings

1 tablespoon ghee or coconut oil
2 boneless free-range chicken breasts, cut into cubes
½ teaspoon sea salt, or more, as needed
1 small onion, diced
4 celery ribs, cut into ¼-inch slices
4 cups chicken stock, mineral broth, or filtered water
2 teaspoons grated fresh ginger
1 teaspoon ground coriander
1 bunch chard or kale, stems removed and cut into thin strips
1 cup cooked brown rice (optional)
freshly ground pepper, to taste

Heat a medium pot on medium-high heat, and melt the ghee or coconut oil.

Add chicken pieces and brown them on all sides. Season with sea salt.

Add all the rest of the ingredients except the kale and simmer for about 30 minutes.

Add kale or chard, and continue to cook on low heat for 10 minutes more. Add the rice at this point if you want a thicker soup.

• •

SUSPECT THYROID OR ADRENAL TROUBLES?

Thyroid: Ask your healthcare practitioner for a complete thyroid panel test, which includes:

- TSH
- free T4 and total T4
- free T3 and total T3
- thyroid-binding globulin
- reverse T3 and T3 Uptake
- anti-TPO

Adrenals: Levels of cortisol, DHEA, and other stress-related hormones can be measured through a saliva test. Most healthcare practitioners can provide you with access to testing.

There are many symptoms related to thyroid and adrenal

problems that are beyond the scope of *Happy Foods*. However, following the guidelines on healthy eating and habits in this book is the path to maintaining or recovering your endocrine system's health.

• •

SNOOZE SOLUTION

Good, deep sleep is another factor that profoundly influences our energy level and sense of wellness. In fact, sleep is so important that I am devoting an entire chapter to it (chapter 4). Meanwhile, here are a few salient sleep tips to help you enter slumberland, so that you can awaken refreshed and ready to tackle the day.

- Get to bed by 10:00 p.m. Why? Because we need to follow nature's circadian rhythm. A normal cycle means that cortisol rises in the morning, and drops to its lowest point at night. If you "burn the midnight oil," the cycle will get out of sync. Staying up late causes cortisol to surge again, giving us that "second wind." It may feel good temporarily, but this prevents a good night's rest, and you pay for it in the morning and the rest of the day.
- Set an alarm to go off at 9:00 p.m. to remind yourself to wind down. Dim the lights and turn off the TV and all electronic devices. Do something soothing, such as deep breathing exercises, meditate, or read a calming book before snuggling into your bed.
- If you have trouble falling asleep, add a few drops of lavender oil and Epsom salts or Dead Sea salts to your bath. To a hot bath, add two to four cups of Epsom salts and three to five drops of lavender oil. Slip in and feel the relaxation! How does it work? Epsom or Dead Sea salts contain magnesium that will be absorbed through your skin, helping relieve muscle tension and aches and pains. Epsom salts contain magnesium and sulfates, while Dead Sea salt also has other minerals such as potassium and calcium.
- Get adequate physical activity during the day, but refrain from intense exercise after 5:00 p.m. Why? Again, it has to do with circadian rhythm. Intense exercise, such as jogging

or weight lifting, are a form of stress to the body, and trigger the upsurge of cortisol. Remember, we want cortisol to taper off at night. A good option is to take a slow, relaxing stroll, or do calming yoga stretches.

· Keep your cell phone and other wired devices out of your bedroom. Why? The EMF (electromagnetic field) interferes with release of melatonin from the pineal gland.[6] Melatonin is a powerful hormone that regulates deep sleep, acts as an antioxidant, facilitates tissue repair, and calms inflammation, which in turn helps prevent cancer.

See chapter 4, page 119, for more sleep tips.

EXERCISE RIGHT

There's not a doubt that regular exercise helps us stay fit and happy. However, if you are plagued by low energy and sad mood, exercise may be the furthest thing from your mind. But know that exercise increases circulation and oxygen and boosts our happy hormones, such as GABA and serotonin. So, tear yourself away from your laptop, your big screen TV, and other sedentary temptations. Even just a daily twenty–minute walk around your neighborhood is a good start.

Be creative and discerning with exercise. What you want is an activity that increases blood flow, brings fresh air into your lungs, tones your muscles, and maintains flexibility. Don't add more stress by engaging in activities that are grueling or debilitating.

Yoga, breathing exercises, tai chi, swimming, fast walking, dancing, and Pilates are wonderful choices. And remember, making love is also a form of exercise that brings deep joy, plus physical and emotional rewards.

ENERGY-ZAPPING FOODS

Hopefully, by now, you fully appreciate the importance of eating well to nourish your thyroid and adrenals, so that they can work in concert to provide you with vitality and elation. But just in case you still want to pick up a meal at your local drive-thru, let us take a closer look at what happens when you down junk food.

Here are two ingredient labels from a well-known fast-food giant:

Soybean Oil, Buttermilk, Water, Avocado, Enzyme Modified Egg Yolk, Distilled Vinegar, Garlic Juice, Sugar, Salt, Garlic,* Onion,* Natural Flavor, Spice, Cornstarch, Lactic Acid, Potassium Sorbate and Sodium Benzoate Sodium Added as Preservative, Xanthan Gum, Lemon Juice Concentrate, Disodium Guanylate, Disodium Inosinate, Lime Juice Concentrate, Propylene Glycol Alginate, Sodium Acid Pyrophosphate, Sodium Alginate, Ascorbic Acid, Citric Acid, Calcium Disodium EDTA Added to Protect Flavor, Blue # 1. *Dehydrated CONTAINS: MILK, EGGS

And that's just the dressing! Of the 28 ingredients listed, 12 are preservatives that have been linked to cancer or are endocrine disruptors.

Water, Enriched Flour (Wheat Flour, Niacin, Reduced Iron, Thiamin Mononitrate, Riboflavin, Folic Acid), Apples, High Fructose Corn Syrup, Shortening (Partially Hydrogenated Soybean and/or Cottonseed Oil With TBHQ And Citric Acid To Protect Flavor), Modified Food Starch, Sugar, Brown Sugar, Canola Oil With TBHQ (Preservative). Contains 2 percent Or Less Of: Ascorbic Acid, Baking Soda, Caramel Color, Cellulose Gum, Citric Acid, Dextrin, Dextrose, Dough Conditioner (Sodium Metabisulfite), Maltodextrin, Margarine (Palm Oil, Soybean Oil, Salt, Mono- and Diglycerides, Annatto Color, Calcium Disodium EDTA [Preservative], Artificial Flavors, Vitamin A Palmitate), Natural and Artificial Flavor (Natural and Artificial Flavor, Flour, Sugar, Cornstarch, Unsalted Butter, Salt, Soy Lecithin, Dextrose, Polysorbate 80, Xanthan Gum, Annatto Color), Nonfat Dry Milk, Salt, Whey, Xanthan Gum. Oil: High-Oleic Low-Linolenic Canola Oil, TBHQ (To Protect Flavor), Dimethylpolysiloxane (An Antifoaming Agent). CONTAINS: WHEAT, MILK, SOYBEANS

This second list of ingredients is for a kind of hot apple pie. I don't know about you, but when I crave an apple pie, I just want sweet apples and a nice crispy crust.

When there are so many types of artificial preservatives, coloring, flavor enhancers, and processed oils in a "food," the liver and kidneys, which are involved with filtration and detoxification, are burdened with a huge toxic load, which adds to overall stress for your thyroid and adrenals. Not to mention the blood sugar yo-yo havoc brought on by the presence of high-fructose corn syrup and other starches.

In short, all those man-made chemicals will accumulate as toxins and damage your body, causing weight gain, hormonal disruption, and yes, even depression.

Note: Worried that you have accumulated toxins and extra fat cells? Don't worry—learn how to detox in chapter 6.

. . . .

THE LIVER AND KIDNEYS CONNECTION

This is a short list of how these two organs work together to keep us clean and healthy.

Waste Removal: In addition to our digestive system, the liver is instrumental in breaking down the foods we eat into energy. During this process, ammonia is formed and is converted to a compound called *urea*. Urea travels through the blood to the kidneys, which excrete it as urine.

Blood Pressure Balance: Our blood pressure depends on the concentrations of water and sodium in the blood. When the kidneys sense a decrease in blood flow, it will signal the liver to produce a hormone that tells the kidneys to retain sodium and water.

Vitamin D and Calcium: When we enjoy sunshine without suntan lotion, skin cells react with the sun and make a chemical that the liver converts into a form of vitamin D. This chemical travels to the kidneys via the bloodstream. In the kidneys it is converted to a hormone called *calcitriol*. Calcitriol helps us absorb calcium from food.

. . . .

WHY FOOD ALLERGIES SUCK YOU DRY

Most allergies, including ones caused by food, involve the release of histamine. This infamous substance is produced when the body senses an allergen. Histamine causes swelling (inflammation) so that our immune defense cells can transport themselves to the allergens and zap them. In a normal response, when histamine is released, cortisol follows to bring down inflammation.

So, the more histamine is released, the more cortisol is needed. The demand for cortisol depletes your adrenals, causing adrenal fatigue, which then affects your thyroids. Clearly, it becomes an endless depleting cycle if you keep exposing yourself to allergenic foods. The sad thing is that many people live for years without recognizing that they have food allergies and just assume that discomforts such as indigestion, bloating, or excess gas after eating are normal.

Foods That Trigger Allergies

While the list of foods that trigger allergies is different for everyone, the top six that seem to be most problematic are: gluten-containing grains (wheat, rye, barley, and cross-contaminated oats), soy, dairy, eggs, corn, and peanuts/ tree nuts.

Gluten

It is very hard to digest the protein portion of gluten-containing grains (barley, wheat, rye), and gluten can cause leaky gut and celiac disease.

Symptoms: Bloating, brain fog, irritability, weight gain, joint pains

Soy

An endocrine disrupter that also blocks thyroid function. About ninety percent of soy is GMO.

Symptoms: Feeling cold all the time, sluggish, digestive issues, thyroid problems

Dairy

Modern commercial dairy production uses pasteurization and homogenization, which damage protein and enzymes, making dairy products a challenge to the digestion and the immune system.

Symptoms: Asthma, eczema, psoriasis, and other skin issues. Increased production of phlegm and constant nasal drip are also common symptoms. (Some people may be okay with yogurts and goat or sheep dairy products. Raw dairy may also be an option because it contains the enzyme *lactase* to help break down the milk protein *lactose*.)

Eggs

While eggs are one of the most nutritious foods in the world, many people are allergic to them and they are very difficult to avoid. Choosing eggs from chickens that are not fed GMO soy or corn products and that are one hundred percent pasture-raised or free-range may help. (See sidebar, page 5.) In baked-goods recipes, a flax slurry can be substituted for eggs. (See recipe for Banana & Cherry Muffins, page 56, for directions.)

Symptoms: Digestive discomfort, inflammation, rashes and other skin problems

Corn

GMO, hard to digest, very high carbohydrate content.

Symptoms: Indigestion, skin rashes, constipation, weight gain

Peanuts or Tree Nuts

Peanuts are actually in the legume family, but they present one of the major food allergies in children and adults. Tree nuts include Brazil nuts, cashews, almonds, pecans, hazelnuts, and many others. (If you suspect that you have a nut allergy, the best way to identify it specifically is to do a blood test through your health practitioner.)

Symptoms range from mild discomforts to anaphylactic attacks that require immediate emergency care such as epinephrine shots

As you can see from the list of symptoms, eating foods that you are allergic to is incredibly debilitating and requires a lot of energy from your body to deal with the onslaught.

You can do a blood test to identify specific foods to which you are allergic, or try the detox protocol in chapter 6. The protocol includes removing gluten, soy, and dairy: the major food allergens.

JAVA ROULETTE

If God didn't want us to drink coffee, why are there coffee beans? Good question.

Allow me to present all the reasons why coffee is not good for energy and health, and then you can decide for yourself:

- Impairs liver function. (Your liver needs to detoxify and break down caffeine.)
- Impairs digestion and absorption of nutrients by damaging the lining of your stomach.
- Causes muscular tension that can lead to pain and inflammation.

- Leaches out minerals such as magnesium, calcium, and potassium from the body, increasing the risk of heart disease and osteoporosis.
- Contributes to aging by creating free radicals.
- Weakens the adrenal glands, which can cause fatigue, weight gain, sugar cravings, and anxiety.
- Weakens the immune system, making you more vulnerable to viruses, infections, and cancer.
- Conventionally grown coffee beans are heavily sprayed with pesticides and chemical fertilizers, both of which are toxins that damage our endocrine system.
- Negatively affects sleep patterns.
- Causes depression by depleting B vitamins.

• •

HOW TO WEAN YOURSELF OFF THE BEAN

Days 1–2: Make a blend of ¾ of your regular coffee with ¼ herbal coffee (e.g., Teechino) in a drip coffeemaker or coffee press.

Days 3–4: Blend ⅔ coffee with ⅓ herbal coffee.

Days 5–6: Blend ½ coffee with ½ herbal coffee.

Days 7–8: Blend ⅓ coffee with ⅔ herbal coffee.

Days 9–10: Blend ¼ coffee with ¾ herbal coffee.

Day 11: Drink one hundred percent herbal coffee.

- Swiss water process decaf is okay, but an herbal blend is ideal.
- Use coconut, almond, or hemp milk instead of cream in the herbal blends—yummy!

• •

WHY BOOZE IS BAD

A glass of red wine now and then may be good, but drinking alcohol every day can have a huge negative impact on your energy by upsetting blood sugar balance, resulting in either increased or decreased blood glucose. It also interferes with the assimilation of nutrients from food and can cause deficiencies. In particular, alcohol impairs fat absorption, which means that the fat-soluble vitamins—A, D, E, and K—can become depleted. Like coffee, alcohol also drains the body of B vitamins, which can lead to low mood. Alcohol consumption, especially at night, affects sleep. Needless to say, moderation is a priority. Make it a habit to stop after one drink, and substitute sparkling water in order to rehydrate and to deflect mindless drinking.

Fermented beverages such as kombucha or sparkling water kefirs (recipe, page 49) are excellent alternatives to alcohol.

MACA MOCKTAIL
YIELD: 4 servings

2 cups coconut water (unsweetened)
⅓ cup unsweetened pomegranate juice
1 tablespoon maca root powder
1 tablespoon fresh lime juice
3 cardamom pods, crushed
¼ teaspoon cayenne
2 teaspoons honey
pinch of sea salt
a few ice cubes

Put all ingredients into a blender and blend well.

Strain into cocktail glasses and garnish with a slice of lime.

SPARKLING WATER KEFIR

The first step is to get some water kefir grains. You can order online or get them from someone who is already making them.

The following instruction is from www.culturesforhealth.com. It is for water kefir grains that need to be activated first.

To activate water kefir grains:

Heat 3–4 cups filtered water.

Pour into glass jar.

Dissolve ¼ cup cane sugar in the water.

Cool to 68°–85°F.

Empty entire packet of dehydrated water kefir grains into cooled sugar water.

Cover with a coffee filter or cloth secured by a rubber band.

Put in a warm spot, 68°–85°F, for 3–5 days.

After 5 days, grains should be plump and translucent. They are now ready to make water kefir. Strain off the sugar water and discard it.

To make water kefir beverage:

Heat 3–4 cups filtered water. To make larger batches, use up to 8 cups water.

Pour into glass jar.

Dissolve ¼ cup cane sugar per quart of water.

Cool to 68°–85°F.

Add water kefir grains.

Cover with a coffee filter or cloth secured by a rubber band.

Put in a warm spot, 68°–85°F, for 24–48 hours.

After culturing is complete, prepare a new batch of sugar water (steps 1–4 above).

Separate kefir grains by straining them from the finished water kefir.

Add kefir grains to the new batch of sugar water.

The finished water kefir is now ready to consume. You can add flavorings to it. Store it in the refrigerator.

Avoid aluminum utensils when making water kefir. Stainless steel is acceptable.

Now that we have looked at the reasons why we can be depleted in oomph, let's get to the fun part of what to eat and what habits to embrace for vim and vigor.

WAYS TO ENERGIZE

I begin this section with another quote from legendary nutritionist Adele Davis.

Eat like a King for breakfast, a Prince for lunch,
and a Pauper for dinner.

For those of you who skip breakfast, or think that a cuppa joe fortified with sugar and cream is adequate to start your day, you are in serious trouble!

By the time you wake up, it has been around eight to twelve hours since your last meal, depending on when you finished dinner. While you slumber, your body is working hard to digest your dinner, produce enzymes and growth hormones, facilitate detoxification, and keep your heart pumping, lungs breathing, and brain dreaming.

That takes a lot of energy! So, when you get up, you need to recharge to face the day. Skipping breakfast lowers your metabolism, because your body has very little fuel left for the long day ahead. Not eating breakfast also sets you up for cravings, especially for carbs, which in turn contributes to weight gain and malaise.

Research shows that weight loss is sustained when dieters have breakfast compared to those who don't. Eating breakfast can heighten your metabolism by as much as twenty-five percent.

But not any old breakfast will do. A high-carb/high-sugar breakfast will cause an insulin surge, which leads to high cortisol, which leads to stress.

Breakfast Nos

- No refined, high-carb foods such as bagels, donuts, Danishes, sugar-coated and pressed cereal flakes, or leftover pizza
- No high-glycemic fruits such as mangoes, pineapples, and papaya, including fruit juices or smoothies made from them, especially without adding a high-quality protein powder
- No skipping breakfast

FIVE ENERGIZING BREAKFASTS

MUSHROOM AND HERB SCRAMBLE
YIELD: 1 serving

1 tablespoon butter or coconut oil
6-8 cremini or shiitake mush-
  rooms, sliced
¼ cup chopped fresh dill,
  cilantro, or parsley (or a
  mixture)
2-3 large eggs, pasture-raised or
  free-range, lightly beaten
sea salt and freshly ground
  pepper, to taste

Heat a cast-iron or omelet pan on medium-high heat and add the butter or coconut oil.

Add the sliced mushroom pieces and sauté for about 2 minutes, then add the herb(s).

Pour the eggs onto the mushroom mixture and season with salt and pepper.

Using a wooden spoon, stir or scramble until eggs are cooked through.

AVOCADO COCOA SMOOTHIE
YIELD: 1 serving

1 serving protein powder (see the
  Shopping Guide at the end of
  chapter 8 for best choices)
½ avocado
1 tablespoon tahini
1 tablespoon ground flax seeds
¼ cup coconut milk
1 teaspoon unsweetened cocoa
  powder
¼ teaspoon ground cinnamon
8 ounces filtered water
pinch of sea salt

Put all ingredients into a blender and blend until smooth.

TURKEY SAUSAGES AND SWEET POTATO HASH
YIELD: 1 serving

2 tablespoons coconut oil or ghee
2 cups grated sweet potato
1 green onion, thinly sliced
⅛ teaspoon cayenne (optional)
sea salt and freshly ground
*   pepper, to taste*
2 links turkey sausage, cooked

Heat a cast-iron pan on medium-high heat. Add the oil of your choice.

Mix grated sweet potato, chopped green onion, and cayenne. Put into the pan. Using a spatula, flatten the mixture to a round pancake shape. Allow to cook on one side for about 3 minutes, then flip over and allow to cook for another 3 minutes.

Season with sea salt and pepper.

Remove from pan and serve with the turkey sausages.

AMARANTH PUDDING WITH YOGURT AND WALNUTS

1 cup amaranth, whole grains
3½ cups filtered water
pinch of sea salt
¼ cup yogurt (or coconut milk if
*   you are dairy sensitive)*
¼ cup walnuts, lightly chopped
¼ teaspoon ground cinnamon
1 tablespoon maple syrup

Put first three ingredients in a pot and bring water to boil.

Lower heat to a simmer and cook amaranth, stirring occasionally, until thickened and soft, about 20 minutes. Add more water if it becomes too thick.

Spoon into a serving bowl and top with yogurt or coconut milk, nuts, cinnamon, and maple syrup.

Note: The cooked amaranth will make 2-3 servings. The recipe's topping ingredients are for one serving. Leftover amaranth makes a wonderful afternoon snack. You can try using different nuts, dried fruits, and raw honey instead of maple syrup.

· ·

AMAZING AMARANTH

Amaranth is an ancient grain used by the Aztecs, who believed that these tiny seeds contain magical powers. Well, amaranth is rather special in that it has the highest amount of *lysine* (an important amino acid) and also outshines other cereal grains in protein content. In fact, just 150 grams of amaranth supplies the daily minimum requirement for protein in adults. **Note:** Each individual's requirements may vary, depending on level of activity and state of health.

· ·

SAVORY LENTIL PANCAKES WITH GREEN ONION
YIELD: approx. 12 3-inch pancakes

1 cup green lentils and water for soaking
pinch of sea salt or 1 teaspoon lemon juice
½ teaspoon ground coriander
½ teaspoon ground cumin
¼ teaspoon sea salt
freshly ground pepper, to taste
1 cup filtered water
1½ teaspoons baking powder
2 green onions, thinly sliced
coconut oil or ghee for cooking the pancakes
salsa, chutney, or yogurt, for serving

Put the lentils in a bowl and cover with water by 2 inches. Add the salt or lemon juice. Allow to soak overnight (8–9 hours).

Drain lentils and put in a blender along with all seasoning ingredients, baking powder, and water and blend until smooth.

Pour the lentil mixture into a bowl and fold in the sliced green onions.

Heat a cast-iron pan on medium heat with about 1 tablespoon cooking oil of your choice and spoon a dollop of the batter into the pan to make a 3-inch round pancake. Repeat, making 2 or 3 more, depending on the size of your pan.

Cook on one side for about 5 minutes, then flip to the other side and cook for about 4–5 minutes more. Be patient here, as it takes time to thoroughly cook the lentils. It is helpful to use a paper towel to wipe the pan clean after each round of pancakes.

Serve with salsa, chutney, or yogurt.

Note: These savory pancakes are great for snacking, and also freeze well if you want to make a bigger batch. If you want to do a smaller batch, simply cut the amounts in half.

PICK-ME-UP SNACK IDEAS

- ½ avocado with pinch of sea salt and Dijon mustard
- a slice of turkey or ham wrapped in a leaf of romaine or butter lettuce
- ½ cup cow or goat yogurt with nuts (only if you are not allergic to dairy)
- celery sticks with tahini or other nut butters
- protein smoothie
- handful of sprouted nuts and seeds

• •

BRAIN POWER

Although the brain takes up only two percent of total body weight, it needs over twenty percent of the energy and oxygen that we make to maintain its function.[7] One of the most important omega-3 essential fatty acids for the brain is DHA (*docosahexaenoic acid*). It is found in seafood, eggs, and chickens that are raised on pasture. The amount of DHA greatly depends on what the animals are fed. Studies show that one hundred percent free-range or pasture-raised eggs have anywhere from twenty to fifty percent higher DHA than conventional eggs.[8]

DHA is a structural fat, making up approximately thirty percent of the structural fats in the gray matter of the brain.[9]

• •

HAPPY-BRAIN GRAINLESS SAVORY MUFFINS

YIELD: 6 large muffins

½ cup coconut flour
1 teaspoon baking powder
¼ teaspoon sea salt
⅛ teaspoon cayenne (optional)
5 large eggs, pasture-raised or
  free-range
4 tablespoons coconut oil or
  organic butter, softened
3 ounces zucchini, grated
1 teaspoon grated fresh ginger
¼ cup chopped dill
1 teaspoon lemon zest

Preheat oven to 350°F. Prepare a large muffin pan by lining it with 6 large unbleached paper muffin cups.

In a small bowl, mix the dry ingredients together.

In another larger mixing bowl, lightly beat the eggs.

Add the softened coconut oil or butter to the eggs and mix. Don't worry if the mixture clumps together.

Sift the dry ingredients into the egg mixture a little at a time until well incorporated.

Fold in the grated zucchini, ginger, dill, and lemon zest.

Divide the mixture into the prepared muffin cups.

Bake for about 30 minutes. Test by inserting a toothpick into a muffin; if it comes out clean, they're ready.

BANANA AND CHERRY MUFFINS

YIELD: 12 muffins

These moist and tasty muffins are gluten-free, dairy-free, and egg-free.

Dry ingredients
1½ cups quinoa flour
½ cup brown rice flour
¼ cup tapioca flour
½ teaspoon xanthan gum
1 teaspoon baking powder
1 teaspoon ground cinnamon
½ teaspoon nutmeg
½ teaspoon allspice
¼ teaspoon sea salt

Wet ingredients
2 tablespoons whole flax seeds
6 tablespoons filtered water
½ cup almond, rice, or coconut
　　milk
2 medium bananas, very ripe,
　　with brown spots on the peel
1 tablespoon coconut oil, melted
1 teaspoon vanilla extract
1 cup frozen pitted cherries (keep
　　frozen until ready to add to
　　batter)
1 cup chopped walnuts (optional)

Preheat oven to 350°F. Line a muffin pan with paper liners.

Mix all the dry ingredients together and sift into a medium bowl.

Grind the flax seeds in a spice/coffee grinder.

Make a flax slurry* by mixing the ground flax with the water in a small bowl until it looks gelatinous. Put slurry in the fridge and allow it to set for 30 minutes.

Put flax slurry into a blender, then add the rest of the ingredients (except the cherries and walnuts, if using) and continue to blend for about 30 seconds.

Fold the blended dry ingredients into the wet, then carefully fold in the cherries and walnuts.

Divide the batter into the prepared muffin pan and bake for 35–40 minutes.

* A flax slurry gives binding qualities when eggs are not used. To substitute one egg, use 1 tablespoon ground flax to 3 tablespoons water.

FIVE ENERGIZING LUNCHES

CHICKEN SALAD WITH ORGANIC GREENS AND A MUSTARD-HONEY DRESSING

YIELD: 1 serving

5 ounces cooked chicken, cut into bite-size cubes
4 cups loosely packed organic greens mix
⅓ cup raw sauerkraut (recipe, page 98 or back of book for best brands to purchase)

Put all ingredients in a bowl and toss with about ¼ cup Mustard-Honey Dressing.

MUSTARD-HONEY DRESSING

YIELD: approx. ¾ cup

½ cup extra virgin olive oil
2 teaspoons Dijon mustard
1 tablespoon raw honey
¼ cup apple cider vinegar
1 tablespoon lemon juice
sea salt and freshly ground pepper, to taste
dried herbs or chopped fresh herbs (optional)

Put all ingredients into a clean jar (a recycled nut butter jar is perfect for this task).

Screw the lid on tightly and shake vigorously until dressing is well mixed.

Store dressing in the jar. Use within 5 days.

SPICY TEMPEH CURRY WITH LEMON QUINOA

YIELD: 3-4 servings

1 package tempeh, cut into 1-inch cubes

2 tablespoons coconut oil

1 small onion, diced

1 small carrot, diced

1 tablespoon grated fresh ginger

½ cup coconut milk

1 cup chicken broth, mineral broth, or filtered water

1 cup frozen green peas, thawed

2 teaspoons curry powder

⅛ teaspoon cayenne (optional)

1 tablespoon fresh lime juice

sea salt and freshly ground pepper, to taste

handful of fresh cilantro leaves, for garnish

Steam the cut tempeh pieces for 20 minutes. Set aside.

In a heavy-bottom pot, heat the coconut oil on medium-high heat.

Add the onion, carrot, and ginger. Sauté for about 5 minutes.

Add steamed tempeh pieces, coconut milk, and stock or water.

Lower heat to maintain a gentle simmer. Add the spices, peas, lime juice, and salt and pepper.

Simmer gently for about 15 minutes. If the mixture seems too thick, add a little more stock or water.

Serve over the Lemon Quinoa (recipe follows) and garnish with cilantro.

LEMON QUINOA

1 cup quinoa, rinsed well by placing in a fine mesh colander and run under cold water (If you have time, it is optimal to soak the quinoa for about 4-5 hours with a pinch of salt or a dash of lemon juice. After soaking, drain well.)

1½ cups chicken stock, mineral broth, or filtered water

1-2 tablespoons grated lemon zest

pinch of sea salt

Put the quinoa, liquid of your choice, and salt in a pot.

Bring to a simmer and cover loosely. Cook for 10 minutes. Add the lemon zest.

Remove from heat and put the cover on snugly. Allow to rest for 10 minutes. Fluff with a fork when ready.

LETTUCE CUPS WITH CHICKEN AND AVOCADO

YIELD: 1 serving

4-5 leaves of butter or bibb lettuce, washed and patted dry
4 ounces cooked chicken, cut into cubes
½ avocado, cut into cubes
1 tablespoon extra virgin olive oil
½ teaspoon Dijon mustard
sea salt and freshly ground pepper, to taste
2 tablespoons chopped fresh cilantro or dill
⅓ cup toasted pumpkin seeds

Put all the ingredients except the lettuce in a small bowl and mix well.

Arrange the lettuce cups open side up on a plate and spoon the chicken mixture into the lettuce cups.

Top each prepared cup with a few pumpkin seeds.

SEARED SALMON WITH PEAR AND ARUGULA SALAD

YIELD: 1 serving

½ d'Anjou pear, cut into thin slices
3 cups loosely packed arugula
2 tablespoons extra virgin olive oil
½ tablespoon balsamic vinegar
½ tablespoon nutritional yeast
4-5 ounces wild salmon filet, skin on, rinsed and patted dry
2 tablespoons coconut oil or butter
sea salt, to taste
freshly ground pepper, to taste
⅓ cup chopped almonds or pecans
squeeze of fresh lemon or lime juice

Put the pear slices and arugula in a large bowl.

Drizzle the olive oil and balsamic vinegar over the pear and arugula, and season with nutritional yeast and a little sea salt and freshly ground pepper. Transfer to a plate.

Heat a cast-iron pan on medium-high heat. Add cooking oil of your choice.

Sear the salmon filet for about 2 minutes on the skinless side.

Using a spatula, carefully flip the salmon to the skin side and cook for another 2–3 minutes. (If you like your salmon well done, put a cover over the pan after you flip the salmon. Lower the heat and cook for about 5 minutes.)

Serve the cooked salmon on top of the prepared pear and arugula salad. Top with chopped nuts, and finish with a squeeze of lemon or lime juice.

HAM AND MUSHROOM QUICHE (DAIRY AND GLUTEN FREE)
YIELD: 6–8 servings

For the crust:
1 cup brown rice flour
⅔ cup almond meal
⅓ cup quinoa flour
1 teaspoon xanthan gum
⅛ teaspoon sea salt
6 tablespoons coconut oil, at
    solid state
6 tablespoons cold filtered water
    (or a little more, if needed)

Prepare a 9-inch pie pan by lightly coating it with coconut oil and dusting with brown rice flour. Set aside.

Put the dry ingredients in a bowl and mix well using a fork. Transfer flour mixture to a food processor.

Measure the coconut oil into a small bowl. Be sure that it is at a solid state. (Coconut oil will become liquid when the ambient temperature is too warm.)

Flake the coconut oil in small chunks into the flour mixture.

Pulse a few times, adding water one tablespoon at a time, until the mixture looks like cornmeal. The dough should be moist and just hold together, without being too dry or too wet. It should feel like putty, and should not stick to your hands.

Lightly flour a clean countertop with brown rice flour and turn the dough onto the prepared surface. Very gently knead and shape dough into a disk about 5 inches in diameter. Transfer dough to a large piece of waxed or parchment paper, about 12 inches x 12 inches.

Lightly flour a rolling pin with more brown rice flour and gently roll the dough until it is about ¼ inch thick.

Place the pie pan over the dough and flip the dough onto the pan. Using your fingers, gently press the dough into the pan, trimming off excess dough around the rim.

Using a fork, pierce the dough in several places. This will prevent the dough from rising up when baking.

Chill in the fridge for 30 minutes. Preheat oven to 325°F.

Prebake the crust for 20 minutes.

While the crust is baking, make the filling.

For the quiche filling:

5 large eggs, pasture-raised or free-range

1 cup cooked ham, cut into small cubes

2 green onions, finely chopped

2 cups full-fat unsweetened coconut milk

¼ teaspoon sea salt

¼ teaspoon freshly ground pepper

⅛ teaspoon ground nutmeg

2 tablespoons nutritional yeast

½ tablespoon lemon zest

⅛ teaspoon cayenne (optional)

In a large bowl, beat the eggs until fluffy. Add the rest of the ingredients and whisk together.

When the prebaked crust is ready, remove from the oven and allow it to cool for about 15 minutes. Raise the oven temperature to 350°F.

Carefully pour the filling into the crust and bake for about 35 minutes, or until the filling is set.

Allow the quiche to cool before cutting it.

Serve with a small salad or some raw sauerkraut.

FIVE RELAXING DINNERS

HERBED TURKEY MEATBALLS WITH SPAGHETTI SQUASH
YIELD: 3-4 servings

For the spaghetti squash:
1 spaghetti squash, cut in half lengthwise
1 tablespoon extra virgin olive oil

Preheat oven to 375°F.

Brush the cut sides of the spaghetti squash with olive oil.

Cover a baking sheet with parchment paper, and put squash, cut side down, on the prepared sheet.

Bake for about 30 minutes. The squash is tender when the strands of squash come out easily with a fork.

While the squash is baking, make the meatballs.

For the meatballs:
1 pound ground turkey
2 teaspoons dried sage, or 5-6 fresh sage leaves, finely chopped
2 teaspoons dried oregano
1 large egg, pasture-raised or free-range
1 teaspoon sea salt
freshly ground pepper, to taste
1 tablespoon butter, coconut oil, or lard
1 small onion, diced
1 garlic clove, minced
8 ounces organic tomato sauce (choose one that comes in a glass jar)
1 cup chicken stock or filtered water
¼ teaspoon sea salt
freshly ground pepper, to taste
handful of chopped parsley, for garnish

In a large bowl, mix the ground turkey, herbs, egg, and salt and pepper.

Wet your hands and form the turkey mixture into small round balls about 1½ inches in diameter. Set them on a plate.

Heat a large sauté pan on medium-high heat and add the cooking oil of your choice.

Toss in the onion and garlic, and sauté until the onions are translucent, about 3 minutes.

Add the tomato sauce and chicken stock or water. Add the additional salt and pepper.

Bring to a simmer, then add the meatballs.

Cover loosely with a lid, and allow dish to gently simmer for 20-25 minutes, or until the meatballs are done.

While the meatballs are cooking, check the spaghetti squash. When it is done, remove the strands of cooked squash with a fork into a bowl, and season with a little salt if desired.

To serve:

Portion the spaghetti squash onto individual plates, and top with the meatballs and sauce.

CAULIFLOWER AND CASHEWS WITH NIGELLA SEEDS OVER BASMATI RICE

YIELD: 2 servings

½ tablespoon nigella seeds
2 tablespoons coconut oil or ghee
½ cup chopped onion
1 teaspoon grated fresh ginger
1 small cauliflower, cut into small pieces or florets
½ cup cashews (best if soaked for 3-4 hours in water with a pinch of salt or ½ teaspoon lemon juice)
1 cup frozen peas, thawed
⅓ cup chicken broth or mineral broth
sea salt and freshly ground pepper, to taste
handful of cilantro leaves, for garnish
1-2 cups cooked basmati rice

In a small pan, toast the nigella seeds on medium heat for about 1 minute. Remove the toasted seeds immediately to a small bowl, so as not to overtoast them.

Heat a sauté pan on medium-high heat, and add the cooking oil of your choice.

Add the onion and ginger. Sauté until the onion is translucent, about 2 minutes.

Add the cauliflower pieces, toasted nigella seeds, cashews, peas, and broth. Add sea salt and pepper.

Cover the pan with a lid and allow to cook on medium-low heat until the cauliflower is tender, About 8-10 minutes. Check to make sure that the ingredients are not too dry; add a little more liquid if needed.

Serve over cooked basmati rice, and garnish with cilantro leaves.

THREE-MUSHROOM MEDLEY WITH BROWN RICE
YIELD: 2 servings

*2 tablespoons butter, coconut oil,
or extra virgin olive oil*
2 garlic cloves, minced
1 small onion, diced
*6–8 medium shiitake mushrooms,
sliced*
*8–10 medium cremini mush-
rooms, sliced*
*2 ounces oyster mushrooms, torn
into small pieces*
*1 small bunch kale, stems
removed, cut into strips*
*sea salt and freshly ground
pepper, to taste*
*1 tablespoon lemon juice or apple
cider vinegar*
*1 cup cooked brown rice (recipe,
page 97)*

Heat a large sauté pan on medium heat. Add the cooking oil of your choice.

Add the garlic and onions and sauté until the onion is translucent, about 3–4 minutes.

Toss in the mushrooms and add the salt and pepper. Cook for about 2 minutes.

Add the kale and lemon juice or vinegar.

Cook, stirring, until the kale is wilted and tender.

Serve over brown rice.

PAD THAI RICE NOODLES: *HAPPY FOODS* VERSION
YIELD: 2 servings

2 ounces dried Pad Thai rice
    noodles
2 tablespoons coconut oil
2 garlic cloves, minced
8–10 raw wild shrimp, deveined,
    or 3 ounces raw chicken, cut
    into small cubes
1 large egg, pasture-raised or
    free-range, lightly beaten
2 teaspoons fish sauce (see the
    Shopping Guide at the end of
    chapter 8 for best brand)
2 teaspoons Sucanat
⅛ teaspoon sea salt
2 cups bean sprouts
¼ cup chopped green onion
1 tablespoon lime juice
1 wedge of lime, as garnish
¼ cup toasted pecans or walnuts
    (peanuts are the traditional
    topping: use them if you not
    allergic)

Soak rice noodles in warm water for 10–15 minutes; drain well.

Heat a wok or large sauté pan on medium-high heat and add the coconut oil.

Add the garlic, shrimp, and egg. Stir really well with a wooden spoon until eggs are almost set.

Add the drained noodles to the pan along with the rest of the ingredients except the lime wedge and nuts.

Using two wooden spoons or heat-proof spatulas, stir and toss the noodles while mixing the ingredients together.

Cook until the noodles and bean sprouts are soft.

Transfer to a plate and top with nuts and lime wedge.

EASY ROAST CHICKEN WITH MASHED CELERY ROOT AND SWEET POTATO

YIELD: 4–6 servings

For the chicken:
1 whole chicken, pasture-raised or free-range
1 tablespoon sea salt
2 tablespoons dried dill or 1 tablespoon chopped fresh dill
2 garlic cloves, minced
freshly ground pepper

The secret to a tasty, juicy bird is to rub the seasoning under the skin.

Preheat oven to 425°F.

Mix the salt, dill, and garlic in a small bowl.

Begin by gently inserting your index finger between the skin and the flesh at the breast. Insert a little of the salt, dill, and garlic mixture and rub it in while lifting the skin, working from the base toward the neck.

Repeat the same with the other breast and back of the chicken, then sprinkle freshly ground pepper all over the skin.

With scissors or a paring knife, cut a slit in one leg, just above the last joint (or knuckle) of the leg, and insert the other leg through the cut slit. Doing this will keep the bird nice and tight while roasting to keep in moisture, and to retain its shape.

Line a roasting pan with parchment paper and place a rack over the pan. Lay the seasoned bird on the rack and put in the oven.

After 15 minutes, lower the temperature to 375°F and continue to roast chicken for about 50 minutes, or until the internal temperature reaches 165°F.

For the mashed vegetables:
1 whole celery root, unpeeled
1 sweet potato,* unpeeled
sea salt, to taste
white pepper, to taste
butter or extra virgin olive oil

(Exact quantities are not given with this recipe because celery roots and sweet potatoes come in different sizes. The ratio should be about 50/50. Use your own good taste to determine the amount of salt, pepper, and fat.)

* If you want your mashed vegetables to look like mashed potatoes, get the Japanese or Hannah sweet potatoes, which have a creamy-beige interior. Jewels or Garnets have orange-red interiors.

Bring a large pot of water to a boil.

Put the celery root and sweet potato into the pot, making sure that they are both covered to the top with water. Add more water if needed.

Put the cover onto the pot, slightly ajar to allow steam to escape.

Boil until very tender. The sweet potato will cook a little quicker than the celery root, so check the doneness with a paring knife.

Peel both roots. You may want to run them under cold water so that they are easier to handle.

Rough-cut the vegetables and put the chunks in a large bowl, or back in the pot (minus the water, of course).

Add a good hunk of butter or olive oil, and mash until the mixture is well mashed. You can also mash the chunks in a food processor. The mixture will be very smooth and more starchy done this way.

Season with sea salt and pepper, to taste. If the mixture has cooled too much, simply reheat it in the oven in a heatproof dish until nice and hot. Serve with more butter on top, or an additional drizzle of extra virgin olive oil.

Note: You will notice that these dinner dishes contain more carbohydrates than the breakfast and lunch recipes. Why? During the day, it is absolutely necessary to keep your blood sugar steady with protein and fats. In the evening, a measured amount of carbohydrates, along with foods that provide tryptophan, alkalinizing minerals, and B vitamins will encourage your body to produce serotonin.

FIVE TRULY SUPER SUPERFOODS THAT BOOST ENERGY

Bee Pollen

Contains twenty-two amino acids, minerals, vitamins, and fatty acids along with enzymes. Because bee pollen also has a mild detoxifying effect, some individuals may experience mild allergic reactions when they take it initially.

- Start with a small amount, then build up to about a tablespoon per day.
- Can be added to smoothies, or sprinkled on cooked, gluten-free cereals.
- Avoid pollen that has been dried at temperatures above 130°F.

Maca Root Powder

Made from the root of a radish that is grown on the highlands of Peru at elevations of between eight thousand and 14,500 feet. It is a hardy perennial and was domesticated by the Incas two thousand years ago. It is used by the native Peruvians as food *and* medicine. It is an adaptogen that helps balance the adrenals. Regular use enhances memory, improves immunity, and increases production of sex hormones. Maca is known as the Peruvian ginseng and is touted as a natural Viagra.

- Maca can be very stimulating for some people, so start with a very low dose (about ¼ teaspoon), and build up to no more than one tablespoon a day.
- Unlike some other superfoods that are best in their raw state, maca needs to be roasted for optimal digestion and therapeutic benefits, so choose a maca powder that is toasted and then ground.

Nutritional Yeast

Excellent source of B vitamins (except B_{12}) and also provides amino acids and minerals, including chromium, which helps balance blood sugar. Choose a nutritional yeast that is processed under low heat.

- Great sprinkled over salad for a "cheesy" flavor, or add to soups.

Cod Liver Oil

Important for both children and adults. Cod liver oil provides vitamins A, D, and EPA (eicosapentaenoic acid), an omega-3 fatty acid. All these nutrients are needed for brain function, the nervous system, bone health, and good vision.

Capsules are a good choice for those who cannot muster up the taste buds to deal with the strong and distinct flavor of cod liver oil.

Blue-Green Algae, Spirulina, and Chlorella

These three green superfoods are related and all grown on bodies of freshwater around the world. Indigenous cultures such as the Aztecs of Mexico consumed them as staple foods. They are high in protein, minerals, and carotenoids. Although some producers claim that these algae have vitamin B_{12}, it is not in a form that we can absorb.

- Add these green superfoods to your morning smoothie, or make your own power bar with them.
- Note: They should never be heated.

Summary

- Stress comes in many guises, including a poor diet or the S.A.D. (Standard American Diet), which causes inflammation and nutrient deficiencies.
- Two main endocrine glands, thyroid and adrenals, affect your well-being and energy. Nourish and protect both to ensure vitality and good mood.
- Good-quality sleep is paramount for a steady supply of energy and overall health.
- Breakfast is the most important meal of the day to give you your get-up-and-go.
- Allergies are very draining.
- If nothing else, get off gluten and processed sugar and feel the difference.
- Said it before, I'll say it again! The quickest way to energize is to cut the sugar and carbs, and enjoy high-quality protein and healthy fats with lots of vegetables thrown in.
- Use superfoods to boost nutrients in your diet.

A Perfect Energizing Day

6:30 a.m.: Warm water with fresh lemon juice

Exercise options: Fast walk, burst training, Pilates

7:30 a.m. Breakfast: Avocado Cocoa Smoothie

10:30 a.m. Snack: Apple with Tahini

1:00 p.m. Lunch: Lettuce Cups with Chicken and Avocado

3:30 p.m. Snack: Handful of Crispy Nuts

7:00 p.m. Dinner: Three-Mushroom Sauté with Brown Rice

9:30 p.m.: Alarm rings to wind down

Take bath with Epsom salts and lavender oil

10:30 p.m.: In bed, lights out, and sweet dreams

Case Study

Becky came to see me because she had been taking thyroid medication for a few years. Although she initially felt great on Synthroid, she was now experiencing fatigue and weight gain. In fact, she was suffering from extreme dips of energy throughout the day. She said that sometimes in the middle of her workday she would secretly go to her car in the parking lot, set the alarm on her cell phone, and doze off for twenty minutes so that her coworkers wouldn't find her asleep at her desk. After her snooze, she would guzzle down a strong cup of coffee with cream and sugar to pull her through until 5:00 p.m.

In addition, Becky was a single mom to a mildly hyperactive eight-year-old son, so she needed the energy to keep up with him.

I explained to Becky that gluten negatively affects thyroid health and causes inflammation, digestive troubles, and weight gain. And that she also needed to support her adrenals with herbs and adequate sleep. I asked her to shop for organic meats, vegetables, and healthy cooking oils, such as coconut oil and butter. I designed a one-month menu plan for her and emphasized that she must have a protein-based breakfast every single day. I also asked her to drink coffee only in the morning and then switch to green tea in the afternoon if she absolutely needed some caffeine.

The first few days were rough—she was craving carbs, especially in the afternoon—but she stuck with our protocol because she was sick of feeling tired and puffy all the time. After a month of going gluten-free and eating well, she reported to me that she had lost eight pounds and could get through the day without needing to nap. She was also sleeping a lot better.

At this point, I encouraged her to seek the help of a holistic doctor, who put her on a natural thyroid supplement instead of Synthroid, which is synthetic, and to also use herbs to support her adrenals.

I continued to coach Becky on her menu plans while she worked with a naturopathic doctor. After about three months, her weight stabilized at a healthy point for her physique, and she no longer felt those bouts of fatigue. What's even better is that Becky also got her son off gluten. He is less hyper and is doing much better at school. He has learned from his mom to be aware of what he eats and loves eggs or sausages for breakfast, not a bowl of sugar-laden cereal.

Notes for Chapter 2
1   National Research Council, "Fluoride in Drinking Water: A Scientific Review of EPA's Standards" (Washington, DC: National Academies Press, 2006).
2   Fluoride Alert, "Pineal Gland," http://fluoridealert.org/issues/health/pineal-gland/

3   Christopher Bryson, *The Fluoride Deception* (New York: Seven Stories Press, 2004), 39–40.

4   Donna Gates, *"Is Your Thyroid Healthy? 5 Signs of an Underactive Thyroid,"* http:// bodyecology.com/articles/is-your-thyroid-healthy

5   Datis Kharrazian, DC, *Why Do I Still Have Thyroid Symptoms? When My Lab Tests are Normal* (New York: Morgan James Publishing LLC, 2010), 139.

6   University of Melbourne, Department of Electrical and Electronics Engineering, ePub, October 10, 2012.

7   Michael A. Schmidt, *Brain-Building Nutrition: How Dietary Fats and Oils Affect Mental, Physical, and Emotional Intelligence* (Berkeley: Frog Books), 23.

8   Cheryl Long and Tabitha Alterman, "Meet Real Free-Range Eggs," October 2007, http://www.motherearthnews.com/real-food/free-range-eggs-zmaz07onzgoe. aspx#axzz3I7QSckGW

9   Blaylock, Russell MD, "DHA Supports Brain Development and Protects Neurological Function," January 2008, http://www.lef.org/magazine/2008/1/report_dhafishoil/ Page-01

Chapter 3
Banish Bingeing, Welcome Satisfaction

A diet of overprocessed food goes hand in hand with living an overprocessed life.
—CHARLES EISENSTEIN

CAUSES OF BINGE EATING

Who hasn't wrangled with the demon of gluttony at one time or another? You know, that relentless nagging driving you to grab those slices of leftover pizza, then that piece of cheesecake, then maybe just a few spoonfuls of ice cream, and then rip open that bag of chips for a hit of salt and crunch to round things off.

Most of us have experienced binge eating on some level. I certainly have. There was a time when I would open the fridge door, position myself in front of it, gorge on anything that I could shove into my mouth, and move on to whatever was left in the cupboards.

When I examine my hedonistic food behavior, it presents itself as a parade of boxed cereals, chips, cookies, and takeouts. A dastardly irresistible lineup of processed foods that held me prisoner to an endless cycle of cravings, followed by a tug-of-war with willpower, only to succumb to another gorge-a-thon and then the dark, heavy shadow of remorse and self-loathing settling overhead. It was an exhausting and seemingly endless cycle.

As the title of this book suggests, foods should bring us happiness. But when you are stuck on the binge eating cycle, food is the addiction you hate but can't stop desiring, and instead of being a source of nourishment and joy, it becomes the enemy that inflicts emotional and physical distress.

Fortunately, many health experts and even allopathic doctors are now beginning to realize that binge eating is not simply "mind over matter," but a combination of many factors stacking the odds against us. However, when you learn what these factors are and take action to remove them, you can conquer bingeing and boot it out the door, for good!

We will first look at six major causes of binge eating and then, in the second part of the chapter, learn how to alleviate those bingeing baddies so that balance is restored and food is allowed to bring true comfort and satisfaction.

SIX CULPRITS THAT CAUSE BINGEING
Hormonal Imbalances

You may be surprised that we start off by talking about hormones. Now, everyone's familiar with estrogen and testosterone, but when we look at the big picture of food addiction, there are other hormones that govern our motivation and desires.

Humans produce about fifty different types of hormones. Basically, we are a walking organic laboratory that pumps out clusters of molecules we call hormones. And these hormones are messengers that give instructions to our cells, which then affect the way we behave and feel. Let's take a look at four that are intricately linked with eating.

Dopamine

We want it, we need it, and will do anything to get it! No, it's not an illicit drug, but the hormone dopamine. Strictly speaking, dopamine is both a hormone and a neurotransmitter. It influences well-being, alertness, learning, creativity, attention, and concentration. Dopamine also affects brain processes that control movement, emotional response, and our feeding behavior. Its many powerful effects mean that we constantly need to produce more. However, the conundrum is that it can be increased by healthy means, such as certain whole foods, exercise, or romantic encounters; or unhealthy ways, such as taking heroine, cocaine, and overdosing on junk food.

Dr. David Kessler, author of *The End of Overeating*, says of the food industry:

> By strengthening our sense of anticipation, dopamine gets us to engage in a complex set of pursuit-and-acquisition behaviors so we can recapture the remembered pleasure of a favored food.[1]

74

The link between processed foods and binge eating is no accident. It is a carefully orchestrated science where men and women in white coats move about in sterile labs, engineering foods that will trigger constant craving in us so that we get in our cars, drive to the supermarket and "forage" up and down the supermarket aisles for fake foods that produce transitory pleasure and long-lasting health problems. This is of course aided by billions of dollars worth of swanky advertising. Commercials with attractive actors and hypnotic music seduce us into believing that processed foods are desirable and delicious and trigger the anticipation/reward circuitry in our brains that heighten dopamine. It is one of the sinister ways in which the industrial food giants cause addiction in the gullible consumer.

In essence, the act of acquiring and then gorging on food functions as a drug, or opioid.[2] What's worse, with prolonged overeating the receptors for dopamine can become insensitive, which means that it takes more eating for the binge eater to feel the same "high" as before. How depressing! But don't be too depressed. The second part of this chapter will show you how to take control of your dopamine needs and elevate it with wholesome, real foods, instead of lifeless, chemical-laden fake foods, drenched with additives and cloaked in colorful packages.

Leptin

Also known as the hormone of satiety, leptin is made in fat cells and its message is received in the brain (hypothalamus). In a person with healthy metabolism, when a meal is eaten and fat storage initiates, leptin gives the signal to stop eating. It's a well-designed feedback loop that curbs desire for food because the body has enough fuel. The more fat cells there are, the more leptin will be released. The strange thing is that overweight and obese individuals, who do have plenty of fat and who also have more leptin, are constantly struggling with hypereating. Their brains are not telling them to stop. Why?

There are several factors causing this dangerous disconnect. One is that when too much leptin is made, receptors become resistant to them, leading to leptin resistance. When this happens, the feeling of satiety doesn't set in, causing constant craving for food. Lack of proper sleep also contributes to a leptin handicap, and most insidious of all is the consumption of sugar and high-fructose corn syrup,[3] which we will look at a little later.

• •

YOUR THYROID AND LEPTIN RESISTANCE

Adding insult to injury, when leptin resistance occurs, the thyroid may also take a hit and slow down overall metabolism, because without the cue from leptin, your thyroid won't convert a needed hormone to its active form (T4 to T3). This slowdown of metabolism leads to fatigue and weight gain.[4]

• •

Ghrelin

The counterhormone to leptin is ghrelin, which is made in the stomach. It tells us to eat when the stomach is empty. Constant intake of sugar, high-fructose corn syrup, and high-carb foods, and inadequate sleep and stress can all heighten the gnawing cry of this hunger hormone. And if you combine the negative duo of leptin resistance and nonstop ghrelin, it's a dire situation indeed.

Insulin

Leptin resistance increases insulin resistance. Both cause inflammation in the body and, more importantly, can affect our brain chemistry, leading to mood issues such as depression.[5]

A low-carb diet composed of protein, fats, and plenty of vegetables, along with cutting out sugar and getting adequate sleep will help correct both leptin and insulin resistance.

Processed/Engineered Foods

So, now that you know how powerfully certain hormones can affect our relationship with food, you may fully appreciate why processed/engineered foods are one of the major culprits that enslave many to binge eating.

> *In the twenty-first century, our taste buds, our brain chemistry,*
> *our biochemistry, our hormones, and our kitchens have been*
> *hijacked by the food industry.*
> —DR. MARK HYMAN[6]

The food industry is not only generating billions of dollars for itself by designing hyperpalatable combinations of sugar, fat, and salt—it's also creating products that have the capacity to rewire our brains, driving us to seek out more and more of those products.[7]

An example of how the processed food giants engineer

foods to manipulate our desires is Coca-Cola. Did you know that Coke has very high sodium content?—55 mg of salt, in fact. So the sugar is there to mask the salt. Why so much salt? Because it is a diuretic, which means that it will cause you to lose water and make you thirsty for—another Coke! Along with all that salt, a single serving of regular Coke also has about 9½ teaspoons of sugar.[8]

—DR. ROBERT LUSTIG

· ·

CANNABIS IN YOUR CORN CHIPS?

Industrial food production depends on mass amounts of vegetable oils, because they are cheap. However, cost is not the only reason why manufacturers use them to fry chips, make dressings, swirl into dips, etc. You see, omega-6 oils (vegetable oils are mainly composed of omega-6), create *endocannabinoid* compounds.[9] These are our very own natural cannabis-like chemicals that are produced when omega-6 oils are ingested. They are very similar to the cannabinoids found in marijuana. This leads to addiction, which means repeat business.

Potheads are known for sitting about listlessly, watching endless reruns, and indulging the munchies. A person on a binge-a-thon does just about the same, minus the giggles.

Vegetable oils, such as corn, soy, canola, and cottonseed, also cause inflammation that can lead to heart disease.[10] In short, high intake of omega-6 will cause us to binge, bulge, and become inflamed.

· ·

High-Sugar/High-Carb Diet

We have already touched upon the many negative consequences of sugar consumption in the previous two chapters. However, since sugar is such a highly addictive substance, let us examine it again. The goal here is to convince you for good that overintake of sugar, in its many forms, and carbohydrates (remember, they turn into sugar in your bloodstream) causes bingeing, weight gain, and hormonal imbalance, and can even mess up your brain and thus your mood.

Dr. Richard Lustig, an endocrinologist who has done extensive research on the current obesity epidemic in America, states that white sugar and high-fructose corn syrup are the two most addictive and deadly substances around. His conclusion is that both sugar and HFCS contribute to the disruption of our endocrine system, especially affecting the two hormones associated with hunger and satiety: ghrelin and leptin.[11]

Recall that ghrelin is produced in the gut and tells the brain to eat when the stomach is empty. Leptin is produced in fat cells, and signals us to stop eating when adequate amounts of food have been consumed. The villainous feature of both white sugar and HFCS is that they disrupt the communication between these hormones and our brains and cause constant hunger even when plenty of calories have been chomped down.

Lack of Healthy Fats and Protein

Healthy fats provide a feeling of satiety, and proteins are the raw materials we need to make hormones. With good fats, the body feels nourished and does not trigger you to think that you are persistently hungry. The bonus is that healthy fats help us to be more energetic and fuel our brains to produce more uplifting chemicals.[12]

When you overconsume carbohydrates and fall short on good fats and protein, insulin spikes and a blood sugar imbalance causes cravings and bingeing.

Bad Gut Ecology

Did you know that your gut is host to trillions of microbes?

Unsettling as it may seem, we all have bacteria living in our gut, and we actually depend on them for our existence. Just as the health of our planet depends on a harmonious ecosystem, so it goes with our very own interior terrain. When there's *dysbiosis*—bacterial imbalance in the gut caused by antibiotics, candida yeast overgrowth, or lack of good bacteria like *lactobacilli*—intense craving for sugar and carb-laden foods can easily override any willpower you can muster up. Those bad bugs love, and live off, sugar. They want you to eat junk and lots of it!

Studies being done on the microbes in our digestive tract have made headlines lately, as researchers are beginning to realize that individuals with an out-of-balance gut biome may suffer problems with overeating, bingeing, and obesity.[13]

Recently, a study conducted in Denmark showed that individuals who had "gut bacterial richness" were much healthier. In contrast, "individuals with a low bacterial richness are characterized by more marked overall adiposity, insulin resistance...and a more pronounced inflammatory phenotype when compared with high bacterial richness individuals. The obese individuals among the lower bacterial richness group also gained more weight over time."[14]

In everyday lingo: lots of good gut microbes help us eat right and stay fit.

Lack of Sleep

We touched on sleep in chapter 2 and there'll be much more on this important topic in the next chapter. For now, know that when you are not spending enough time in slumberland, production of several key hormones becomes compromised:

- Insulin stays high at night, when it should be flat.
- Cortisol stays high too far into the night and falls when it should be high in the morning.
- Not enough melatonin is made. (It can only be made in the dark.)
- When melatonin is low, the signal from leptin (which tells you to stop eating) becomes much less effective.
- And ghrelin (which signals you to eat) stays high.

In short, lack of sleep will increase your cravings, especially for carb-heavy and sugary foods.

• •

GET OUT OF BED, NATURALLY

As of May 2013, Binge Eating Disorder (BED) is now included in the DSM-5, the official manual of mental health diagnosis, published by the American Psychiatric Association. According to the manual's description, BED is characterized by recurrent and persistent episodes of binge eating.

Binge eating episodes are marked by the presence of at least three of the following symptoms:

- Eating much more rapidly than normal.
- Eating until feeling uncomfortably full.
- Eating large amounts of food, when not feeling physically hungry.
- Eating alone because of being embarrassed by how much one is eating.

- Feeling disgusted with oneself, depressed, or very guilty after overeating.
- Marked distress regarding binge eating.
- Absence of regular compensatory behaviors, such as purging.

Although binge eating is a "disorder," don't let this categorization deter you from taking the steps to wholesome and healthful eating. Food *is* your best medicine.

• •

SIX WAYS TO END BINGEING

Now that we know some of the major causes of out-of-control eating, we can utilize many healthy strategies to reverse it. In this section, we will look at delicious and uplifting ways to bring satisfaction and happiness with every meal.

Up Dopamine with Real Foods

As we have already learned, the behavioral patterns around desiring, acquiring, and then eating junk food causes a surge in dopamine, which is one of the reasons why we get addicted. Other unhealthy and destructive ways to get dopamine going is by using drugs like cocaine, heroine, and amphetamines. The good news about dopamine is that healthy eating, sex, kinship, and all forms of social bonding also elevate it.

The most critical thing to appreciate about dopamine is that it can be made from foods rich in the amino acid tyrosine. When we consume such foods, our metabolic system first converts tyrosine to L-dopa and then to dopamine. It is a pathway created by the process of digestion and assisted by folic acid and iron.

So, load up on tyrosine-rich foods such as turkey, chicken, eggs, tempeh,* beets, avocados, artichokes, blueberries, spirulina, tahini, almonds, pumpkin seeds, and yogurt.

*Caution: Although soy-based foods have tyrosine, they are not well absorbed by the body and can also negatively affect the functioning of your thyroid. Fermented soy edibles, miso and tempeh, are healthy choices.

• •

CATECHOLAMINE CONNECTION

Norepinephrine, adrenalin, and dopamine are catecholamines: hormones that are part of our sympathetic, or fight-or-flight, system. And dopamine is the parent to norepinephrine and adrenalin.

Julia Ross, author of *The Mood Cure*, refers to the catecholamines as "cats" and describes them this way: "They enthuse you in the face of positive news and alarm you in the face of threats. They prime you to take action and even program your physical movements. They are your internal cheering squad and drill sergeant combined."[15]

If you are low on them, you may be drawn to stimulants such as coffee, chocolates, and tobacco, or binge eating in an attempt to raise your "cats."

• •

CHICKEN AND BEET SALAD WITH SPIRULINA DRESSING
YIELD: 2 servings

1 medium beet
6 ounces cooked chicken, cut into cubes
2 cups diced cucumber
1 cup cooked chickpeas
⅓ cup chopped parsley

For the dressing:
⅓ cup extra virgin olive oil
1 tablespoon apple cider vinegar
1 teaspoon spirulina powder
½ teaspoon maple syrup or raw honey
sea salt and freshly ground pepper, to taste

Put the beet, unpeeled, in a pot and cover with water. Bring to a boil and simmer until cooked through. Run under cold water and peel. Cut crosswise into thin slices.

Put the dressing ingredients in a recycled glass jar or mason jar, screw the lid on, and shake for about 10 seconds, until well mixed.

In a bowl, mix the chicken, cucumbers, chickpeas, parsley, and dressing.

Line two plates with the sliced beets, placing them in an overlapping circle for each plate.

Divide the chicken salad into two portions and serve on the prepared plates.

BRAISED STAR ANISE TEMPEH OVER CARDAMOM-SCENTED RICE

YIELD: 2-3 servings

1 packet tempeh (8 ounces)
2 tablespoons untoasted sesame
  oil
3-4 garlic cloves, sliced
1 small onion, sliced
1 tablespoon grated fresh ginger
8-10 shiitake mushrooms
2 whole star anise
2 tablespoons tamari
1 tablespoon mirin
1 cup filtered water
sea salt, to taste

For the Cardamom Rice:
1 cup brown basmati rice
3-4 cardamom pods
1¾ cups filtered water
pinch of sea salt

Cut the tempeh into 1-inch cubes and steam for 20 minutes. Set aside.

Heat a medium pot on medium heat with the sesame oil, and toss in the garlic, onion, and ginger. Sauté for a few minutes until the onion is translucent.

Add the shiitake mushrooms, the steamed tempeh pieces, and the rest of the ingredients.

Bring to a simmer and allow to cook for about 20–25 minutes.

Soak the rice overnight in water with a little lemon juice or a pinch of sea salt.

Drain the rice and put into a pot. Add the other ingredients and bring to a simmer.

Cover the pot tightly and turn the heat to low. Let rice cook for about 30 minutes, or until all the liquid is absorbed and the rice is tender.

Serve the Braised Tempeh over Cardamom Rice.

TURKEY MEAT LOAF AND MASHED CAULIFLOWER
YIELD: 4 servings

1½ pounds ground turkey
2 teaspoons dried sage, or 6–7 fresh sage leaves, finely chopped
1 tablespoon dried oregano
1 large egg, pasture-raised or free-range
1½ teaspoons sea salt
freshly ground pepper
6 ounces canned organic tomato sauce, for topping (you can skip this topping if you are nightshade sensitive)

Preheat oven to 375°F.

Put the ground meat in a large bowl and thoroughly mix in all the ingredients (except the tomato sauce) with a spoon or your hands. (It's quite okay to dig in with your hands and have fun mixing and squishing the mixture through your fingers, but please wash your hands before and after.)

Pack the turkey mixture into a loaf pan and top with the tomato sauce. Put in the oven on a sheet pan and bake for 60 minutes, or until a meat thermometer registers 165°F.

Allow to cool slightly and cut into 1-inch slices to serve.

Mashed Cauliflower
YIELD: 4 servings
1 medium head cauliflower
3–4 large garlic cloves, peeled (more if you want to ward off vampires)
1 cup filtered water, or stock
¼ teaspoon sea salt
freshly ground pepper, to taste
2 tablespoons nutritional yeast (optional)
¼ cup extra virgin olive oil or organic butter

Wash and trim the cauliflower and cut into rough pieces.

Heat a pan and pour in the cup of water or stock, then toss in the cut cauliflower and cloves of garlic. Bring to a simmer, add salt and pepper, and cover the pan. Allow to cook for about 10 minutes, until the cauliflower is soft.

Transfer mixture, including the liquid, to a blender. (You may want to do this in two batches.) Add the nutritional yeast, olive oil, and a little more salt. Puree until it resembles the consistency of mashed potatoes. You may need to add a little more water/stock to facilitate the blending, but be careful not to add too much liquid. (You could also be super daring and try adding some coconut or almond milk for extra richness and flavor.)

Adjust seasoning as needed. Please don't eat all the mashed cauliflower before the turkey loaf is done!

Say Goodbye to Bad Highs

Did you know that certain foods contain *opioids* that cause a reaction similar to taking morphine? Two of the most consumed foods in North America, wheat and dairy, contain these opiate-like compounds, and they are also two of the most allergenic foods around. Gluten contains *gluteomorphine*, and dairy contains *casomorphine*. These foods can make you "high," but the long list of negative consequences far outweigh the fleeting few moments of euphoria. Allergenic foods damage the digestive tract by causing constant inflammation, and repeated exposure can lead to leaky gut, IBS, celiac disease, and autoimmune diseases. Ouch!

Gluten is one of the strongest triggers of the constant desire to eat. When a person with gluten intolerance consumes gluten-containing foods, it sets off a feel-good endorphin rush, which can lead to overeating. So, the tragedy is that we become addicted to foods that we should avoid in an attempt to experience that rush again. That giddy moment is a protective mechanism because the gluten-protein is actually doing damage to our intestinal lining. The release of endorphins is our body's way of protecting us from pain. Casein, the protein found in dairy products, causes the same reaction.

Dr. Daniel Kalish, a holistic health practitioner and author of *Your Guide to Healthy Hormones*, tells his patients, "Eating gluten is like exposing the interior of your digestive lining to a sunburn, day after day. Eventually, you'll burn a hole in your gut!"[16]

And the hurt doesn't stop there. When your gut lining is damaged, it leads to malabsorption of key nutrients such as calcium, iron, B vitamins, and trace minerals. Lack of vital nutrients also leads to overeating because your body is not getting the sustenance it needs to maintain itself, and it will call you to eat more in an attempt to satisfy its needs. Poor digestion also depletes serotonin, and low serotonin leads to cravings for carbohydrates and dairy, especially in the evening, because eating these foods temporarily raises serotonin. This can lead to an unhealthy dependency that is ultimately ruinous to well-being, while bringing on feelings of anxiety and depression as you spin around and around in an endless cycle of depletion.

COW VS. GOAT

Goats' milk is much more digestible than cows' milk. For one thing, the fat molecules found in goats' milk are only a fraction of the size of the fat globules found in cows' milk. This means that the fat molecules in goats' milk are broken down easily. Another reason why goats' milk is better for digestion is the fact that goats' milk contains a higher amount of medium-chain triglycerides, or MCTs. MCTs assist in speeding up your metabolism and can also help lower your cholesterol levels.

Dairy allergies are most often caused by a certain protein found in cows' milk called alpha S1 casein protein, which is not found in human or goats' milk.

EAT GLUE?

It's interesting to note that Elmer's Glue is made from milk casein, and industrial adhesives can be made from gluten, soy, and corn. All four (casein, gluten, soy, corn) are troublemakers for our digestion because they can sure stick things together!

HOMEMADE ALMOND MILK

YIELD: approx. 3 cups

To make almond or other nut milks, it is best to get a nut milk bag, which you can easily purchase online or at a good kitchen supply store.

1 cup raw almonds and 1
teaspoon lemon juice, soaked
in 2 cups water overnight
3 cups filtered water
1 teaspoon vanilla extract
pinch of sea salt

Drain the almonds and put in a blender. Add the water, salt, and vanilla extract. Blend until almonds are pulverized and the mixture is silky.

Pour half the contents into a nut milk bag and squeeze the liquid out into a bowl.

Remove the remaining solids from the milk bag and repeat the squeezing with the rest of the almond mixture.

You can now use the almond milk in lieu of regular milk for most recipes.

NONDAIRY CHEESY SPRINKLE

YIELD: 1 cup

1 cup raw walnuts
⅓ cup nutritional yeast

Preheat oven to 325ºF.

Pour walnuts onto a parchment lined baking sheet and bake until toasted and fragrant.

Allow the nuts to cool, then transfer to a food processor.

Add nutritional yeast and pulse a few times until the mixture looks like cornmeal.

This is a great cheese alternative to sprinkle over any dish.

GLUTEN-FREE ALMOND CAKE WITH STRAWBERRY COULIS

1½ cups almond meal

1 teaspoon baking powder

½ teaspoon salt

4 large eggs, pasture-raised or free-range, separated

1 tablespoon vanilla extract

¼ cup Sucanat or natural cane sugar

Preheat oven to 350°F. Prepare an 8-inch cake pan by lining with parchment and greasing the sides.

In a large bowl, combine the almond meal, baking powder, and salt.

Whisk the egg yolks in a small bowl with the vanilla extract and Sucanat for about 3 minutes, or until smooth and creamy. Add the yolk mixture to the almond meal mixture.

Whisk the egg whites in a large bowl until stiff peaks form. Fold into the almond-yolk mixture in thirds until well incorporated.

Pour batter into the cake pan and bake for about 25 minutes, or until a toothpick inserted in the middle comes out clean.

Allow to cool and serve with Strawberry Coulis.

For the Strawberry Coulis:

2 cups fresh strawberries (organic is very important because conventional berries contain a lot of pesticide)

¼ teaspoon vanilla extract

1 tablespoon maple syrup or raw honey

¼ cup filtered water

pinch of sea salt

Put all ingredients in a blender and blend until smooth.

You can strain the coulis for a super-silky texture, or use as is.

You can also use other berries or ripe stone fruits to make a coulis.

Throw Out Sugar, Bring in Fat and Protein

Pure, white, deadly, and more addictive than cocaine: that's sugar. And yet despite numerous press releases and literature warning us about the dangers of sugar, we are still ingesting way too much! The latest statistics show that the average American consumes over 140 pounds of sugar per year.

According to Dr. Lustig, our Paleolithic ancestors got their sweet fix from fruits and vegetables. Estimates put their daily consumption at about fifteen grams of mainly fructose that was bound to plenty of fiber and nutrients, because they ate only whole foods (not to mention that they had to expend physical energy to forage for their "treats").[17] Evolution in humans is slow, so physically we haven't changed much from our hunter-gatherer ancestors, but we have dramatically increased our intake of sugar.

Greater of Two Evils

Table sugar (sucrose) is composed of two monosaccharides: glucose and fructose. When we ingest sugar, our digestive tract pumps out enzymes that breaks sucrose down into glucose and fructose, which are then absorbed into the body. High-fructose corn syrup is also composed of the same two monosaccharides. However, the percentage of fructose is high and also in a form that requires more work from the liver. And that's where the big, fat problem lies. When fructose enters the liver it prompts *lipogenesis*, a pleasant sounding word for the production of triglycerides and cholesterol, which are definitely not pleasant when made in excess. Toxic compounds such as acetaldehyde and acetic acid are also produced. The same process also occurs with alcohol intake. And that is why someone who regularly consumes foods or beverages with HFCS can develop fatty liver, just like a person who drinks too much booze.[18]

To make things even worse, HFCS blunts the message from leptin and increases ghrelin. In other words, your brain will think you are starving when you have already consumed plenty of calories.

Food manufacturers know that we are slaves to our sweet tooth and HFCS is cheap, much cheaper than sugar made from beets or cane. More addiction means more sales, which means more profits with less production cost, which means even more profits!

Are you getting the picture? There's a conspiracy going on, and that big binge problem that you thought was all about willpower is also about greed. So, the logical step is to disengage from the processed, fast food paradigm and join the organic, whole foods revolution. And learn to cook! Learn to love to cook! Cook as if your life depended on it, because it does.

· ·

SUGAR-FREE IS EXPENSIVE

So you think that switching to sugar-free soda and snacks is better? Think again.

Artificial sweeteners actually confuse our brain and body by tricking us into thinking that we are consuming real sugar when it's fake. This deception leads to metabolic confusion and overconsumption. Wait—what's happening here? You see, even though we know that sugar is bad, it does provide fuel in the form of glucose and fructose. So, when you drink a diet soda your taste buds sense sweetness and send a signal to your brain that energy is on its way. However, since artificial sweeteners are devoid of nutrients and filled with toxic chemicals, your entire physiology gets whacked out. Your cells are expecting fuel, but there's nothing coming, so you will start to crave more and overeat in order to compensate for the fraud. What's worse, researchers found that, just as with regular soda, the consumption of artificially sweetened beverages is associated with obesity, type 2 diabetes, metabolic syndrome, and cardiovascular disease.[18]

· ·

Why Protein and Fat Are Good

If you have a gooey sugar-drenched pastry for breakfast instead of a wholesome protein-based breakfast of, say, poached eggs with spinach and mushrooms, then leptin doesn't get activated and ghrelin will remain high. "Eat more, eat more, eat more," is the mantra that will constantly hum in your head. Simply put, banishing sugar is one of the most powerful and effective ways to banish bingeing!

On the other hand, the combination of fat and protein in a meal promotes satiety, while also prompting release of fat storage for energy and good digestion. Because this is an essential point to understand, we will need to get a little technical. Let's take a brief look into biochemistry to learn the many good things about these two macronutrients.

In addition to insulin, the pancreas makes another hormone: glucagon. When we eat protein and fat, glucagon is released, driving very different results from that of insulin.[19] This chart compares the different actions of insulin vs. glucagon.

Insulin	Glucagon
Lowers high blood sugar	Raises low blood sugar
Signals cells to go into storage mode	Signals metabolism to go into burning mode
Converts fat you eat into fat storage in your cells = more fat cells	Converts fat you eat into ketones that are used in the tissues for energy
Increases the body's production of cholesterol	Decreases the body's production of cholesterol
Cause retention of excess fluids, aka bloating	Causes release of excess fluids
Stimulates the use of glucose for energy	Stimulates the use of fat for energy
Released by the beta cells of the pancreas	Released by the alpha cells of the pancreas

Information on chart from **Protein Power.** [20]

The main thing to recognize is that insulin stores fat, while glucagon releases fat from cells to be used as energy. Obviously, if you want to shed the pudge from around your waist, a diet that encourages the release of glucagon is preferred. How do we make that happen? By eating protein and fat in higher proportion than carbohydrates.

POACHED EGGS WITH SAUTÉED GREENS
YIELD: 1–2 servings

For the Sautéed Greens:
1 tablespoon extra virgin olive
oil, coconut oil, or butter
1 garlic clove, minced
1 bunch kale, chard, or spinach,
washed, stems removed, cut
into 1-inch strips
sea salt and freshly ground
pepper, to taste
2 teaspoons lemon juice

Heat a sauté pan on medium heat. Add the cooking oil of your choice.

Add the garlic and cook for about 10 seconds, then add the greens.

Stir to rotate the greens, then add the seasoning and lemon juice.

Lower the heat and cover the pan. Allow the greens to cook for about 5–6 minutes.

Check for seasoning. Add more salt or pepper as needed.

Remove from the pan to a plate and set aside.

POACHED EGGS, STEP BY STEP
2 large eggs, pasture-raised or
free-range
5 cups filtered water
1½ teaspoons white wine vinegar
or 1½ tablespoons fresh
lemon juice

In a small stainless-steel pot, bring 5 cups water to a boil with vinegar or fresh lemon juice.

Crack one egg and put it into a small bowl or ramekin.

When the water comes to a full boil, tilt the vessel containing the egg over the bubbling water and gently slide the egg in.

Immediately repeat with the other egg. (Don't worry about the trailing egg whites; the acid from the vinegar or lemon juice will coagulate it as the egg cooks in the water.) Lower the heat slightly to maintain a happy simmer.

Cook 3 minutes for a runny yolk; 3 minutes and 30 seconds for a slightly firmer one. (My absolute favorite texture is at 2 minutes and 45 seconds.)

Get ready with a slotted spoon and folded paper towels to dry off the eggs when they are ready to exit the simmering water.

When the eggs are cooked to your liking, carefully lift the eggs out with the slotted spoon and put them on the paper towel to dry.

Turn the eggs onto the cooked greens. You can easily tuck in the sides for a neater look. Drizzle with extra virgin olive oil and season with sea salt and freshly ground pepper.

THREE-SPICE SHAKE 'N BAKE CHICKEN

YIELD: 4 servings as a snack or 2 servings as a meal

This recipe is a healthy, gluten-free version of the popular Shake 'n Bake breadcrumb coating that comes in a box with ingredients you can't pronounce. These chicken nuggets are great on a salad for lunch, or they make a wonderful snack.

12 ounces boneless chicken, thigh or breast, cut into approximately 2-inch chunks
¾ teaspoon sea salt
1 teaspoon ground coriander
1 teaspoon ground cumin
1 teaspoon ground chipotle powder
½ cup ground almonds or hazelnuts

Preheat oven to 375°F. Line a baking sheet with parchment paper.

In a bowl, mix the seasoning and ground nuts.

Put the chicken pieces in a medium pot, add the spice and nut mixture, and put the lid on.

Keeping one hand firmly on the lid, grab the handle with your other hand and shake the pot up and down until the chicken pieces are coated. (You can also do this with a ziplock bag, but I discourage using plastic.)

Transfer the coated chicken to the prepared baking sheet and set the chunks about an inch apart.

Bake for 20–25 minutes, or until the internal temperature reaches 165°F.

BACON-WRAPPED PORK TENDERLOIN WITH DATES

YIELD: 2–3 servings

1 pork tenderloin, about 1½
  pounds
5–6 dates, pitted
½ teaspoon sea salt
1 teaspoon ground cumin
2 garlic cloves, minced
4 strips bacon (nitrate-free)

On a cutting board, cut the loin lengthwise with a chef's knife, stopping an inch before reaching the "spine," so that the loin remains in one piece and opens like a book.

Season the inside of the loin with salt, cumin, and garlic.

Place the dates end to end along the length of the loin.

Roll the loin back into a cylinder.

Lay the bacon strips on the board, next to each other, perpendicular to you.

Place the stuffed loin onto the bacon strips and roll the strips up to wrap the loin completely.

Put the wrapped loin, seam side down, on a parchment-lined baking sheet.

Bake at 400°F for about 25 minutes, or until the internal temperature reaches 145°F on a meat thermometer.

Remove from the oven and allow to cool for about 5 minutes.

Cut the loin into 1-inch slices and serve.

Delicious with a salad or sautéed greens.

More Roots, Less Grains

While going gluten free is certainly a good start, cutting down on gluten-free grains can bring a faster end to bingeing, especially for those who are hormonally sensitive. Recall that carbohydrates turn into sugar in the blood-stream, which causes an insulin surge and cravings.

All grains pose problems to digestion because they contain *lectins* and *phytates*. Lectins are a class of sticky proteins, found in all grains and legumes, that are very challenging for our gut. The undigested particles can cross through our digestive lining into the bloodstream, causing allergies and autoimmune diseases.

Phytates, or phytic acid (found in all grains) is an organic acid to which phosphorus is bound. While this is good for plants, since they need phosphorus to spur energy for growth, phytic acid is bad for us because it binds to calcium, magnesium, iron, and zinc, taking them out of our bodies. Now, since all these minerals are vital to good health, consuming a high-grain diet can cause a serious depletion. Lack of calcium and magnesium can cause osteoporosis as well as acidity; lack of iron leads to anemia, and lack of zinc weakens the immune system.

So, in addition to cutting out gluten, try a diet that reduces or eliminates gluten-free grains as well. Instead, substitute root vegetables, such as sweet potatoes, turnips, celery root, and parsnip that contain satisfying amounts of carbohydrates without the bothersome lectin and phytates.

• •

SOAK YOUR GRAINS, NUTS, SEEDS

There is a way to remove the phytic acid from grains: soaking them in water overnight before cooking. Although this will not remove all the phytates, it does help make the grain much more digestible and the nutrients contained within them available to us. Nuts and seeds also contain phytates, so they should be treated the same way.

See recipes at the end of this chapter.

• •

. . . .

POTATOES ARE NIGHTSHADES

Although potatoes are root vegetables and do contain a lot of nutrients, they belong in the nightshade family, which means they can cause inflammation for some sensitive individuals and especially for those with arthritic conditions. Potatoes are also rather high on the glycemic index, which means that they will trigger high insulin.

Substitute sweet potatoes, which are not from the family of nightshades. They contain more fiber with less calories and plenty of beta-carotene.

. . . .

ROASTED ROOT VEGETABLES

Here's how to roast root vegetables the super-easy way.

root vegetables: turnips, parsnip, rutabaga, beets, sweet potatoes
baking sheet
parchment paper
extra virgin olive oil
sea salt
freshly ground pepper
herbs such as thyme, rosemary, or oregano

Preheat oven to 350°F. Line a baking sheet with a piece of parchment. Peel and cut the root vegetables of your choice into cubes or squares. Cut all the pieces approximately the same size to ensure a uniformed roasting time.

Spread the cut vegetables on the prepared baking sheet and drizzle a generous amount of olive oil over them. Season with salt and herbs. Cover with another piece of parchment paper. (Be sure to cover the veggies fully, but do not crimp the edges of the parchment.)

Roast for about 30 minutes, or until vegetables are tender. If you want to take it one step further and brown the cooked roots for a richer flavor, turn on the broiler, remove the parchment paper, and allow to brown (caramelize) for a few minutes.

Caution: Keep your attention on the veggies while they are under the broiler because the browning process happens very quickly!

SLOW-COOKER CINNAMON LAMB STEW WITH CAULIFLOWER "COUSCOUS"

YIELD: 4–6 servings

For the Lamb Stew:
2 pounds deboned lamb shoulder
2 tablespoons ghee or coconut oil
1 onion, chopped
1 teaspoon grated fresh ginger
1 teaspoon ground cinnamon
1 cinnamon stick (optional)
1 bay leaf
1 teaspoon sea salt
freshly ground pepper
8–10 dried apricots or figs
filtered water
handful of chopped parsley, for
garnish

Cut the lamb into 2-inch pieces.

Heat a large sauté pan on high heat. Add the cooking oil of your choice.

Toss in the lamb pieces and brown on all sides. Season with a little sea salt and freshly ground pepper.

Transfer the browned lamb to a slow cooker.

Add the rest of the ingredients to the cooker with just enough water to cover the contents.

Turn the slow cooker to a medium setting and allow to slow-cook for 8 hours, or until the lamb is tender.

Note: If you do not have a slow cooker, you can do this in a pot. It will take about 2–2½ hours on a gentle simmer.

For the Cauliflower "Coucous":
1 small head cauliflower, stem
*   removed.*
2 tablespoons ghee or coconut oil
½ cup finely chopped onion
sea salt and freshly ground
*   pepper, to taste*

Chop the cauliflower florets into large chunks and put in a food processor.

Pulse a few times until the cauliflower has a rough cornmeal or grainy consistency. Set aside.

In a large sauté pan, heat the oil of your choice and add the onion. Cook until it is translucent, about 3–4 minutes.

Add the cauliflower and season with salt and pepper. Stir well and allow to cook until it softens, about 6–8 minutes. If the mixture looks too dry, add a little water a tablespoon at a time.

Serve with the Lamb Stew.

SWEET AND SPICY NUTS

*3 cups raw pecans, walnuts, and/
or almonds (a mix or just one
type)*
2 tablespoons maple syrup
½ teaspoon ground cumin
½ teaspoon ground coriander
½ teaspoon cayenne
½ teaspoon sea salt

Soak the nuts in water with 1 teaspoon lemon juice or ⅛ teaspoon sea salt overnight, or for least for 4–5 hours.

Drain the nuts and pat dry with a paper towel.

Mix the dried spices and salt together in a small bowl.

Transfer the nuts to a large bowl and coat with the maple syrup.

Add spice mixture and gently mix.

Pour the coated nuts onto a baking sheet lined with parchment paper. Take care to spread the nuts into a single layer.

Bake for about one hour at 250° F, or until the nuts are crispy.

PERFECT BROWN RICE

YIELD: 2-3 servings

The trick to tasty and digestible brown rice is to soak it overnight. Adding a small piece of kombu and using chicken broth or mineral broth to cook the rice will add not only flavor, but additional nutrients as well.

1 cup brown rice
filtered water for soaking the rice
*1 teaspoon fresh lemon juice or
pinch of sea salt*
1½ cup filtered water or broth
*1 piece kombu, approx. 1 inch x 2
inches, soaked in cold water
for 5 minutes*
pinch of sea salt (optional)

Soak the rice overnight in water with lemon juice or salt.

Drain well. Put the rice into a medium pot and add water, kombu, and salt.

Bring to a simmer and turn the heat to the lowest setting. Put the cover on.

Cook until the water has been absorbed, about 30-35 minutes.

Remove from heat. Allow the rice to rest, with the cover on, for about 5–10 minutes before serving.

Note: You can also cook the rice in a rice cooker after soaking the grains overnight.

Load Up with Probiotics from Fermented Foods

We already know that when your gut has more bad microbes then good microbes, addiction to sugar and high-carb foods can rule your day and night and drive you to overeat.

The importance of good gut ecology cannot be overstated. Load up on probiotic-rich foods such as kefir and yogurt and lacto-fermented vegetables, such as sauerkraut and kimchi. These delicious fermented goodies have been enjoyed by different cultures from around the world for centuries. Now they are being appreciated anew, since modern science has validated that many strains of bacteria contained in these foods, such as *lactobacilli bifidus* or *bulgaricus,* feed the good bacteria in our gut, helping to sustain and balance our internal ecosystem and boost immunity.

Taking a probiotic supplement will also help, though it won't be nearly as satisfying as eating real food's rich, live cultures.

CLASSIC SAUERKRAUT

1 head cabbage, about 1½ pounds, cored and finely shredded
1 tablespoon caraway seeds
1½ tablespoons sea salt
1 wide-mouth quart mason jar

Put the shredded cabbage in a large bowl. Sprinkle salt over the cabbage and massage for about 5 minutes by squeezing handfuls between your palms and fingers with a medium-firm pressure. The purpose of the massage is to help release juice from the cabbage. The longer you do it, the more cabbage juice will be released.

Mix in the caraway seeds and transfer the mixture to the mason jar. Really pack it in. Use a spoon, pestle, or the end of a rolling pin to tamp down the cabbage and to help build up more liquid. Be sure to leave at lease 2 inches of clearance between the top of the cabbage and the opening of the jar. Depending on the quality of the cabbage, you may or may not get a lot of juice.

If needed, add enough filtered water to cover the sauerkraut-to-be by about an inch.

Now you will need to keep the cabbage submerged underneath the brine. A small mason jar will fit nicely into a quart mason jar and serve as a weight. Loosely close the lid and leave the filled jar in a cool, dark spot. (68–72°F is ideal.)

Allow the fermentation process to do its magic for 10–14 days.

After 2 weeks, store the jar in the refrigerator. Enjoy your probiotic-rich sauerkraut as a condiment with meals. About ⅓ cup is a good serving size.

CHOPPED ROMAINE AND HAM SALAD WITH SAUERKRAUT

YIELD: 2–3 servings

1 small head romaine lettuce, chopped into thin slivers
4 ounces cooked ham, sliced
⅓ cup chopped black olives
⅔ cup raw sauerkraut (home-made or store-bought)
2 tablespoons raw sauerkraut juice
⅓ cup chopped dill
4 tablespoons extra virgin olive oil
sea salt and freshly ground pepper, to taste
2 tablespoons dulse* flakes (optional)

Put all ingredients into a large bowl and toss well.

Top with dulse flakes, if using.

*Dulse is a type of seaweed with a very mild flavor. It has a lovely deep purple color, and can be found in many organic grocery stores. It can easily be crumbled, or you can put it into a processor and pulse a few times to make flakes.

KEFIR PROTEIN SHAKE

YIELD: 1 serving

⅓ cup kefir (dairy or coconut)
1 serving protein powder (see the Shopping Guide at the end of chapter 8 for best brand)
1 tablespoon almond butter
½ pear or peach
¼ teaspoon grated fresh ginger
1 tablespoon ground flax seeds
1 teaspoon bee pollen or spirulina (optional)
8 ounces filtered water
pinch of sea salt

Put all ingredients into a blender and blend until smooth.

Sleep Well

Our ancestors averaged 9 to 12 hours of sleep per night. Now we are lucky to sneak in 7 hours. Our inability to connect with the sandman is costing us a lot! Sound sleep brings down cortisol and heightens melatonin, which then regulates leptin, so that we feel full after a meal and are free of constant hunger signals.

See chapter 4 to learn all about sleep and good slumber tips.

MORE TIPS TO BANISH BINGEING

- When you feel a binge attack coming on, pour yourself a big glass of room-temperature water and sip it all, slowly. We often think we are hungry when we are actually dehydrated and need water, not food. (Flavor the water with lemon or cucumber slices to perk it up.)
- Engage mindful eating. That means don't have your meals in front of the computer or TV. When your attention is distracted by a reality show or reading emails rather then truly enjoying your food, the tendency to overeat is greatly increased.
- Chew your food well. And that means chewing each bite of food at least thirty-five times. Does that seem excessive? Well, researchers have studied the metabolic differences between chewing thirty-five times per bite against ten times per bite and found that participants experienced a higher feeling of "comfortably full" and lost more weight, to boot. So, exercise your jaw when you eat.
- Get plenty of sunshine, without suntan lotion, to ensure that you have adequate levels of vitamin D. Deficiency in D interferes with secretion of leptin, the hormone that signals satiety. (For instructions on how to enjoy the sun safely without suntan lotion and optimize production of vitamin D, see page 144)
- Studies show that loneliness and feeling isolated can lead to overeating and low moods, so make an effort to be engaged in your community.
- Take classes at your local community center, or become a volunteer. Make an effort to know your neighbors.
- Practice positive self-image and stay away from fashion magazines that create unrealistic expectations.

- Psychotherapy or Cognitive Behavioral Therapy (CBT) have been shown to be effective treatments for binge eating.

Summary

- Binge eating is not all about willpower. There are unwholesome ingredients in processed foods that cause addiction.
- Engage in a healthy diet that promotes functioning of leptin, ghrelin, dopamine, insulin, and glucagon.
- Foods rich in tyrosine help elevate dopamine.
- Sugar and high-fructose corn syrup not only sabotage your efforts to end bingeing, they also cause serious health issues.
- In addition to eating organic, whole foods, increase your intake of probiotics by adding lacto-fermented vegetables or cultured dairy products to your diet.

A Perfect "End Bingeing" Day

Upon waking: Glass of warm water with lemon

Breakfast: Poached Eggs over Sautéed Spinach

Drink: Green tea

Snack: 2 sliced cooked ham or handful of Sweet and Spicy Nuts

Lunch: Roasted Beets and Chicken Salad with a Spirulina Dressing

Snack: ½ avocado

Dinner: Bacon-Wrapped Pork Loin with Dates and steamed vegetables

Drink: Chamomile or valerian tea after dinner to help relaxation and sound sleep

Refrain from eating three hours before bed.

Get moderate exercise during the day, preferably outdoors to soak up some vitamin D, and get to bed by 10:00 p.m.

Case Study

Jerry reluctantly took a cooking class from me. His physician had just told him he was borderline diabetic and advised him to lose about twenty pounds. His girlfriend also gave him an ultimatum: shape up, or she was going to say goodbye. (She was also the one who gave him a certificate to my class.)

Because Jerry was only in his mid-thirties, he wasn't concerned about his health up to this point. He ran a very successful graphic and web design business with two college buddies and was completely focused on his career—spending ten to twelve hours in front of his computer and eating most meals while looking at the screen. He and his colleagues drank multiple lattes daily and always ordered Chinese, Mexican food, or pizzas to be delivered to their office for lunch. Then they would snack on chips, Goldfish crackers, and Red Hots all day. At night, Jerry would down a pint of ice cream or have a bowl of cereal before going to bed. The only healthy meals were the ones his girlfriend cooked for them once or twice a week. Without being conscious of it, Jerry had become addicted to junk food and the result was excess weight and blood sugar imbalance.

After the cooking class, Jerry came up to me and asked if I could coach him on how to eat right. I conducted a session with him to learn more about his lifestyle and decided that the best way to motivate him was to get his colleagues and girlfriend involved. So we launched a thirty-day, no-processed-sugar, no-gluten, no-junk-food challenge. The goal for Jerry was to lose ten pounds. The challenge was for everyone else (his buddies and his girlfriend) to support him by eating the same way. If Jerry hit his goal, all three of his supporters would get $250 each! The gauntlet was thrown down, and they started on the first day of March. His two buddies at work agreed to order their lunches from an organic caterer, and they also agreed to toss out all the bad munchies and only have nuts and low-glycemic fruits as snacks. His girlfriend agreed to cook more dinners, and to make sure that Jerry stayed gluten-free and sugar-free when they ate out. To help Jerry balance his blood sugar, I put him on a food-based multivitamin, chromium, vitamin D, and probiotics. I also insisted that he had a protein-based breakfast before heading to work.

The results on the 31st of March were dramatic! Jerry lost twelve pounds and his blood sugar dropped back to normal range. He also had to fork out $750 bucks as a happy loser.

(Side note: His girlfriend thanked me for his weight loss, but told me that the other great side benefit was that Jerry didn't snore at night anymore!)

Over the next few months, Jerry continued with his new eating habits, and had dropped another ten pounds when we did a follow-up in July.

Notes for Chapter 3

1   David A. Kessler MD, *The End of Overeating* (New York: Rodale Press, 2009), 41.

2   Ibid, 54.

3   Joseph Mercola, "Clinical Scientist Sets the Record Straight on Hazards of Sugar," 1/5/2014, http://articles.mercola.com/sites/articles/archive/2014/01/05/dr-johnson-leptin-resistance.aspx

4   Kent Holtorf, "Long Term Weight Loss—More Than Will Power? 6/13/2009, www.huffingtonpost.com/kent-holtorf/long-term-weight-loss---m_b_192933.html

5   Ibid.

6   Mark Hyman MD, http://www.azquotes.com/author/36883-Mark_Hyman_M_D.

7   Kessler, *The End of Overeating*, 137.
8   Robert Lustig MD, "The Complete Skinny on Obesity," 10/28/2013, www.uctv.tv/shows/
     The-Complete-Skinny-on-Obesity-25717
9   Emily Deans, "Omega 6, Obesity, and Endocannabinoids (Again)," September 28, 2012,
     http://evolutionarypsychiatry.blogspot.com/2012/09/omega-6-obesity-and-endocan-
     nabinoids.html
10   Mary Enig, *Know Your Fats: The Complete Primer for Understanding the Nutrition of
     Fats, and Cholesterol* (Silver Spring: Bethesda Press, 2000).
11   Lustig, "The Complete Skinny on Obesity."
12   Michael A. Schmidt, *Brain-Building Nutrition: How Dietary Fats and Oils Affect Mental,
     Physical, and Emotional Intelligence* (Berkeley: North Atlantic Books, 2001), 22.
13   Michael Pollan, "Some of My Best Friends are Germs," 5/15/2013, http://www.nytimes.
     com/2013/05/19/magazine/say-hello-to-the-100-trillion-bacteria-that-make-up-your-
     microbiome.html
14   Emmanuelle le Chatelier et al. "Richness of the Human Gut Microbiome Correlates
     with Metabolic Markers," http://www.nature.com/nature/journal/v500/n7464/full/
     nature12506.html
15   Julia Ross, *The Mood Cure* (New York: Penguin Books, 2002), 56.
16   Dr. Daniel Kalish, quoted.
17   Lustig, "The Complete Skinny on Obesity."
18   Ibid.
19   Ibid.
20   Michael and Mary Eades MD, *Protein Power* (New York: Bantam Books, 1999).

Chapter 4

Sweet Dreams and Serenity

That we are not much sicker and much madder than we are is due exclusively to that most blessed and blessing of all natural graces, sleep.
—ALDOUS HUXLEY

The Fountain of Youth is not found in a mythical tropical paradise off the coast of Florida, or hidden in the verdant jungles of South America. It is your bed. To put it more precisely, it is you sleeping soundly in your bed for many hours, night after night.

The benefits of deep, restful sleep can fill volumes, but all one has to do to truly appreciate the positive effects is to experience the opposite. Don't sleep for twenty-four hours and see how you feel. Chances are you'll suffer dizziness, irritability, and inability to concentrate or master basic tasks such as driving, simple arithmetic, or putting your eyeliner on straight.

WHY SLEEP?

Our nocturnal sojourn to the Land of Nod is the golden thread that connects our mortal plane to that of the Divine. Numerous artists, writers, and scientists have credited sleep and dreaming as the inspiration or source for their great works of art or inventions.

Paul McCartney credits his inspiration for the song "Yesterday" to a dream. The famous Russian chemist, Dmitri Mendeleyev, created the Periodic Table based on solutions that came to him while he slept. And the unforgettable tale of *Dr. Jekyll and Mr. Hyde* was revealed to Robert Louis Stevenson through his phantasmagorical meanderings while slumbering in bed.

Beyond the creative potentials, the sheer physical benefits derived from snooze time are enough to demand that we honor sleep by endeavoring to do it well each night. If you miss just a few nights of good sleep, you become insulin resistant, and your other hormones such as cortisol and melatonin will get out of kilter, causing you to crave carbohydrates, suffer a sluggish brain, and lowering your immunity. Lack of sleep is a major form of stress on your body. So, it should be quite obvious that sleeping well is one of the most important things we can do to be happy, healthy, and fit, and to prevent premature aging and cancer.

With all these clear benefits, why is it that we rob ourselves of this most precious gift every night? Instead of making an effort to foster sound slumber, we stay up late watching brainless reruns, shopping on QVC, or surfing the Internet for junk we don't really need. Such health-sabotaging behaviors are signs that we are not truly appreciative of the incredible healing qualities of sleep.

· ·

EIGHT IS NOT ENOUGH

In our current competitive world, most people are working ten-hour days and trying to get by with a paltry six to seven hours of sleep. There are perhaps the lucky few who are clocking eight hours. But even that really isn't enough. While everyone's individual needs are different, consider that just a short century ago the average adult was sleeping nine to ten-hours a night, and we haven't evolved enough in a mere hundred years to adapt to our current state of constant sleep debt.

In *Lights Out*, one of the most informative and well-researched books on the subject of sleep, the authors state, "The ultimate think tanks in America...are proving that we are seasonal eaters and breeders with a feast–famine metabolism who develop diabetes, heart disease, cancer, and severe depression on anything less than nine and a half hours of sleep a night for seven months of the year."[1]

The exception is during the summer months when there's ample sunlight and short nights. And those think tanks include the National Institutes of Health, the National Institute of Mental Health, and NASA.

· ·

STAGES OF SLEEP

Every time we close our eyes, relinquish the seeming control of wakefulness, and cross the border into seemingly uncontrolled sleep, we are actually entering into a realm in which our parasympathetic system takes over and performs tasks that are absolutely vital to our survival. So, it is not a dark void into which we enter, but a powerful rejuvenating portal.

The invention of the electroencephalograph (EEG) made it possible to study how our brains behave during sleep. Thus far, researchers have determined that there are two main types of sleep:

- NREM, or non-rapid eye movement, also known as quiet sleep
- REM, or rapid eye movement, also known as active sleep

Furthermore, it appears that we also cycle through different stages[2] where the brain produces various wave patterns in conjunction with the two main types of sleep.

Stage I

We transition from full wakefulness to feeling drowsy and then to sleep.

Sounds can still be detected. Theta waves, which are very slow, are generated. This stage lasts for approximately five to ten minutes.

Stage II

We enter light sleep or dozing. Sounds are still detectible, but much fainter than in stage I. The brain begins to produce rhythmic, fast waves known as *sleep spindles*. During this stage, body temperature drops and heart rate slows down.

Stage III

This is the transitional stage between light and deep sleep. Here, very slow undulations, known as delta waves, occur in the brain.

Stage IV

We are now in deep, or delta sleep, due to the delta waves that occur during this stage. This cycle lasts for about thirty minutes.

REM (sometimes referred to as Stage V)

We do most of our dreaming in this stage, known as REM sleep. Here, something paradoxical happens. Our respiration, heart rate, and brain activity increase, while voluntary muscles become paralyzed. For this reason, it is also called paradoxical sleep. Researchers have theorized that the temporary paralysis prevents us from physically acting out our dreams.

Throughout our sleep sojourn, we cycle through these stages and enter the first REM sleep approximately ninety minutes after falling asleep. Each REM sequence may become longer throughout the night, and can last for up to an hour. We usually awaken in the morning during a dream episode.

NO SNOOZE, YOU LOSE

If you have sleep troubles, rest assured that you are not alone. Millions of Americans have the same problem; prescriptions for sleeping pills have risen steadily by six percent per year since the start of our new millennium. In 2011 alone, some 60 million prescriptions were filled. It is estimated that 50 to 75 million adults in the U.S. suffer from insomnia or sleep problems several days a week.[3]

Insomnia is Latin for "no sleep." By definition, it means not getting enough sleep to wake up refreshed. All the following symptoms fall under the definition of insomnia:

- Lying awake for a long time and having trouble falling asleep
- Waking frequently and having trouble returning to sleep
- Waking too early in the morning
- Upon waking in the morning, feeling like you haven't slept at all

Insomnia is not considered a disease, but rather a sign of other issues such as stress, poor diet, depression, or, as we will see in the next section, a result of our hypertechno world—in which artificial lights and man-made radiation invade the darkness and disrupt our natural circadian rhythm and hormonal cycles.

· ·

SLEEPING PILLS: A WAKE-UP CALL

In 2012, CBS reported a study done by Dr. Daniel F. Kripke, a professor of psychiatry at the University of California, that revealed rather shocking data on the safety of sleeping pills, also known as hypnotics. It seems that increased risk of death and developing cancer are hazards that endanger people who pop sleeping pills, even as few as eighteen uses per year.

"What our study shows is that sleeping pills are hazardous to your health and might cause death by contributing to the occurrence of cancer, heart disease and other ailments," said Dr. Kripke.[4]

He also states that sleeping pills are as dangerous to health as smoking cigarettes.[5]

The cost of sleeplessness goes beyond matters of personal health. The Institute of Medicine, an independent scientific advisory group, estimates that nearly twenty percent of all fatal motor vehicle accidents are associated with driver drowsiness.[6] The loss in terms of work productivity is another consideration, as well as other less measurable yet profound effects, such as the impact on relationships, participation in social gatherings, and family dynamics. All these activities need energy, and poor sleep leaves one depleted.

If we can't sleep, perhaps it is because we've forgotten how. In premodern times, our ancestors slept quite differently, going to bed at sunset and rising with the break of dawn. Because they couldn't just flip on a light switch, they naturally followed the circadian rhythm and the flow of time as measured by the celestial movements of the sun and moon.

• •

• •

THE CLOCK WITHIN

Although we rely almost entirely on looking at a watch or checking our cell phones to tell time, it may surprise you to learn that all mammals, including humans, have an innate timepiece located deep within our brain. Situated at the base of the hypothalamus, and no bigger than a grain of rice, the suprachiasmatic nucleus (SCN) works like an internal Rolex to help us keep track of the twenty-four-hour cycle. The SCN reacts from the amount of light coming in through our eyes (the retina), and in turn signals the pineal gland (located deep within our brain) to either increase or decrease the production of melatonin.[7]

• •

CAUSES OF SLEEPLESSNESS

Stress

We already know that stress is the villain in practically all chronic diseases, because it causes an overproduction of cortisol. Well, it should come as no surprise, then, that stress will also mess with our ability to sleep well.

In relation to our sleep and wake cycle, cortisol's normal course is to spike up in the morning, around 6:00 to 7:00 a.m. This rise is what wakes us up and gets us going for the day. Then it slowly falls as the day progresses. As evening approaches the drop in cortisol signals us to unwind and to get ready for bed, ideally around 10:00 p.m. However, workaholics, or people who crash during the day and are trying to make up for lost time in the evening, often get a second wind and stay up way past midnight. If you engage in this habit, it may seem like a good way to stay ahead, but the "second wind" will blow out your candle, because when you don't heed the call to snuggle in bed and cradle your laptop instead, cortisol shoots back up and your circadian rhythm gets out of sync. High cortisol at night leads to low cortisol in the morning and affects your REM sleep, so that you wake up groggy and can't fully function until you get a hit of caffeine. High cortisol at night will also suppress your immune system, which makes you vulnerable to infections and cancer.[8] Overall, high cortisol will lower production of DHEA, also known as the "mother" hormone because it is the precursor to estrogen, progesterone, and testosterone. A shortage of DHEA will negatively affect your sex hormones and cause weight gain, low libido, and low mood.

So, all you nocturnal overachievers out there, be forewarned that burning the midnight oil, night after night, is a sure way to age quickly and feel crappy doing it.

Hormone Imbalances

We know that it is not good to elevate cortisol at night. But the hormone and sleep connection doesn't end here. Most women think about hormones in association with having PMS, or when suffering the hot flashes brought on by menopause; while most men think that the only hormone they need is testosterone. However, there are over fifty of them produced in the body, and several key hormones can't do their jobs properly when we fall short on sleep.

Melatonin

Often called the "hormone of darkness," melatonin is the star that takes top billing in our sleep story. Its highest output is around midnight to 2:00

a.m., provided that we are able to be asleep in a dark room, free of artificial light and wireless gadgets. The reason for this is because melatonin is released by the pineal gland, and since this gland is exquisitely sensitive to light variations, radiation, and electromagnetic fields, keeping your bedroom dark and radiation free helps boost melatonin.

Cells throughout our body have melatonin receptors. As melatonin peaks during the night, it can attach to breast cancer or prostate cancer cells and cause the culprits to self-destruct by fighting off excess estrogen, which stimulates cancer cell growth.

· ·

LIGHT KILLS MELATONIN

When you switch on a light at night, melatonin production plummets. As light travels through your optic nerves to your pineal gland, your biological clock thinks it's day and signals melatonin to stop. If you need a navigational light in your hallway or bathroom, use a low-wattage lamp that emits yellow, orange, or red wavelengths, because white or blue bandwidths shut down melatonin.

In addition, consider switching off your fluorescent/ halogen lights after sundown, and relax in the glow of warm-spectrum lightbulbs, or use candles and salt lamps.[9]

· ·

Prolactin

This hormone is most associated with nursing mothers, as it helps induce milk for their babies, but it is also another major player that affects sleep and health for both women and men.

Prolactin activates our T-cells and natural killer cells, which are part of our immune defense system. They zap foreign invaders, such as pathogens and harmful bacteria, and are our first line of defense against cancer.

A little known fact is that in order for prolactin to be released, melatonin has to be in circulation first for several hours. Therefore, we need those long dark hours of sleep for both of these hormones to do their best work, at the proper time. If prolactin is secreted during the day instead, because you routinely go to bed too late, it can quickly turn into weight gain, and even diabetes. Prolactin shuts down leptin, our satiety hormone (see page 75), and makes us crave sugar/carbohydrates.[10]

Erythroprotein

When it comes to feeling energized throughout the day, having plenty of red blood cells to deliver oxygen to your entire body is pretty important. And that's where erythroprotein (EPO) comes into play. It is a hormone released by the kidneys, which stimulates production of red blood cells by your bone marrow. The power of EPO to galvanize energy and increase stamina is well appreciated by high-performance athletes. So much so that a few famous ones have been caught doping with injections of EPO.

Hey, but you don't need to be doping up. All you need to do is get some good-quality shut-eye and your body will naturally produce this vital hormone.[11]

Growth Hormone

This hormone is released by your pituitary gland and is at its highest point about one hour after falling asleep.[12] As the name implies, growth hormone helps increase muscle mass, while facilitating repair of tissues. It optimizes the uptake of calcium into bones, stimulates the immune system, and also encourages the liver to reduce storage of glucose.

Low growth hormone is one reason why people who do not get enough sleep carry excess weight and have weak muscle tone and weak bones.

Testosterone

This hormone is correlated with the production of melatonin. Low melatonin during the night means low testosterone during the day, which leads to fatigue, depression, low libido, and weight gain.[13]

Although associated with men, testosterone is also needed by women (in much smaller amounts) to maintain lean body mass, libido, energy, concentration, and overall vitality.

Now that you know the delicate balance of all these hormones, and how they affect each other, and us, I hope that you will make sleep a priority.

Bad Diet

As mentioned in other chapters, a bad diet can bring on the blues, pile on the pounds, and usher in disease. Now we will learn why eating junk foods can also cause you to stare at the ceiling all night even after counting trillions of sheep.

I like to use the term *alchemy* to illustrate the relationship between food and sleep. According to the Merriam-Webster dictionary, alchemy is:

- a science that was used in the Middle Ages with the goal of changing ordinary metals into gold
- a power or process that changes or transforms something in a mysterious or impressive way

Alchemy: transforming common substances into gold. That is what our bodies do every single day at every single meal. It really is magic, if we consider the incredible process of our own internal natural alchemy. We take in nutrients and transform them into precious substances, such as hormones and neurotransmitters, that confer many benefits, including serene sleep. And the familiar, yet mysterious province of sleep in turn grants us the vitality and power to live life with purpose and enthusiasm during our waking hours. Yes, a healthy diet enables the process of turning edibles into "gold" that sustains and enriches our lives.

Here are just a few examples of what bad food choices can do to impede the "alchemic" process:

- Drinking sodas, which are high in phosphorus and sugar, will deplete magnesium and calcium reserves, both of which are needed for maintaining alkalinity and relaxation, so that you fall asleep faster. (Low magnesium and calcium levels can also lead to heart disease and osteoporosis.)
- Alcohol consumption, especially in the evening, can interrupt REM sleep. Excessive alcohol intake will also overtax the liver and deplete fat-soluble vitamins: A, D, E, and K.
- A high-carbohydrate diet, especially refined carbs, requires a lot of B vitamins to process. This means that they can quickly become depleted. Lack of B_3 and B_6 deters serotonin production. Lack of folic acid is connected with insomnia. Lack of B_{12} can lead to anemia, and low iron can trigger restless leg syndrome, in which twitching leg muscles disturb sleep.
- Inadequate intake of good-quality protein and healthy fats could cause a deficiency in all the necessary amino acids needed to make hormones such as serotonin.
- Stress and processed foods (which contribute to more stress) deplete us of vitamin C. This critical vitamin helps relieve stress, regulate sleep patterns, promote sound sleep, and lower our risk of having anxiety attacks. Vitamin C can also lessen the effects of caffeine, which is a common cause of insomnia.

• •

HAVE YOUR CAKE AND NIGHTMARES TOO

So you're feeling a bit hungry and nibble on a slice of carrot cake before going to bed.

The cloying sweetness lingers in your mouth as you drift off to sleep, but in about two hours you are awakened by a terrifying nightmare, and you're sweating and feeling mildly nauseous. You get up, exhausted, but also wanting to eat. You head to the kitchen and grab a cookie. Now you are fully awake and can't get back to bed until 4:00, and you need to get up by 6:00 to get to work...

That nightmare wasn't caused by the scary movie you saw, but by a severe drop in blood sugar due to that piece of cake. Anything sugary before bedtime is a trigger for blood sugar imbalance, which can lead to hypoglycemia (a drop in blood sugar). The nightmare alarms you to get up and get some glucose, thus you feel the urgency to wake up and eat. If this is happening to you, stop eating for at least three hours before going to bed.

• •

WIRELESS WRECKS YOUR ZZZZS

Since the advent of the wireless age, we have been inundated in a sea of invisible electrosmog. From huge cable towers to Wi-Fi routers and our own personal wireless devices, we have created an invisible electromagnetic field (EMF) that surrounds us day and night. Scientists are only now beginning to learn the multitude of negative health effects that persistent radiation causes.

EMFs suppress the production of melatonin. That alone is enough to sound the alarm. Furthermore, researchers at the University of Malaga found that significant exposure to EMFs increases the chance of developing depression fortyfold.[14]

Another study done by the renowned Karolinska Institute in Sweden found that using cell phones just before going to bed caused people to take longer to reach deeper stages of sleep.[15] They also linked EMFs, or electrosmog, to headaches, irritability, unusual tiredness, and sleeping disorders.

I'm sorry to report that it's not only wireless devices that cause problems with sleep. Old-fashioned electrical appliances and outlets that emit "dirty electricity" can also cause those who are sensitive to suffer restless nights. (See chapter 8 for information about how to reduce these invisible menaces in your home.)

• •

LIGHT BULBS: LIBERATION OR HEALTH HAZARD?

Every evening as the sun goes down, lights get switched on around the world. They are the ultimate symbol of man conquering nature. The ability to defy the night and extend our workday without limit has been heralded as the greatest advancement since humans discovered fire. But though we have achieved so much, what is the cost?

There's a reason why the night shift is also known as "the graveyard shift."

Long-term exposure to artificial light has been associated with an increased risk of cancers, cardiovascular disorders, and diabetes. In 2007, the International Agency for Research on Cancer classified shift work that disrupts normal circadian cycles "as a probable carcinogen."

- Melatonin suppression due to prolonged exposure to light at night among female nurses has been associated with an increased risk of breast and colorectal cancer.
- Women with previous or current breast cancer should be advised not to work night shifts because tumor growths may increase when melatonin is suppressed.
- Male night-shift workers have been found to have an increased risk of prostate cancer.

• •

POOR SLEEP AND SAD MOODS

So, now we know all the physical perks to having good sleep, but can this most primal and basic act really help us feel serene and happy? This is an issue that has been well studied and the evidence shows that indeed, sleep and mood are inextricably linked.

Researchers at the University of Pennsylvania rounded up a bunch of test subjects and limited them to a mere 4.5 hours of sleep per night for a whole week. The participants reported feeling more stressed, sad, angry, and mentally exhausted. When they were allowed to resume normal sleep, all the subjects reported a dramatic improvement in mood.[16]

On the flip side, difficulty sleeping can signal the first signs of depression. Studies have found that fifteen to twenty percent of people diagnosed with insomnia will develop major depression.[17]

While there is still much to explore in the connection between sleep and depression, it is interesting to note that if a person doesn't get enough sleep, serotonin levels can build up because it is not being turned into melatonin. *Too much* serotonin can cause cell receptors to burn out, causing a "deficiency"— much like insulin resistance, which occurs when too much insulin is released due to a high-carb/high-sugar diet and the cells become unresponsive.

Here's a summary by T.S. Wiley of *Lights Out:*

> Sleep normalizes serotonin levels because the melatonin produced during sleep can only be made by using up the available serotonin. That's why people who are depressed tend to self-medicate by either sleeping all the time or not sleeping at all. Both options work just like antidepressants. Not sleeping at all in a twenty-four-hour period causes the serotonin to build up to antidepressant burnout levels because it never gets to turn into melatonin. When it (serotonin) gets high enough, it "washes over the top," and the overload causes your receptors to go down and– *voila*–it's just like it's low, or just like you're on Prozac.[18]

· ·

SNORING AND SLEEP APNEA

Laugh and the world laughs with you,
snore and you sleep alone.
—ANTHONY BURGESS

Although there are numerous jokes about people who snore loudly, chronic snoring is no laughing matter. It can disrupt sleep for the person snoring and for their bed partner.

Dramatic snoring can also be a sign of sleep apnea, which is a life-threatening condition because it interrupts breathing.

Ways to help lessen snoring: lose weight, refrain from eating at least two hours before bed, avoid allergenic foods such as gluten, dairy, alcohol, and caffeine, change sleep position (lying on the side is better), avoid sedatives, and use hypoallergenic pillows and sheets.

Signs of sleep apnea include:

- Snoring with pauses in breathing (apnea)
- Gasping or choking during sleep
- Restless sleep
- Daytime sleepiness
- Problems with mental focus
- High blood pressure
- Nighttime chest pain
- Depression
- Morning headache
- Frequent trips to the bathroom at night

Sleep apnea is a serious health problem. If you suspect that you or your bedmate may have this condition, consult with a professional health practitioner.

• •

Now that we have looked at the clear benefits of sleep, are you ready to conk out and greet the sandman?

EAT WELL TO SLEEP WELL

Earlier in this chapter, we went over how poor food choices leads to nutrient deficiencies, robbing us of the necessary raw materials with which we make our own natural chemicals, such as hormones and neurotransmitters. The ebb and flow of our internal metabolism affects our energy levels by day and our ability to enjoy dreamland by night. In other words, what you put in your mouth does affect how well you sleep.

Now let's look at two specific amino acids, *tyrosine* and *tryptophan*. Both of these protein chains are needed by the brain to make hormones that are vital to our daily function. However, they affect us in very different ways. Tyrosine is the precursor to epinephrine (aka adrenalin), norepinephrine, and dopamine—which means it energizes and stimulates. Tryptophan is the precursor to serotonin, which is then converted to melatonin—which means that it has a calming effect and then a sedative effect.[19]

Foods with Tyrosine	Foods with Tryptophan
Poultry: chicken, turkey, duck	Poultry: chicken, turkey, duck
Meat: beef, lamb, pork	Meat: beef, lamb, pork
Fish	Fish
Eggs	Eggs
Milk	Milk
Cheeses	Cheeses
Avocados	Avocados
Pumpkin Seeds	Pumpkin Seeds
Sesame Seeds	Sesame Seeds

Wait, aren't the two lists the same? Yes. And there lies the secret to our sleep solution. You see, both of these amino acids need to get into the brain in order to affect our mood, and they both cross the blood-brain barrier via the same pathway.

A meal with carbohydrates will increase the brain's tryptophan levels—which is what we want in the evening in order to relax and feel tired for bed. If tyrosine crosses the barrier you will feel energized and alert, which is not what you want at night.

The presence of carbohydrates will trigger release of insulin, which sends other amino acids, including tyrosine, into cells in the body before they reach the brain. This gives the opportunity for more tryptophan to get across the blood-brain barrier.

Please remember that not all carbohydrates are the same. So only consume gluten-free, complex carbohydrates with your late afternoon or evening meals. As always, in the evening, stay away from processed sugar and anything that is too sweet, since a blood glucose spike will increase both insulin and cortisol. And another point to keep in mind is that after you've made serotonin, you need to sleep (in the dark), so that melatonin can be made. Remember, a buildup of too much serotonin can have negative effects on mood and health.[20]

Here are the basics of eating well to sleep well:
- Enjoy plenty of good-quality protein and healthy fats, along with lots of vegetables (both cooked and raw) during the day. This encourages tyrosine to be active.

- Cook with healthy fats such as coconut oil, organic butter, or ghee. We need fats in order to fully absorb the amino acids from protein.
- Snack on low-carb, low-glycemic foods, such as nuts, avocados, or cold cuts.
- Fruits are fine during the day, as long as they are low in sugar, such as berries.
- The optimal way to get serotonin going is to eat complex carbohydrates with foods containing tryptophan at night.

STEPS TO SERENE SLEEP

Suffering from insomnia or other sleep troubles can make one feel desperate and frazzled. Luckily, there are many things that we can do to help relax the body and mind and prepare ourselves for the luxurious gift of rejuvenating slumber. Twenty-seven steps are listed below: if you can do them all, you will be well rewarded with radiant health and happiness! However, it's perfectly fine to start with whichever steps feel easy and good to do.

- Get to bed by 10:00 p.m. (Set the alarm to *go* to bed. Set it for 9:00 p.m. Turn off all electronics, dim the lights, and wind down.) The time between 11:00 p.m. and 1:00 a.m. is when the liver is most active, effectively detoxifying all the gunk we absorbed throughout the day. If you stay up beyond the "liver" hours, toxins back up and flow back into your bloodstream.
- Sleep in complete darkness. (Remember our "hormone of darkness," melatonin, from earlier in this chapter?) When any light, especially artificial light, is detected by the pineal gland, release of melatonin comes to a halt. (Get blackout curtains if you are living in an area where streetlights penetrate your window treatments. See the Shopping Guide at the end of chapter 8 for resources.)
- Keep your bedroom free of any electronic and wireless devices, such as TV, wireless router, and computers. Do not put your cell phone by your bed. Put it in another room where you can still hear it, but far enough away so that the radiation does not disturb your pineal gland.
- Digital clocks that show time in the dark should also be

removed, or you can put a towel over them to mask the artificial light.

- Refrain from eating three hours prior to bed.
- Avoid caffeine after 3:00 p.m. It can take six or more hours to clear caffeine from the body.
- Avoid alcohol three to four hours before bed. Alcohol intake disrupts REM sleep and will also upset blood sugar balance, and cause dehydration.
- Keep your bedroom cool at around 60–70°F.
- Wear socks in bed when the weather is chilly. Since circulation to our feet is poor, they tend to feel cold, which can prevent sound sleep.
- Organic bedding matters! Especially if you have allergies. Synthetic mattresses and foam pillows release harmful petrochemicals. This *off-gassing* can cause breathing problems and accumulation of toxins.
- Exercise during the day and refrain from doing so at night to prevent cortisol from edging back up, which may cause poor sleep and a desire to eat late at night.
- Unwind by listening to relaxing music or reading something soothing to help you go to bed.
- Turn your bedroom into a sanctuary; avoid eating in bed or working in the bedroom.
- If your bed buddy snores, sleep in separate rooms! It's really worth it.
- If your partner has sleep apnea, that needs to addressed. (See page 116.)
- Get at least twenty minutes of sunlight during the day. Take a walk for lunch, sit down in the sun for a cup of tea, enjoy a walk with your dog, or grab your rays of sunshine in a park before heading to work. Exposing ourselves to daylight helps with the production of serotonin and also attunes our pineal gland to the circadian rhythm.
- Turn off the TV and get off computers and other electrical devices at least an hour before bed. You'll find that you can sleep much better, because watching a screen or answering an email can trigger a rise in cortisol. In addition, the neurons in our brain get revved up and can take as much as an hour to return to a calm state.

- Dim the lights after sunset. When your eyes are exposed to blue and white light spectrums your pineal gland (a tiny endocrine organ in your brain) will not secrete the melatonin you need for a good night's sleep.
- Do deep breathing for ten to twenty minutes before bed. This helps calm your central nervous system and relax the mind into a state of meditation.
- Take a hot bath with Epsom salts before bed. The magnesium contained in Epsom salts will help your body relax and also facilitate detoxification. Add three to four cups to a hot bath, and soak for at least fifteen minutes. Add a few drops of essential oil, such as lavender or rose, to make it a sensual experience.
- Use a sleep sachet (recipe, page 128).
- Ask someone to give you a foot massage, or do it yourself. Meridians on the feet are directly linked to different parts of the body. Massaging your feet at night can help calm your mind and lower cortisol.
- Make a list of all the things you are grateful for and find joy in.
- If you have noisy neighbors, wear earplugs.
- To help relaxation and calm anxiety, brew yourself a cup of chamomile, valerian, or oat straw tea and drink it one hour before bed.
- Make it a habit to gaze at the moon every night. City dwellers seldom follow the changing lunar phases throughout the month. By being aware of the waning and waxing cycles, we can better align ourselves to the natural biorhythms.
- Instead of being shocked awake by the jarring noise of a conventional alarm clock or the beep from you smart phone, use a *dawn simulator*, which will cast a rich glowing light, simulating the coming of dawn, and then chime gently. (See the Shopping Guide at the end of chapter 8.)

Summary
- Deep, restful sleep is a self-healing and rejuvenating process.
- We should strive to sleep for at least eight hours, though nine and a half is optimal.
- Melatonin, a powerful hormone that is made from serotonin,

is released in the dark. So make your bedroom as dark as possible and remove all gadgets that emit EMFs.

- Food choices have profound effects on how well you sleep.
- Lack of adequate sleep is linked to many chronic diseases and negative mood issues.

A Perfect Day Leading to Sweet Dreams and Serenity

7:00 a.m. Rise and shine after 9½ hours of sleep.

Drink a glass of room temperature water with fresh lemon.

7:30 a.m. Have a protein-rich breakfast and refrain from eating carbs (Rev Up Omelet recipe follows).

8:00 a.m. Walk or bike to work.

11:00 a.m. Snack on handful of nuts or avocado.

12:30 p.m. Protein-based lunch with vegetables.

Walk for 20 minutes in the sunshine.

3:30 p.m. Snack on an apple with almond butter.

6:30 p.m. Dinner with protein and gluten-free complex carbohydrates, plus veggies (Saffron Chicken Noodle Soup recipe follows).

9:00 p.m. Alarm sounds for you to wind down. Dim lights.

Take an Epsom salt bath with lavender oil.

10:00 p.m. Put your Sleep Sachet (recipe, page xx) next to your pillow.

Wishing you beautiful dreams saturated with melatonin!

RECIPES FOR RESTFUL SLEEP

REV UP OMELET

YIELD: 1 serving

This protein- and tyrosine-rich breakfast will provide you with lift and verve to start your day. (No carbs here, because we want to encourage tyrosine to travel across the blood-brain barrier.) Your blood sugar will also be very stable, so you won't be tempted by donuts in the break room.

1 tablespoon coconut oil or ghee
2 large eggs, pasture-raised or free-range, beaten
sea salt and freshly ground pepper, to taste
⅓ cup soft goat cheese, crumbled
⅓ cup chopped fresh dill
½ avocado, sliced, for topping (optional)

Heat a cast-iron pan with the cooking oil of your choice.

Season beaten eggs with sea salt and pepper.

When the pan is hot, pour in eggs and swirl them around to coat the pan.

When the eggs start to set, about one minute, add the cheese and fresh dill on one side of the omelet. Gently fold the other side to make a half-moon shape.

Flip folded omelet over to cook the other side for just about 10 seconds. Serve with slices of avocado and additional salt and pepper, to taste.

MELLOW CHERRY MOCKTAIL

YIELD: 2-3 servings

A mocktail is just as sexy as a cocktail, minus the alcohol. Sour cherry juice also contains melatonin and other powerful antioxidants that help calm inflammation.

8 ounces sour cherry juice
2 tablespoons fresh lime juice
4 ounces coconut water
2 teaspoons maple syrup
¼ teaspoon cardamom powder
¼ teaspoon ground cinnamon
4 whole pitted fresh cherries, for garnish (optional)

Pour the liquids and spices into a blender and blend well.

Serve in martini glasses, or over ice in tumblers. Garnish with lime slices or cherries as desired.

CALMING CHAI

YIELD: 2 servings

This recipe has all the flavor and richness of classic chai without the caffeine and dairy. A perfect afternoon treat that tastes great hot or cold.

3-4 rooibos tea bags
12 ounces filtered water
1 cinnamon stick
2 slices fresh ginger
3 cardamom pods, lightly
  crushed
1 star anise
½ teaspoon vanilla extract
⅓ cup coconut milk
2 teaspoons honey or maple
  syrup (optional)

Put the tea bags, water, spices, and vanilla extract in a small pot and bring to a boil.

Lower heat and allow mixture to simmer gently for 8–10 minutes.

Add coconut milk and sweetener, if using.

Strain and serve immediately.

EMERALD DREAMS SOUP

YIELD: 3-4 servings

Romaine lettuce has a high magnesium content, which helps with relaxation. Although usually eaten raw in salads, romaine makes a beautiful emerald-colored soup when cooked. The addition of chamomile is extra soothing. Serve this soup in the evening with a piece of grilled chicken or fish for the tryptophan.

1 head romaine lettuce, roughly
  chopped
2 garlic cloves, crushed
1 medium onion, diced
3 cups chicken broth or mineral
  broth (recipe, page xxv), or
  filtered water
2 chamomile tea bags, steeped
  in one cup hot water for 10
  minutes (tea bags removed)
1 small parsnip or potato, diced
sea salt and freshly ground
  pepper, to taste
⅓ cup chopped dill

Put all the ingredients except the chopped dill in a medium pot and bring to a simmer.

Cook for about 20 minutes, until parsnips are tender.

Pour into a blender and puree until smooth. (For safety, since the soup is hot, puree in two batches.)

Adjust with more sea salt and pepper as needed.

Garnish with dill and serve.

SAFFRON CHICKEN NOODLE SOUP (GLUTEN FREE)

YIELD: 3-4 servings

The combination of tryptophan from the chicken and carbohydrates from the gluten-free pasta will help optimize the production of serotonin, which is the precursor to melatonin.

2 ounces (dried weight) gluten-free pasta (see the Shopping Guide at the end of chapter 8 for a recommended brand)
1 tablespoon coconut oil, ghee, or butter
1 small carrot, cut into small dice
1 small onion, diced
2 celery ribs, chopped
1 garlic clove, peeled and mashed
8 ounces cooked chicken breast or thigh meat, shredded
5 cups chicken stock
5-6 strands of saffron, soaked in ¼ cup water for about 5 minutes; reserve soaking water (If you feel like being extravagant, put in a few more strands. Saffron helps brighten dark moods and is also soothing for frayed nerves.)
Celtic sea salt and freshly ground pepper, to taste
½ cup chopped cilantro or parsley

Cook the pasta according to manufacturer's directions. Drain and cut into shorter strands. Set aside.

Heat a large pot on medium-high heat and add the cooking oil of your choice.

Add carrot, onion, celery, and garlic. Sauté until the vegetables are aromatic and translucent, about 5 minutes.

Add the stock, shredded chicken, and saffron strands plus the soaking water. Season with a little sea salt and pepper.

Simmer for about 20 minutes. Add the cut pasta.

Simmer for about 5 minutes more. Add more sea salt and freshly ground pepper as needed.

Turn off the heat and add the fresh herbs.

Serve immediately in soup bowls.

MEDITERRANEAN BAKED HALIBUT WITH POTATOES

YIELD: 2 servings

This super-simple dish combines tryptophan found in fish with nongrain carbohydrates from potatoes, made delectable with the addition of olives and sun-dried tomatoes. Serve with an organic salad to boost vitamin C and B complex.

2 garlic cloves, mashed
10 Kalamata olives, pitted and chopped
⅓ cup chopped sundried tomatoes
2 small potatoes, peeled and cut into ⅛-inch slices
2 tablespoons extra virgin olive oil
¼ teaspoon sea salt and freshly ground pepper, to taste
2 6-ounces filets of halibut or cod
1 tablespoon extra virgin olive oil or butter

Preheat oven to 375°F. Mix the garlic, chopped olives, and sun-dried tomatoes. Set aside.

Brush a Pyrex dish or similar ovenproof baking vessel with some of the olive oil, then line with the potato slices, fanning them out to make a thin layer. Drizzle the rest of the olive oil over the layered slices.

Bake the potatoes for about 12–15 minutes.

Place the fish filets on top of the potatoes.

Season filets with sea salt and pepper, then drizzle with olive oil or dab with butter.

Top the filets with the olive mixture and bake for about 10 minutes more, or until filets are done.

Serve immediately.

WARM MILK WITH ROSES

YIELD: 1 serving

Roses are not only beautiful to behold, but their essence has been used by healers to calm frayed nerves, dispel melancholia, and to invite opening of the heart. Milk contains tryptophan and calcium, both of which help with sleep. Drink this one hour prior to bed.

8 ounces organic cows' or goats' milk

2 tablespoons organic dried roses, or organic rose petals, if you are lucky enough to have them

1 teaspoon honey or maple syrup (optional)

Gently simmer the roses in the milk for about 8–10 minutes.

Strain. Be sure to press down on the roses to extract more flavor.

Sweeten with honey or maple syrup if desired.

Please do not be tempted to add more sweetener, because the glucose will cause cortisol to rise.

GOLDEN COCONUT MILK TONIC

YIELD: 1 serving

This is a warming drink for those who are allergic to dairy. Coconut milk is combined with turmeric and ginger, all of which are anti-inflammatory and soothing.

4 ounces cup coconut milk

2 ounces filtered water

¼–½ teaspoon turmeric

2 slices fresh ginger, lightly crushed

½ teaspoon honey or maple syrup (optional)

Heat the coconut milk, water, turmeric, and ginger in a small pan.

Simmer gently for about 5–6 minutes.

Strain out the ginger and pour into a cup.

Add sweetener if desired.

Please do not be tempted to add more sweetener, because the glucose will cause cortisol to rise. Since coconut milk is naturally sweet, try it without extra sweetener first.

SLEEP SACHET

This is not for eating, but to be placed near your pillow for sound sleep and sweet dreams.

1 part dried organic roses
1 part dried organic lavender
1 part dried organic chamomile
2–3 drops essential lavender oil

In a bowl, mix the dried herbs together, then add the essential oil.

Stuff mixture into a small silk or linen pouch, and put it by your pillow.

You can refresh your sleep pillow by emptying out the contents and adding fresh drops of lavender oil every few days.

Other dried herbs that you can use are hops, poppy flowers, and oat straw.

Case Study

Megan was an account executive who used to travel for about eight months of the year.

When she turned forty, she decided to take a leave of absence from her work because she was feeling absolutely run-down. She had gained about twenty pounds and noticed that she was losing a lot of hair, while unwanted facial hair was causing her embarrassment. In addition, her periods were very erratic and she often experienced severe cramps without menstruation. She was diagnosed with PCOS (polycystic ovarian syndrome) by a naturopathic doctor, who recommended that she consult with me about changing her diet.

Three red flags went up after our initial intake: she was on a low-fat diet; she ate a very heavy diet of carb-based foods; and she only slept about four to five hours a night.

Taking those three important factors as the starting point to help Megan address her health issues, I asked her to increase her fat intake by adding coconut oil, organic butter/ghee, and extra virgin olive oil, and to increase her protein intake with every meal. Then I got her off gluten, because of the link between gluten intolerance and insulin resistance, which exacerbates PCOS. Finally, I coached her on how to get a good night's sleep.

It wasn't easy at first, but after a lot of handholding and reassurance that we could turn things around if she could just stick with the protocol, Megan saw the possibilities and jumped into her new routine.

Within about three weeks, she lost five pounds and noticed a lot less discomfort with cramping and fatigue. During this time, she also took herbal and nutritional supplements prescribed by her naturopathic doctor. I also got her to give up dairy, sugar, and coffee.

Megan even took cooking lessons from me and learned to whip up many gluten-free dishes. Her family and friends were surprised at how good they tasted.

After about eight months, hormonal tests showed that her androgen hormones and thyroid were back into balance. Her periods gradually became less painful, and her cycles were more normal. She also dropped all the excess weight, began the process of becoming a certified Pilates instructor, and started a new career with a PR firm. Megan felt like a healthy, vibrant woman entering a new decade of life.

Notes for Chapter 4

1   T.S. Wiley and Bent Formby, *Lights Out* (New York: Pocket Books, 2000), 5.
2   Stanley Coren, *Sleep Thieves* (New York: Free Press Paperbacks, 1996), 30.
3   Elijah Woflson, "The Rise of Ambien: Why More Americans are Taking the Sleeping Pill and Why the Numbers Matter," 5/8/2013, www.huffingtonpost.com/elijah-wolfson-/ambien_b_3223347.html
4   Ryan Joslan, "Prescription Sleeping Pills Tied to Increased Risk for Death, Cancer," 2/28/2012, www.cbsnews.com/news/prescription-sleeping-pills-tied-to-increased-risk-for-death-cancer/
5   Ibid.
6   Pete Bigelow, "Drowsy Driving Involved in 21 percent of Fatal Car Accidents," 11/5/2014, www.autoblog.com/2014/11/05/drowsy-driving-underreported-aaa/
7   Coren, *Sleep Thieves*, 87–90.
8   Wiley, *Lights Out*, 157.
9   Joseph, Mercola MD, *Dr. Mercola's Total Health Program* (Schaumburg, IL: Mercola.com), 54.
10   Wiley, *Lights Out*, 64–66.
11   Elizabeth Quinn, "EPO and Blood Doping in Sports," 5/28/2014, http://sportsmedicine.about.com/od/performanceenhancingdrugs/a/EPO.htm
12   Pamela Hanson, "Deep Sleep Tied to Hormone Production," 8/16/2000, http://articles.chicagotribune.com/2000-08-16/news/0008160337_1_eve-van-cauter-sleep-hgh
13   Abraham Harvey Kryger MD, *A Woman's Guide to Men's Health* (Berkeley: RDR Books, 2006), 86.
14   Alasdair Philips, "Is Wi-Fi Frying Our Brains? Fears that Cloud of 'Electrosmog' Could Be Harming Humans," 11/30/10, www.dailymail.co.uk/sciencetech/article-1334291/Is-Wi-Fi-frying-brains-Fears-cloud-electrosmog-harm-humans.html
15   Ibid.
16   D. Dinges et al., "Cumulative Sleepiness, Mood Disturbance, and Psychomotor Vigilance Decrements During a Week of Sleep Restricted to 4-5 Hours Per Night," *Sleep* 1997 Apr; 20(4):267-277.
17   D. Neckelmann et al., "Chronic Insomnia as a Risk Factor for Developing Anxiety and Depression," *Sleep* 2007; 30(7):873-880.
18   Wiley, *Lights Out*, 108.
19   Julia Ross, *The Mood Cure* (New York: Penguin Books, 2002), 123.
20   Wiley, *Lights Out*, 108.

Chapter 5

Say Goodbye to Sad

Happiness is like a butterfly which, when pursued, is always
beyond our grasp, but, if you will sit down quietly, may alight
upon you.
—NATHANIEL HAWTHORNE

Life's incessant stresses can really bring us down. From unfulfilled relationships to financial worries to environmental degradation: the barrage of woe-
inducing travails can cause physiological and emotional damage that leads
to a downward spiral where a permanent dark cloud looms overhead day after
day after day.

There exists a connection between external events causing us to feel
depressed and internal bodily processes. For example, you may receive
some devastating news, which causes sleepless nights and lack of appetite. If
this goes on for an extended period of time, it will wear down your ability to
take in nourishing substances from food and make vital hormones. Without
adequate sleep, you cannot make melatonin or growth hormone, both of
which contribute to a sense of well-being (See chapter 4 on Sleep), and with
lowered caloric intake due to diminished appetite, certain amino acids and
fats, which are needed as raw materials for hormones, energy, and metabolism, may become deficient.

On the flip side, if you have been indulging in junk food feasting, drinking
too much alcohol or coffee, smoking, or all of the above, it is sure to drain your
reserves of necessary vitamins and minerals required to make neurotransmitters such as serotonin or dopamine, which are needed for a positive and
joyful disposition.

While the trials and tribulations of life are beyond our control, the happy news is that an awareness of what to eat and what to avoid, along with changing bad habits, can boost your mood, whether the blues are caused by external circumstances or by eating the S.A.D. (Standard American Diet).

SEVEN CAUSES OF THE BLUES

In chapter 2, we looked at the links between digestive, thyroid, and adrenal health in regard to energy. In this chapter, we will deepen our understanding by exploring the connections with mood when these same channels are not functioning well. In addition, we will also look at the all-important liver and dietary nutrients, both of which also have a profound effect on whether we can enjoy the "alightment" of happiness, or suffer the dark encroachment of gloom.

Blues by Bad Gut

There's a saying in traditional Chinese medicine: "Above all, protect your digestion." And Hippocrates said it over 2,000 years ago: "All disease begins in the gut."

Today, we are just beginning to realize the wisdom of the ancients. Intriguing new studies are showing that how we digest and the quality of microbes in our gut actually affect not only our physical health, but also how we feel. But you don't really have to delve into the mysteries of millennia-old healing practices or be up on the latest scientific research to know that when your tummy is upset, the rest of your body feels bad too, including your brain.

Even if we ate the most organic and well-prepared foods available, we would still need robust digestion to help assimilate the nutrients contained within them. We are energetic, light-loving beings who depend upon sustenance from nature to obtain our energy, or *qi*, through eating plants and animals that have captured the rays of the sun. It is via the process of digestion that we can transform Nature into building blocks that become the foundation of our existence.

The core of good digestion is composed of two main parts: the gut barrier and gut microbes. Let's take a more detailed look.

A Break in the Wall

One of the most harmful gut conditions is a *leaky gut*. Just as it sounds, the protective barrier of your intestinal lining has been compromised through eating allergenic foods, ingestion of toxins, or ongoing stress. When our protective barrier has been breached, particles of undigested foods can sneak into our bloodstream. At that point, our ever-vigilant immune system mounts a response by attacking the "foreign" pathogens. This immune defense reaction can cause bloating, gas, inflammation, and fatigue, though sometimes there may be no overt symptoms. Leaky gut is linked to eczema or psoriasis, heart failure, autoimmune conditions affecting the thyroid (Hashimoto's disease) or joints (rheumatoid arthritis), autism spectrum disorder, depression, and mental illness.

Gut Bugs Are Our Friends

The celebrated writer and activist Michael Pollan published an article in the *New York Times* titled "My Best Friends are Germs."[1] Pollan fully appreciates his relationship with his gut bugs because he knows that good gut ecology depends on the existence of trillions of microbes in our digestive tract. They help digestion, fight off harmful bacteria, and strengthen our immune system.

What's more incredible, our gut microbes actually help rebuild the epithelial lining (the interior skin) of the digestive tract and are also involved in the production of nutrients such as vitamins B_{12} and K.[2]

Another person who understands the critical symbiotic tango between us and our countless microbiota is Dr. Natasha Campbell-McBride, author of the groundbreaking book *Gut and Psychology Syndrome*.

> A human body is like a planet inhabited by huge numbers of various micro-creatures. The diversity and richness of this life on every one of us is probably as amazing as the life on Earth itself! Our digestive system, skin, eyes, respiratory and excretory organs are happily coexisting with trillions of invisible lodgers, making one ecosystem of macro- and micro-life, living together in harmony. It is a symbiotic relationship, where either party cannot live without the other. Let me repeat this: we humans cannot live without these tiny micro-organisms, which we carry on and in our bodies everywhere.[3]

When our microbiome is out of balance, with too many bad microbes taking the helm, it can cause not only physical malaise, but a gamut of cognitive and emotional problems including ADHD, psychosis, and depression.[4]

• •

WHAT IS THE MICROBIOME?

The microbiome is defined as the collective genomes of microbes (composed of bacteria, bacteriophages, fungi, protozoa, and viruses) that live inside and on the human body. We have about ten times as many microbial cells as human cells.

• •

No Joy with Low Thyroid

When this butterfly-shaped, tiny gland is not functioning well, it can also lead to emotional and cognitive issues, because the brain has many receptors for T3, an active hormone we need. There are also other hormones involved with the thyroid; however, we will concentrate on how T3 is made, as it directly affects how we feel.

Dr. Christiane Northrup MD, a luminary physician who specializes in hormonal health, states:

> T3 is found in large quantities in the limbic system of the brain, the area that is important for emotions such as joy, panic, anger, and fear. If you don't have enough T3, or if its action is blocked, an entire cascade of neurotransmitter abnormalities may ensue and can lead to mood and energy changes, including depression.[5]

The T4 to T3 Transformation

- The brain (pituitary) secretes thyroid-stimulating hormone (TSH), which signals the thyroid gland to make the thyroid hormones T4 and T3. They are so named for the number of iodine molecules that are attached to them.
- Although the majority secreted is T4, our body can only use T3, so we must convert T4 to T3 using various pathways. The liver, gut, cells located in the heart, muscles, and nerves are all involved. (Note: twenty percent of T4 is converted to T3 in the intestines, BUT only with good gut flora! Even a single use of antibiotics can mess up your good vs. bad gut ecology and set you up for thyroid problems down the road.[6])
- A whopping sixty percent of T4 is converted to T3 in the liver. Not enough T3 will be produced if it is congested from too many toxins.[7]

- After T3 is made, it enters the nuclei of cells to orchestrate their activities.

When T3 levels are low, organs and internal systems slow down, creating a wide range of symptoms—including depression.

Signs of low thyroid function include feeling cold, exhaustion, loss of outer eyebrows, weight gain, lethargy, and brain fog.

If you suspect that you have a thyroid problem, consult with your health-care practitioner to run a full panel thyroid test. Many signs and symptoms of depression may be corrected when the thyroid and adrenal health is restored.

• •

WHAT IS HASHIMOTO'S DISEASE?

Hashimoto's is an autoimmune condition, in which the tissues of the thyroid are being destroyed by the body's own immune system. It is estimated that Hashimoto's accounts for ninety percent of adult cases of hypothyroidism in the U.S.[8]

• •

Woe with Weak Adrenals

Linked to our thyroid are the adrenal glands, which produce our stress and sex hormones. Here is what Dr. Christiane Northrup says:

The adrenal glands are your body's primary "shock absorbers." These two little thumb-sized glands sitting on top of your kidneys produce hormones including norepinephrine, cortisol and DHEA, which allow you to respond to the conditions of your daily life in healthy and flexible ways.

When one is suffering a perpetual slump, it is a stressful situation that can further deplete hormonal production. And with cortisol remaining constantly high, our sex hormones suffer because the demand to keep cortisol up depletes the master hormone, *pregnenolone*. When there isn't enough pregnenolone to go around because cotisol is demanding most of it, symptoms such as accel-erated aging, lackluster sex drive, fatigue, and constant infections can occur.[9] Now, that's quite enough to make anyone feel down and out!

· ·

THE PREGNENOLONE STEAL

Pregnenolone is the master hormone because virtually all other hormones are made from it. Two branches of hormones need it. One converts the pregnenolone to progesterone, and then cortisol. The other converts it to DHEA, and then into other sex hormones including estrogen and testosterone. If you are stressed, pregnenolone will feed the branch that turns into cortisol, thereby starving, or "stealing" from the other branch, leaving you depleted of vital sex hormones, which affects not only our libido, but also our mood.

· ·

· ·

STIMULANTS ZAP YOUR ADRENALS

Caffeine, alcohol, recreational drugs, sugar, and energy drinks all affect the adrenals by spiking cortisol. If you rely on any of these substances to get going, or to enhance a low mood on a daily basis, know that depending on the amount and level of dependency, you could be harming your adrenals in a big way. The best way to gauge a possible addiction is to refrain from the items that you consume the most for at least one week.

· ·

Stagnant Liver Suppression

While the heart gets all the attention because of its association with passion and romance, the organ that we really need to love is our liver! It is responsible for filtering out everything that enters our body; it stores the fat-soluble vitamins (A, D, E, and K) it converts sixty percent of the inactive T4 hormone into the active T3; it makes cholesterol, which is needed to make adrenal hormones; and it also makes bile, which is integral to proper digestion.[10]

And it does so much more! Healers from antiquity highly valued the liver. The Romans and Greek physicians considered the liver to be the seat of emotions, and Chinese doctors have thought the same for centuries. In particular, they associate the liver with anger. When one cannot properly express anger or frustration, the suppression can lead to depression.

When the liver is out of balance, the following symptoms can occur:

emotional problems, rib pain or fullness, dizziness, headaches, tendon problems, menstrual problems, jaundice, weak or blurry vision, and digestive disorders.

A healthy, uncongested liver is the foundation for physical vitality and emotional well-being. (See chapter 6 for how to do a detox to support your liver.)

Sad by Sugar

Do you remember the Mammoth Mega Rush extreme roller-coaster ride from our Introduction? I used it as a metaphor for what happens when we eat sugary foods that send our blood sugar and insulin skyrocketing and the inevitable crash that follows, when all that glucose gets swept up, leading to hypoglycemia. Constant demand on insulin will lead to insulin resistance. When you are resistant to the hormone, your glucose levels rise, but your cells starve, including the cells in your brain that are involved in making those feel-good neurotransmitters such as serotonin, dopamine, and GABA. Of course, insulin resistance also leads to Type 2 diabetes. Multiple research data shows that developing depression is twice as likely for people with diabetes compared to those without and that depressed adults have a thirty-seven percent increased risk of developing diabetes.[11]

Bad Diet Despair

A bad diet can refer to a diet full of processed foods, laden with highly refined carbohydrates, and laced with additives, but it can also be a diet where trigger foods are being eaten day and night, causing allergies and inflammation.

Still reluctant to give up your bagel and cream cheese? Perhaps reading what Dr. Perlmutter, neurologist and author of *Grain Brain*, has to say about gluten and the brain will shift your stance.

> Depression and anxiety are often severe in patients with gluten sensitivity. This is primarily due to cytokines that block production of critical brain neurotransmitters like serotonin, which is essential in regulating mood. With elimination of gluten and often dairy, many patients have been freed from not just their mood disorders but other conditions caused by an overactive immune system, like allergies and arthritis.[12]

Over the course of five years, researchers in Britain looked at depression and diet in more than three thousand middle-aged office workers. The results showed that people who ate a junk food diet—one that was high in processed meat, desserts, fried food, refined cereals, and commercial dairy products— were more likely to report symptoms of depression.[13]

Consuming allergenic foods such as gluten (found in wheat, barley, rye, and cross-contaminated oats), soy, dairy, corn, and peanuts can lead to leaky gut, which then starts the domino effect of maldigestion, leading to immune disorders, leading to disease.

Get Puffy and Dumpy with PUFAs

No, "Puffy" and "Dumpy" are not two of Snow White's dwarfs, nor is PUFA a cute name for a stuffed toy. *Puffy* is a term I am using to describe inflammation, and *dumpy* refers to being down in the dumps. PUFA is actually an official acronym that stands for *polyunsaturated fatty acid*, otherwise also known as omega-6 and omega-3 oils.

When it comes to calming inflammation and feeling good, the critical point with PUFAs is one of ratios. As everyone knows, omega-3 oils (EPA and DHA) are needed for heart and brain health; however, not many people understand that high consumption of vegetable oils and factory-farmed animal products skews the ratio and can lead to inflammation, which is the genesis for a long list of diseases, including cardiovascular disease, arthritis, depression, and even cancer.

Researchers have found that many hunter-gatherer populations consume less than one percent of calories from omega-6 fatty acids. Whereas, in the U.S., more than seven percent of our calories are from omega-6 PUFAs.[14]

PUFA oils to avoid include: corn, safflower, sunflower, soybean oil, and canola.

How it all connects: Now that we know some of the physical and dietary causes that can bring on depression, let's look at how to turn things around so we can bust the dark clouds and bring on the sunshine!

SIX WAYS TO OVERCOME SAD MOODS

Good Gut for Good Mood

It bears repeating that our gut and brain developed together in utero, and they are still connected by the vagus nerve and share many of the same hormones and neurotransmitters. Therefore, if we want to support the brain, we must also support digestion.

- Remove gluten and other foods you may be allergic to, including corn, dairy, soy, peanuts, etc.
- Heal the gut with bone broth, probiotics, fermented vegetables (sauerkraut, kimchi, etc.), yogurt, and kefir.
- Remove processed sugar.
- Soak all grains, nuts, and seeds.
- Chew slowly: at least thirty-five times each bite.
- Give your digestive juices a boost by using digestive bitters or apple cider vinegar before a meal. (one teaspoon raw apple cider vinegar in one half cup room temperature water taken fifteen minutes before a meal helps with digestion and acid reflux.)
- Don't eat when stressed.
- Eat organic and free-range foods.
- Include and enjoy healthy fats, especially saturated fats from coconut oil, butter, and ghee.
- Appreciate your cholesterol and don't try to lower it with drugs. It is the raw material for hormones and bile production, and it supports the immune system.

· ·

CHEERS FOR CHOLESTEROL

Some researchers theorize that low levels of cholesterol alter brain chemistry, suppressing the production of serotonin and other neurotransmitters in the brain.

According to Dr. Thomas Cowen, author of *The Fourfold Path to Healing,*

> One of the most interesting findings to emerge from hundreds of studies on cholesterol and heart disease is the fact that whenever cholesterol levels are successfully lowered through diet or drug therapy,

there is a corresponding significant increase in depression and aggressive behavior in those whose cholesterol has been lowered the most.[15]

• •

Thyroid and Adrenal Health for Happiness

Both the thyroid and adrenals work in tandem with the brain and receive messages directly based on your reactions to your surroundings and situations at any given moment. They respond by making the appropriate hormones that will regulate metabolism and energy. The thyroid is very sensitive to environmental toxins, such as fluoride[16] and ingestion of gluten, which may lead to Hashimoto's disease. The adrenals are particularly affected by sugar intake, caffeine, and other stimulants such as alcohol and certain prescription drugs.

Ways to support thyroid and adrenals:
- Increasing vitamin C: As stress levels increase, our need for vitamin C also increases. (Because we cannot make our own C, it needs to come from the diet or through supplementation.)
- Buffering minerals such as magnesium, calcium, and potassium
- Going gluten free (to prevent Hashimoto's disease)
- Taking adaptogenic herbs, such as astragalus, rhodiola, and Schisandra
- Minimizing stress
- Going on an alkaline diet
- Increasing sleep
- Appropriate exercise

Love Your Liver

Since the liver needs to filter everything, the cleaner the diet, the better. The liver also needs plenty of protein to do its exhausting work.

Ways to love your liver:
- Eat organic produce and free-range, grass-fed animal products.
- Enjoy bitter herbs and greens such as dandelion, arugula, and chicory.

- Use organic skin care products. Many mass-produced lotions and potions are filled with contaminants that are absorbed through the skin.
- Be mindful of alcohol intake.
- Do not consume beverages or food items sweetened with high-fructose corn syrup. (see page 88 for the reasons)
- Detox at least twice a year (see chapter 6)

Balance Blood Sugar for Bliss

Mood swings, energy fluctuations, and constant cravings for sweets are the hallmark of blood sugar imbalance. So the goal is maintaining a steady flow of energy and feeling even-keeled throughout the day, even if unexpected dramas and traumas come our way.

Ways to Balance Blood sugar:
- No processed sugar
- Limit carbohydrate intake
- Eat foods high in chromium: this trace mineral helps optimize the effects of insulin. Foods with chromium include nutritional yeast, broccoli, apples, chicken, and mushrooms
- Eat protein and fat and plenty of vegetables at every meal

Eat Good, Feel Brilliant

There's no way of getting around it: One of the major causes of disease is what we eat, and yet one of the key factors for health is also what we eat. The difference between the two states, disease and health, is obviously the quality of the foods we choose. By sourcing our foods from organic farmers who practice ethical care of their land and animals, we reap the benefits of better nutrients, fewer toxins, and the satisfaction of knowing that we are part of the ecosystem.

· ·

TOMATO VS. TOMATO

There's been an on going debate about whether organic vegetables are truly better than conventional when it comes to vitamin and mineral content. Countless studies have been done, but variables in soil condition, farming practices, and test methodology have made it hard to come to a definitive answer.

However, more recent studies are showing that there are differences—notably, with tomatoes. Organic tomatoes contained 2.4 percent higher levels of phenolic acids and fifty-five percent more Vitamin C. And, of course, organic tomatoes and other produce do not contain harmful chemicals from pesticides, etc.[17]

• •

• •

GRASS-FED VS. FEED LOT

When compared with conventional beef, grass-fed cows provide far superior vitamins, minerals, and fatty acids. When animals are allowed to graze outside in the sun and freely munch on grass, not only are they much happier, but we are also the recipients of that ethical stewardship.

According to a study done by Professor Cynthia Daley, a professor at the College of Agriculture at California State University at Chico, one hundred percent grass-fed beef far surpasses its factory-farmed counterpart. In particular, when animals are allowed to graze exclusively on grass, the end product provides much higher levels of omega-3, zinc, and vitamins A and D, as well as powerhouse antioxidants such as *glutathione* and *superoxide dismutase*. The meat is lower in total fat, but much higher in an important lipid that helps weight management and is anticancer: CLA, or *conjugated linoleic acid.*[18]

• •

Nutrients We Need for Happy Moods

Here is a list of nutrients that we need to ensure a happy mood. All of them should be sourced from organic or environmentally conscious sources.

B Complex

All the members of the B vitamin family are important for good mood. In particular, low levels of vitamin B_{12}, vitamin B_6, and folate may be linked to depression.

Vitamin D

Known as the sunshine vitamin because we need sun interacting with our skin to make it, and also because Seasonal Affective Disorder (SAD) and general depression are linked to insufficient D. Vitamin D can also be found in animal-sourced foods such as liver, butter, milk, and mushrooms (when the gills are exposed to the sun after harvesting). If you need to supplement, use only the D_3 form. What's the difference between the two forms? Vitamin D_3 is also known as *cholecalciferol* and is created by skin cells, along with cholesterol, in response to UVB light. So Vitamin D_3 comes from animal sources. Vitamin D_2, or *ergocalciferol*, comes from plant sources. The best way to get your D is through sunshine. You could accumulate as much as 10,000 IUs in twenty minutes if you exposed yourself fully.

Zinc

This mineral is involved with over three hundred enzymatic processes. It is highly concentrated in the brain (second only to iron) and maintains the blood-brain barrier, or BBB. The BBB surrounds and protects the brain from many things. Studies show that a zinc deficiency in animals reduces the strength of the BBB, thus possibly increasing the risk for Parkinson's and Alzheimer's. Individuals who suffer from depression have lower concentrations of zinc in their circulating blood compared to those without depression, according to the findings of a new meta-analysis published in the journal *Biological Psychiatry*.[19]

GABA and Theanine

These compounds are found in all teas, but especially in green tea. In contrast to the stimulating effects of caffeine, cola, and energy drinks, tea contains theanine and promotes production of GABA. Both these substances are calming, yet help the mind to stay alert. Call it a state of "alert relaxation."

Theanine is a somewhat rare amino acid found only in tea, a specific species of mushroom (*Boletus badius*), and guayusa, a type of holly tree found in the Amazon.[20]

GABA (gamma-aminobutyric acid) is a neurotransmitter that protects brain neurons from becoming overly excited. It also helps open arteries and lower blood pressure. It is not actually found in food, but is made from an amino acid, glutamine (not to be confused with monosodium glutamate, or MSG).

Foods with glutamine include pork, beef, sesame seeds, and tea.

· ·

GET SAFE SUN

The amount of sun-sourced vitamin D you get depends on location and time of year. If you live in the mid-latitudes of North America (35°–50° north—that is, most of the northern U.S., including New York, Chicago, Seattle, San Francisco, Washington, and Boston), there is no UVB to be had during November through February, so supplementation would be a good idea. For the rest of the year, and especially during the summer, get bare and get safe sun.

Here is The Horlick Formula for Safe Sun, created by Dr. Michael Horlick, a renowned vitamin D researcher and author of *The UV Advantage*:

Expose twenty-five percent of your body's surface area to twenty-five percent of 1MED* two to three times per week, without sunscreen, during all times of the year when UVB rays are available where you live. *1MED just means *one minimal erythemal dose,* which in plain English is the time it takes for you to get a mild sunburn, without sunscreen.

Wait, don't be confused! It's rather simple when you do some easy math and locate your coordinates.[21]

Here's an example of how you do it, according to Dr. Horlick's Formula for Safe Sun:

- Go outside in your shorts or bathing suit (ideally before 10:00 a.m. or after 2:00 p.m.), without sunscreen, and see how long it takes for your skin to get mildly pink. This is your 1MED.
- After that, either get back indoors or put on a full-spectrum sunscreen.
- Multiply your personal 1MED by twenty-five percent. For example, if it took fifteen minutes for you to turn pink (your 1MED), fifteen multiplied by .25 gives you approximately four minutes.
- Now get out and enjoy the sun with twenty-five percent of your body exposed (your face, hands, and arms OR arms and legs) for about four minutes, two to three times per week, when UVB rays are available where you live.
- After the desired exposure time to get your vitamin D, use a full-spectrum suntan lotion if you want to stay out longer.

According to Dr. Horlick, this method will provide you with approximately 1,000 IUs of vitamin D. The more skin you expose, the more vitamin D you will make. Keep in mind that though 1,000 IUs is a good amount, individual needs differ greatly and the optimal amount you require per day depends on your existing vitamin status and on the amount of vitamin D in your diet.[22]

• •

• •

THE DARK SIDE OF SUNSCREENS

In the 1960s, companies that made sunscreens only provided UVB protection. Since it is the UVB rays that cause skin to burn, manufacturers promoted their products to sun-worshippers who could now get dark tans without being burned. However, ironically, it is the UVA radiation that causes premature wrinkles and is linked to melanoma. And it is the UVB that provides vitamin D (with the help of our skin, cholesterol, liver, and kidneys).

The Environmental Working Group cautions against using sunscreens that contain *oxybenzone* and *retinyl palminate*. Both chemicals have been shown to have toxic effects and may cause cancer.[23]

• •

Feel Fantastic with Healthy Fats

We learned earlier in this chapter that PUFAs can have either a positive or negative impact on our mood, depending on the ratio. A healthy balance is 1:1. Limit or discontinue use of vegetable oils (at least in your own kitchen), so that you maintain this ratio as closely as possible.

Saturated fats are another form of fat that we need for a happy brain. In fact, our brains *are made of fat*, sixty percent of which is saturated.

Here are some good saturated fats to eat:
- Butter
- Ghee

- Coconut oil
- Red palm oil (Although palm oil is an antioxidant-rich healthy fat, the harvesting of palm oil is linked to deforestation and destruction of animal habitats. If you choose to use it, please be sure that you are getting it from a sustainable source.)
- Lard
- Duck fat
- The fat under the skin on poultry
- The fat on cuts of meat (trim some off, but not too much)
- Full-fat dairy products, if you are not allergic

We need fat to digest protein and to make bile and digestive enzymes.

More Ways to Say Bye-Bye to Sad
- Exercise
- Yoga
- Massage
- Volunteer work
- Community involvement
- Gardening
- Therapy
- Pets

Summary
- A healthy diet can go a long way to help bust the blues.
- Good digestion is one of the key factors for good mood, because the gut and brain are connected and share the same neurotransmitters.
- Sugar and a high-carb diet contribute to mood swings and depression.
- A balance of PUFAs is very important to calm inflammation. The proper ratio is 1:1 (omega-3:omega-6).
- Vitamins and minerals from foods are necessary for maintaining a happy and calm disposition. So eat well by choosing organic, grass-fed, free-range sources.
- In addition to diet, exercise, relaxation practices, and engagement in the community are all good habits to cultivate.

A Perfect "Say Goodbye to Sad" Day

6:30 a.m. Warm water with fresh lemon juice

Exercise options: Fast walk, burst training, Pilates

7:30 a.m. Breakfast: Vitamin D Frittata (recipe, page 153)

10:30 a.m. Snack: Liver Pâté with rice crackers (recipe, page 150) If possible, get out for some sun and fresh air.

1 p.m. Lunch: Green Tea-Poached Fish with Miso Dressing

3:30 p.m. Snack: Gluten-Free Pound Cake with Cardamom ·

5:30 p.m. Shiatsu Massage

7: 30 p.m. Dinner: Grilled chicken and Wild Rice with Tahini and Green Onions

9:30 p.m. Disengage from all wireless devices

Do a short meditation or read something uplifting.

Take a bath with Epsom salts and lavender or rose oil

10:30 p.m. To bed, so you can make plenty of melatonin

RECIPES TO CHEER YOUR SOUL

EDIBLE FLOWERS AND ORGANIC GREENS WITH MUSTARD-HONEY DRESSING

There's nothing quite like edible flowers to dress up a dish. Nasturtiums, pansies, roses, and marigolds are not only beautiful but also contain antioxidants and vitamin C.

6 cups organic salad greens

⅓ cup Mustard-Honey Dressing (recipe, page 57)

sea salt and freshly ground pepper, to taste

7–8 edible flowers

⅓ cup toasted pumpkin seeds

In a salad bowl, toss the greens with the dressing and season with salt and pepper.

Top with the edible flowers and pumpkin seeds.

BACON-WRAPPED ASPARAGUS

YIELD: 4 servings as an appetizer
This super-simple recipe needs only two ingredients! Fat in the bacon will help you to absorb the vitamins in the asparagus. It's a perfect pairing.

12 spears asparagus, trimmed
6 strips bacon (nitrate-free), cut in half crosswise

Preheat oven to 375°F. Line a baking tray with parchment.

Wrap a piece of bacon around a spear of aspargus and place it, seam side down, on the prepared baking sheet. Repeat with the rest. Leave about ½ inch of space between wrapped pieces.

Bake for about 15 minutes, or until bacon is crisp and asparagus is cooked.

COCONUT AND DATE KISSES

YIELD: approx. 24 pieces

15 medjool dates, pitted
⅓ cup raw cashews, soaked for 5 hours
⅔ cup raw walnuts, soaked for 5 hours
2 tablespoons unsweetened cocoa powder
¼ teaspoon ground cinnamon
¼ teaspoon freshly ground nutmeg
¼ teaspoon sea salt
½ teaspoon cayenne (optional)
2 tablespoons filtered water
2 cups unsweetened shredded coconut flakes, for coating

Drain the soaked nuts and put in a food processor along with the other ingredients except the coconut flakes.

Blend until ingredients are well mixed and form a ball.

Add extra water one tablespoon at a time as needed to facilitate blending. The mixture should feel soft.

Pinch off a well-rounded tablespoon of the mixture and roll it between your palms into a ball. Keeping your palms moist with water will prevent sticking and help make smooth, rounded spheres.

Spread the coconut flakes on a large dish and roll the date balls in them to coat.

Once they are well coated, they magically transform into Coconut and Date Kisses! Yummy.

Store in an airtight container.

VICHYSSOISE WITH CRÈME FRAÎCHE

YIELD: 4 servings

This classic French soup contains plenty of healthy fat, along with gluten-free carbohydrates from potatoes, to offer a comforting creamy experience.

2 tablespoons organic butter or ghee (or extra virgin olive oil, if you want to avoid dairy)

3 cups sliced leeks, white parts only (from about 4 large leeks)

½ medium onion, chopped or sliced

¼ cup dry white wine

1 pound Yukon Gold potatoes, peeled and chopped

3 cups chicken broth or mineral broth

1 teaspoon sea salt (more as needed)

white pepper, to taste

⅓ cup heavy whipping cream

½ cup crème fraîche (If you want to avoid dairy, substitute ¾ cup almond milk for the heavy cream and crème fraîche) (recipe, Homemade Almond Milk, page 86)

chopped fresh chives, for garnish

In a heavy stockpot, melt the butter or ghee on medium-high heat.

Toss in the chopped leek and onion. Sauté until translucent, then add the white wine. Allow to cook for about one minute.

Add the chopped potato pieces and stock. Bring to a simmer and allow to cook for about 30 minutes, or until the potatoes are very soft.

Add sea salt and white pepper.

Puree with an immersion blender or in a regular blender (being careful of the hot liquid) until the soup is smooth. If you desire a very smooth/silky soup, strain the pureed soup through a fine sieve.

Allow soup to cool slightly and gently whisk in heavy cream and crème fraîche.

Chill the vichyssoise to around 65°F. (Overchilling the soup will impair the flavor.)

Taste again for seasoning and add more sea salt and pepper as needed.

Serve in chilled soup bowls and garnish with chopped chives.

Note: For a decadent version, serve with a dollop of caviar.

LIVER PÂTÉ YOU'LL LOVE, REALLY

YIELD: 8–10 servings as an appetizer
Liver was prized by many traditional cultures as a sacred, nutrient-dense food. It provides vitamins A and D, as well as essential fatty acids and trace minerals. This recipe is from Laura Knoff,* who was one of my mentors. This recipe is so good that people who often shy away from liver end up loving it!

4 tablespoons organic butter
1 medium onion, diced
2 teaspoons dried thyme
2 teaspoons dried sage
2 teaspoons dulse flakes
1 pound liver from pasture-raised
  chicken or duck, trimmed
freshly ground pepper, to taste
2 tablespoons miso paste

Blend until mixture is smooth.

Heat a large skillet on medium-high heat and melt 2 tablespoons of the butter.

Toss in the onion and sauté until translucent. Add the dried spices.

Add the liver and cook for 8–10 minutes, or until fully cooked through. Add freshly ground pepper, to taste.

Allow the cooked mixture to cool, then transfer to a food processor. Add the miso and the rest of the butter.

The pâté can be served warm or chilled. Wonderful with gluten-free crackers and topped with capers, Dijon mustard, or chopped olives.

* Recipe by Laura Knoff NC, author of *The Whole-Food Guide to Overcoming Irritable Bowel Syndrome*

GLUTEN-FREE POUND CAKE WITH CARDAMOM

YIELD: 8 servings

Cardamom is known as the "queen of spices" and has been used since ancient times to elevate mood and help with digestion. For more on this spice, see chapter 1, page 19.

1 cup white rice flour
½ cup sorghum flour
¼ cup arrowroot flour
2 teaspoons baking powder
1 teaspoon xanthan gum
⅛ teaspoon sea salt
1 cup organic butter, softened
½ cup turbinado sugar
¼ teaspoon stevia* (green powder form)
4 large eggs, pasture-raised or free-range
1 teaspoon vanilla extract
¼ teaspoon ground cardamom or 3-4 drops cardamom essential oil**

Preheat oven to 350°F.

Lightly coat a 9-inch loaf pan with butter and dust with a little rice flour so that your pound cake can turn out easily when done. (I highly recommend using a Pyrex pan, *not* a nonstick pan, to prevent the release of toxic compounds from the coating.)

Put the first six (dry) ingredients in a bowl and mix well.

In a separate bowl, cream the butter, sugar, and stevia powder together with a spatula or wooden spoon. This will take a few minutes. You can also use an electric beater, but I find that doing it manually is much more meditative and gives your arms a little workout.

Add the eggs one by one until well mixed.

Add the vanilla extract and cardamom.

Sift the flour mixture into the batter. Mix well, and pour the batter into the prepared loaf pan.

Bake on the middle rack of the oven for 50-60 minutes, or until the cake has a nice golden-brown top and a toothpick inserted into the middle comes out clean.

*Stevia comes in many forms. I prefer the least processed: green powder, which can be purchased online (see the Shopping Guide at the end of chapter 8).

** If you choose to use the essential oil of cardamom in this recipe, DO NOT add more than 3-4 drops; pure essential oils are very potent and can be harmful when overused for ingestion. There are only a few essential oils that can be used in cooking, so always consult expert sources before using a culinary oil.

GRASS-FED BEEF BURGER WITH PORTOBELLO MUSHROOM

YIELD: 1 serving

Grass-fed beef is a completely different animal than the factory-farmed, corn-fed version. When cows are allowed to graze freely on grass out in the open and under sunshine, they are much happier and also produce meat that contains high levels of vitamins and minerals, especially zinc and omega-3 fatty acids.

6 ounces ground beef, pastured or grass fed

2–3 tablespoons organic butter or ghee

sea salt and freshly ground pepper, to taste

1 slice cheddar cheese (optional)

1 burger bun (gluten-free; see the Shopping Guide at the end of chapter 8 for best brands)

1 tablespoon Dijon mustard

1 slice onion, ¼ inch thick

2–3 slices of portobello mushroom, cut ¼ inch thick

1 slice tomato, ¼ inch thick

Shape beef into a patty about 1 inch thick.

Heat a cast-iron skillet on medium-high heat and melt half the butter.

Put the patty in the hot skillet and season with salt and pepper. Cook on one side for about 3 minutes, then flip over, season, and cook for another 3 minutes, for medium. Add the cheese on top to melt, if using.

While the burger is cooking, toast bun halves and spread them with the rest of the butter and Dijon mustard.

Transfer burger to bottom bun.

Cook onion and portobello mushroom in the same pan for a few minutes, until softened.

Place onion and mushroom on top of the burger. Finish with a slice of tomato and top bun.

VITAMIN D FRITTATA
YIELD: 6 servings

10 large eggs, pasture-raised or free-range
sea salt and freshly ground pepper
2 tablespoons organic butter or ghee
1 small purple onion, thinly sliced
½ medium red bell pepper, seeded and sliced
1 small zucchini, cut into small dice
1 ounce dried shiitakes, soaked in warm water for 20 minutes, then stems removed and sliced
3 ounces fresh shiitake mushrooms, stems removed and sliced

Preheat oven to 350°F.

Break the eggs into a large mixing bowl, beat vigorously with a fork for one minute, and season with about ½ teaspoon of sea salt and freshly ground pepper. Set aside.

Heat an 8-inch cast-iron pan on medium-high heat and add butter. When the butter just begins to bubble, toss in sliced onions and sauté until translucent, about 2 minutes.

Add the rest of the vegetables and the shiitakes and season with about ⅛ teaspoon of sea salt and freshly ground pepper, to taste. Continue to sauté until the vegetables are crisp-tender.

Pour beaten eggs into the skillet and gently mix. Bake for about 20–25 minutes, or until the frittata is springy when you push the top with your finger.

Allow to cool for about 10 minutes.

Cut into six slices and serve with pesto or salsa.

BAKED FISH EN PAPILLOTE (IN PARCHMENT)

YIELD: 2 servings
This is a great way to cook fish and makes a wonderful presentation when brought to the table.

2 tablespoons extra virgin olive oil
½ cup chopped tomatoes*
10-12 pitted Niçoise olives, chopped
2 tablespoons chopped fresh herb (parsley, dill, or cilantro)
sea salt and freshly ground pepper, to taste
2 filets of white fish such as snapper or halibut, about 6 ounces each

*If you are sensitive to night-shades, substitute vegetables such as zucchini or spinach. These will taste better if you sauté them first, since they will still be somewhat raw when baked for only 10-15 minutes with the fish.

Preheat oven to 375°F.

Cut two large pieces of unbleached parchment paper into circles about 12 inches in diameter. Fold them in half to make a crease line.

In a small bowl, combine the olive oil, tomatoes, olives, and fresh herb of your choice. Season with salt and pepper.

Place one filet onto a parchment round, positioning it in the middle of the half closest to you.

Sprinkle a little more salt on the filet and spoon half the tomato mixture over it.

Seal the parchment envelope by crimping the edge or securing it with toothpicks.

Repeat with the other filet. Place envelopes on a baking sheet and bake for 10–15 minutes.

BUTTERNUT SQUASH SOUP WITH SHIITAKES

YIELD: 3-4 servings

1 small butternut squash
2 garlic cloves, peeled
8-10 medium fresh shiitake
mushrooms, stems removed
and sliced
1 tablespoon nutritional yeast
(optional)
sea salt and freshly ground
pepper, to taste
3 cups filtered water
fresh cilantro, for garnish

Cut butternut squash in half and scoop out the seeds and fibers.

Steam for about 30 minutes, or until the flesh is soft. (Or bake in a covered oven dish at 425°F for about the same amount of time.)

Meanwhile, put the garlic cloves and mushroom slices in the water and simmer with a good pinch of salt for about 10 minutes. Strain and reserve the liquid from the mushroom mixture.

When squash is tender, allow to cool slightly. Scoop out the flesh—you want about 3 cups.

Put squash in a blender along with the nutritional yeast, salt and pepper, the reserved mushroom liquid, and the cooked garlic gloves. Puree until smooth. You may need to add a little more water if the consistency is too thick.

Reheat the soup in a pan and garnish with the cooked shiitake mushroom and cilantro.

If you have extra squash, add it to scrambled eggs or mash it up and add to a pancake mix.

GREEN TEA-POACHED FISH WITH MISO DRESSING
YIELD: 2 servings

For the Miso Dressing
½ tablespoon white miso
1 teaspoon mirin
1 teaspoon toasted sesame oil
¼ cup rice wine vinegar

Put all the ingredients in a small bowl and whisk well to combine. Set aside as you poach the fish.

For the Fish
4 cups filtered water
¼ cup cooking saké
½ teaspoon sea salt
2 organic green tea bags
2 wild halibut filets, or similar white fish (about 6 ounces each)

Pour water, saké, and salt into a pan and bring to a simmer. Add the tea bags and allow them to steep for about 5 minutes.

Add filets and poach on a gentle simmer until they are cooked through, about 8-10 minutes.

Remove filets from the poaching liquid and serve with the Miso Dressing.

This dish pairs very well with Wild Rice with Tahini and Green Onions (recipe follows).

WILD RICE WITH TAHINI AND GREEN ONIONS
YIELD: 3-4 servings

1 cup wild rice, soaked overnight in water and ½ teaspoon lemon juice
2½ cups chicken stock, mineral broth, or filtered water
⅛ teaspoon salt
2 tablespoons tahini
⅓ cup chopped green onion

Drain the soaked wild rice and bring to a simmer in a pot with stock or water and salt.

Cover the pot and simmer for 35-40 minutes, or until the kernels pop open and are tender. Drain off excess cooking liquid, if any.

Mix the cooked wild rice with tahini and chopped green onions. Add a little more salt if needed.

COMFORTING COCOA PUDDING

YIELD: 4 servings

16 ounces amazake,* almond
  flavor
2 tablespoons unsweetened
  cocoa powder
pinch of sea salt
3 tablespoons kudzu powder
¼ cup water

Put amazake and cocoa powder in a pot. Bring to a gentle simmer. Add pinch of salt.

Make a slurry with the kudzu powder and water. Add to the simmering mixture and stir with a wooden spoon until mixture thickens to the consistency of pudding.

Spoon into 4 small ramekins or small glasses and chill in the fridge for at least one hour.

Serve topped with a dollop of whipped cream or coconut milk. This pudding is rich, so a little delivers much satisfaction!

*Amazake is a naturally sweetened rice beverage that has its origin in Japan. The sweetness comes from fermentation of the rice starch, and no processed sugar is added. (See the Shopping Guide at the end of chapter 8 for where to get amazake.)

Case Study

Cathy was a student in my culinary class at Bauman College. When she started the program, she told me that her main goal was to learn more about nutrition and cooking so that she could improve her health. Although she was just 28, she was suffering from a long list of physical ailments, including severe acne, which exacerbated her depression.

As a response to her love of animals and how they are treated in conventional farming, she opted to become vegan during her first year in college. Since the hectic life of a student didn't allow time for cooking, she relied mainly on starchy foods such as breads and pastas, with a salad here and there to get her through. Her only sources of protein were tofu and canned beans. She also had to deal with a constant craving for sweets, so to be more "healthy" she ate a ton of bananas and peanut butter. After graduating, she was dismayed to find out that she had gained over twenty-five pounds and her acne, which she thought would go away as she got older, actually got worse. She was also feeling run-down and was constantly struggling with a feeling of hopelessness, in spite of the fact that she had a bright future and had already acquired a job upon graduation.

I designed an anti-inflammatory diet for Cathy, which included getting her off gluten, taking out soy, and introducing some sustainably sourced animal protein (which she was willing to do because she realized that she was eating too many carbohydrate-heavy foods and needed more protein). I also asked her to stay away from dairy products, because they often contribute to acne. Her new protocol also included plenty of good fats, plus omega-3s, probiotics, vitamin D, and vitamin B_{12}. (Vegetarians and vegans often become depleted in this critical B vitamin, which is needed for good digestion and neurological health.) I also included a food-based multivitamin to ensure that she got the "ACESZ," which stands for vitamins A, C, and E and the minerals selenium and zinc, which are all needed for good skin.

Cathy completed her culinary program, which lasted about five months. During that time I saw her steadily lose weight, her skin cleared up, and her mood and energy improved. It was really wonderful to be able to guide her recovery back to good health. It is also a joy to know that she is now cooking organic, health-promoting, and delicious meals as a chef.

Notes for Chapter 5

1 Michael Pollan, "Some of My Best Friends Are Germs," 5/15/2013, www.nytimes. com/2013/05/19/magazine/say-hello-to-the-100-trillion-bacteria-that-make-up-your-microbiome.html?pagewanted=all&_r=0

2 Ibid.

3 Natasha Campbell-McBride MD, *Gut and Psychology Syndrome* (York, PA: Maple Press, 2012), 15.

4 Tori Rodriquez, "Gut Bacteria May Exacerbate Depression," 10/17/2013, http://www.scientificamerican.com/article/gut-bacteria-may-exacerbate-depress/

5 Christiane Northrup MD, "Thyroid Disease," 10/23/2012, www.drnorthrup.com/womenshealth/healthcenter/topic_details.php?topic_id=59

6 Datis Kharrazian, *Why Do I Still Have Thyroid Symptoms?* (New York: Morgan James Publishing, LLC), 4.

7 Ibid.

8 Ibid.

9 Daniel Kalish, *Your Guide to Healthy Hormones*, (Vista, CA: The Natural Path, 2005).

10 Elizabeth Lipski MS, CCN, *Digestive Wellness* (Los Angeles: Keats Publishing, 2000), 51.

11 http://www.nimh.nih.gov/health/publications/depression-and-diabetes/index.shtml

12 David Perlmutter MD, *Grain Brain* (New York: Little, Brown and Company, 2013).

13 Eric J. Brunner et al., "Dietary Pattern and Depressive Symptoms in Middle Age," *Br J Psychiatry*, Nov 2009;195(5):408–413.

14 A.P. Simopoulos, "The Importance of the Ratio of Omega-6/Omega-3 Essential Fatty Acids," *Biomed Pharmacother*, 2002 Oct;56(8):365-79.

15 Thomas S. Cowan MD, *The Fourfold Path to Healing* (Washington, DC: New Trends Publishing, Inc. 2004).

16 Christopher Bryson, *The Fluoride Deception* (New York: Seven Stories Press, 2004).

17 Joseph Mercola MD, "Organic Tomatoes, While Smaller, Are More Nutritious Than Conventional Counterpart, Study Shows," 3/25/2013, http://articles.mercola.com/sites/articles/archive/2013/03/25/organic-tomatoes.aspx

18 Cynthia A. Daley et al., "A review of fatty acid profiles and antioxidant content in grass-fed and grain-fed beef," *Nutrition Journal* 2010, **9**:10, doi:10.1186/1475-2891-9-10.

19 Walter Swardfager et al., " Zinc in Depression: A Meta-Analysis," 12/20/12, www.biologicalpsychiatryjournal.com/article/S0006-3223%2813%2900451-4/abstract.

20 Anna C. Nobre et al., "L-theanine, a natural constituent in tea, and its effect on mental health," *Asia Pac J Clin Nutr* 2008;17 (S1):167–168.

21 Michael Horlick, *The UV Advantage* (New York: ibooks,inc., 2003).

22 Ibid.

23 Environmental Working Group, "The Trouble with Sunscreen Chemicals," www.ewg.org/2014sunscreen/the-trouble-with-sunscreen-chemicals/

Chapter 6

Delights of Detox

WHAT IS DETOXIFICATION?

Detoxing, or cleansing, is a time-honored way of helping our bodies release toxins that have accumulated during our day-to-day existence. We are no longer in the Garden of Eden. Living in these modern times means that we are constantly being exposed to an excessive onslaught of ever-increasing pollutants present in the air, water, food supply, consumer products, and industrial waste. Over time, the accumulation of toxic chemicals weakens our physical and mental well-being, leaving us vulnerable to the vagaries of stress, disease, and depression.

When too much gunk builds up in our internal terrain, we suffer TTO, or total toxic overload. Like the straw that breaks the camel's back, this burden of excessive toxins causes our health to crash. As multiple toxins accumulate, they lodge in vital organs and fat tissues, creating blockages by damaging our cells. And since all diseases start on a cellular level, a healthy and effective detox should release toxins from the cells and usher them safely out of the body.

> The needs of cells are simple. They are not greedy, needy, neurotic whiners. Each cell wants only three things: food (nutrients), a little conversation (cell-to-cell communication that drives the metabolic machinery), and perhaps most importantly, a clean house (proper elimination of toxins and waste products).[1]
> —DRS. PETER BENNETT AND STEVEN BARRIE

Here's just a short list of toxins from each category mentioned above:

Air: carbon monoxide and carbon dioxide, sulfur oxide, lead, cadmium, radioactive pollutants

Water: arsenic, lead, herbicides and pesticides, disinfectant byproducts, nitrates

Food: artificial colorings, MSG, rancid or hydrogenated fats

Consumer products: mercury, formaldehyde, lead acetate, petroleum distillates

Industrial waste: cadmium, lead and other toxic heavy metals, CFCs (chlorofluorocarbons), and nitrogen oxides

On top of chemical pollutants, our bodies also produce internal toxins from biochemical processes and from the accumulation of negative emotional memories.

Given the profound connection between the body and the mind, it is important to decrease the body burden of physical toxins, as well as emotional toxins, by making positive changes in diet and lifestyle choices.

On a physical level, TTO can lead to oxidative stress, which can then threaten our health by damaging our DNA. Damaged DNA is the catalyst for accelerated aging, cancer, and birth defects.

Here are some symptoms associated with TTO:

- Headaches
- Fatigue
- Joint pains
- Insomnia
- Mood swings
- Weakened immunity (frequent colds/flus)
- Chronic digestive issues
- Brain fog
- Excessive weight gain
- Hormonal imbalance

When these symptoms are left untreated, a plethora of diseases may manifest:

- Heart disease
- Hypertension
- Chronic fatigue
- Allergies

- Asthma
- Kidney disease
- Obesity
- Mental illness
- Skin conditions such as eczema and psoriasis

If all this talk about toxic overload, damaged DNA, and disease is dragging you down, please be assured that a holistic, food-based detox is the solution to a healthier, and happier, body and mind. Some of the amazing benefits include clearer skin, better cognitive function, easing of PMS or menopausal symptoms, banishing cravings, better sleep, more energy, and dropping a few pounds as a bonus.

HOW THE BODY DETOXIFIES

Our bodies are amazingly adaptable, keeping toxins in check through sweating, tears, and elimination of urine and feces. The actual organs involved are: lymph nodes, lungs, kidneys, gallbladder, liver, and the digestive tract. Although we have a very sophisticated process for detoxification, the entire system can suffer from TTO (total toxic overload). When one organ of detoxification becomes congested, it will start a cascade that negatively affects your other detoxification pathways.

The liver is, without a doubt, the most important detoxifying organ, doing about eighty percent of the decontamination. It achieves this remarkable feat by transforming toxins into harmless molecules in two distinct phases; the toxins are then eliminated through our urine or feces.

Phase I

Enzymes transform toxins into what are known as *intermediate compounds*. Some of these compounds may be more harmful than the original compound, so they must be neutralized before traveling through your body to make an exit.

Nutrients that support Phase I:

Folic acid and other B vitamins, vitamin D_3, calcium, vitamin C, milk thistle, quercetin, and cysteine (an amino acid).

Phase II

Enzymes convert the intermediate compounds from Phase I and render them harmless so they can be safely excreted.

Nutrients that support Phase II:

Amino acids found in protein, sulfur compounds found in cruciferous vegetables, B vitamins.

. . . .

THE INCREDIBLE LIVER

Many people think that the heart and brain are our most important organs, but it's really the liver that keeps us healthy by performing an incredibly long list of vital tasks.

Dr. Melissa Palmer, author of *Hepatitis and Liver Disease: What You Need to Know,* wrote a wonderful piece on what the liver does by asking the reader to imagine a job description for "hiring" a liver:

> WANTED—One highly reliable, extremely flexible organ that can act as watchdog, grocer, housekeeper, bodybuilder, energy plant, supervisor, and sanitation engineer. Will be required to process and sort gallons of digested food from the stomach and intestines each day. Must discriminate among fats, proteins, and carbohydrates and send them wherever they are needed in the body. Must be able to detoxify thousand of substances—ranging from alcohol to bug spray to turpentine fumes—that may be ingested with food and drink, absorbed through the skin, or breathed in the air. Should be able to dismantle old, worn-out blood cells and recycle whatever parts are salvageable and prepare the rest for elimination. Must transform cholesterol into steroid hormones, such as androgens and estrogens, and share responsibility with the kidneys to control thyroid hormones, which influence metabolism. Must regulate sugar levels for proper energy management and create clotting factors that stop bleeding from cuts and other wounds. Additional duties will include—but are not limited to—building reserves of vitamins A, D, E, K, and B_{12}, as well as

iron and copper. Must be able to accomplish all of
the above without weighing more than 3–4 pounds.[2]

• •

The best time to do a detox is in spring. During the dark and chilly days
of winter, the tendency is to be less active and many of us also tend to eat
more in order to deal with the harsher climate. So by the time the first green
shoots start to sprout and reach toward the sun, we are also ready to shake
off the lethargy of the wintry months and prime ourselves for renewal. And
according to traditional Chinese medicine (TCM), spring is the season of the
liver.

Autumn is also good for a detox. Again, following the ethos of TCM,
this is the season of the large intestine. After indulgences during the hot,
languid days of summer, when we may have eaten too many BBQ spare ribs
and drunk too many mojitos, we should clear out residual wastes stored in the
bowels and ready ourselves for the harvest and the coming of winter.

Thus, when you clear out internal toxins according to the ebb and flow of
the seasons, you also attune yourself to the rhythm of nature, and your mood
and psyche will joyfully dance in step with your body as you move toward
brilliant health.

• •

GRAPEFRUIT

Grapefruit juice, which contains *naringenin*, slows down Phase
I enzyme activity. It decreases the rate of elimination of drugs
from the blood and has been found to substantially alter their
clinical activity and toxicity. Eight ounces of grapefruit juice
contains enough of naringenin to decrease Phase I activity
by a remarkable thirty percent.[3] Other citrus fruits, such as
lemons, limes, and oranges, are fine.

• •

DETOXIFICATION VS. FASTING

Fasting has been used for centuries by many different peoples and faiths (e.g. Lent, Ramadan, Yom Kippur). Periods of abstinence from food can be a very rewarding spiritual and healing experience. Fasting can also be used as a form of detoxification; however, there are many safety factors to consider. Guidelines for fasting are beyond the scope of this book. Should you choose to fast, it is recommended that you do so under the guidance of a healthcare professional.

Here are a few points to consider regarding fasting:

- Many toxins are fat-soluble and are actually stored in your fat cells. Examples include heavy metals such as mercury, pesticides, PCBs, and dioxins.
- When you abstain from food (fasting), your body needs to meet its energy requirements by burning fat. Although this may sound good for those of you wanting to lose weight, know that when fat cells burn, they also release stored toxins. When fasting, you aren't getting the nutrients you need to keep your detoxification system working optimally.
- If your detox system, especially your liver, falters, toxins circulating in your bloodstream can damage body tissues, including the brain and nervous system.
- According to Dr. Michael Murray, "Your liver needs a steady supply of proteins, vitamins, and minerals to produce substances that make detox happen, such as enzymes and bile. Without raw materials, liver cells simply shut down. A fast can cause blood sugar levels to plummet, so people with diabetes are at risk of lapsing into a coma."[4]
- It may surprise you, but protein is actually necessary for a healthy, holistic detox. Protein breaks down into amino acids after digestion and your liver requires amino acids to perform its many critical tasks, the primary one being the filtration of toxins from your body.

HOW TO DETOX HEALTHILY

There are countless cleanses or detox programs out there and it can get very confusing to chose one that is right. The most important thing to remember is that a truly effective detox should be gentle and support your body with all the nutrients that it needs to do the hard work of pulling toxins out. Also, keep in mind that a detox's primary goal is to lighten your TTO. It is not meant to be a weight loss program (though weight loss can be an added bonus), so do not starve yourself during the process: insufficient calories is a form of stress. This adds to your toxic load, plus it will slow down your metabolism.

And remember, as the liver does about eighty percent of the detox work for the body, our number one goal is to support it with good nutrients from food, herbs, and spices.

GUIDELINES FOR A TWENTY-ONE DAY DETOX

This is an excellent, simple, food-based detox that allows for deep cleansing, while also making sure that you will not feel deprived. Instead of causing you fear and apprehension at the thought of cleansing, this is a nourishing protocol, which does not involve starvation or harsh substances that can cause you to dash for the bathroom at awkward moments. Consider this detox a way to pamper your body, so enjoy the process!

If you are on prescription medication, consult with your doctor before detoxing.

Week One: Toss the Junk

This is the foundational phase where you remove junk from your diet, which will give all your organs less "garbage" to deal with, so that they can concentrate on releasing internal debris that is already there.

Things to avoid:
- Gluten (this includes wheat, barley, and rye, along with oats that may be cross-contaminated during processing)
- Processed and artificial sugars (white and brown sugar, Aspartame, Sweet'n Low, Splenda, high-fructose corn syrup)
- Soy products: soy milk, tofu, soy protein isolates (often found in protein bars and protein powders, so read the label carefully), soy burgers and other soy "meats"
- Dairy
- Corn
- Coffee (green tea is okay)
- Alcohol
- Tobacco
- Recreational drugs

．．．．．．．．．．．．．．．．．．．．．．．．

GLUTEN IN DISGUISE

Read food labels carefully. Gluten can be hidden under such names as hydrolyzed vegetable protein, modified food starch, dextrin, and "natural" flavorings.

Depending on your level of sensitivity, even the smallest amount of gluten could be enough to keep you from feeling your best, so take extra care to spot gluten disguises on labels.

Here's a list of some gluten-containing ingredients on labels:

- Vegetable protein/hydrolyzed vegetable protein (can come from wheat, corn, or soy)
- Modified starch/modified food starch (can come from several sources, including wheat)
- Natural flavor/natural flavoring (can come from barley)
- Artificial flavor/artificial flavoring (can come from barley)
- Modified food starch
- Hydrolyzed plant protein/HPP
- Hydrolyzed vegetable protein/HVP
- Seasonings
- Flavorings
- Vegetable starch
- Dextrin and maltodextrin (both can be made of wheat)

．．．．．．．．．．．．．．．．．．．．．．．．

Additional nutrients and habits to embrace during the *entire* detox:

- Probiotic supplement or eating lacto-fermented vegetables such as sauerkraut and kimchi. (Beneficial bacteria from fermented vegetables protect and strengthen the gut and break down chemicals like BPA and pesticides so they can be cleared out.)
- Vitamin C: take in doses of 500 mg, up to 2,500 mg total per day. This supervitamin is excellent in assisting elimination and quells free radicals that are formed during the detox process. Be sure to choose a food-based brand that contains

plants naturally high in vitamin C, such as amla, rose hips, and acerola berries.

- Flax or chia seeds. These seeds ensure adequate fiber and contain omega-3 fatty acids that calm inflammation and are needed for cellular communication.
- Although using natural sweeteners such as honey or maple syrup is allowed during a detox, keeping blood sugar levels on an even keel is one of the keys to a successful detox, so limit adding sweeteners. Besides, the best way to conquer a sweet tooth is to go "cold turkey." Use this as a way to accomplish that and see how good you will feel.
- Dry skin brushing. This stimulates the lymphatic system and helps remove dead cellular debris on the skin. (See the Shopping Guide at the end of chapter 8 for a link to how to do this.)
- Strive to sleep nine and a half hours at night. Melatonin, which is released while we sleep, is a powerful hormone that helps with detoxification.
- Exercise to the point of sweating, which releases toxins. Refrain from exercising after sundown; doing so will cause a rise in cortisol, which will affect your sleep.
- Visit saunas—in particular, infrared saunas—which are wonderful for pulling waste from the body through a slow release of sweat.
- Reduce time with the computer, TV, cell phones, and other wireless devices. It is also very helpful to use orange spectrum glasses to decrease the blue rays from computers. (See the Shopping Guide at the end of chapter 8 for more information.)
- Practice deep breathing and meditation.

Daily Diet Routine for Week One:

Upon waking: eight ounces room temperature water with two tablespoons fresh lemon juice

Breakfast: Scrambled Eggs with Mighty Cilantro Pesto (recipe, page 17)

Green Tea or Rooibos Chai (recipe, page 124)

Snack: Celery Sticks with Tahini

Lunch: Arugula and Sauerkraut Salad with Chicken and Fresh Herb Dressing

Snack: Sweet and Spicy Nuts (recipe, page 97)
Dinner: Creamy Cauliflower Soup
One hour before bed: One tablespoon ground flax or chia seeds
    in six ounces water
Hydration: drink filtered water, herbal teas, mineral broth (recipe,
    page xxv)
Supplements: probiotics, vitamin C

Week Two: Bring on the Herbs

In addition to avoiding the list from Week One, use a good-quality liver tincture and follow instructions for dosage. Use twice a day. A good blend should include any of these liver and kidney-supportive herbs: milk thistle, turmeric, dandelion, burdock root, Schisandra, yellow dock, and nettles. (See the Shopping Guide at the end of chapter 8 for brand recommendations.)

Note: Herbal tinctures are most effective when taken on an empty stomach and about thirty minutes before eating. Therefore, the daily diet routine is scheduled to reflect this.

During this week, add generous amounts of fresh culinary herbs and spices, especially ones that assist detox.

Daily Diet Routine for Week Two

Upon waking: eight ounces room temperature water with two
    tablespoons fresh lemon juice
twenty to thirty minutes before breakfast: Liver tincture
Breakfast: Turkey patties with steamed broccoli drizzled with
    Green Goddess Dressing (recipe, page 183)
Snack: Apple with almond butter
Lunch: Roasted Beets with Diced Ham over Romaine and Basil
    Salad
Two Hours after lunch: Liver tincture
Snack: One Hard-Boiled Egg with Celtic Sea Salt
Dinner: Baked Fish topped with Basil and Capers
One hour before bed: One tablespoon ground flax or chia seeds
    in six ounces water
Hydration: drink filtered water, herbal teas, mineral broth (recipe,
    page xxv)
Supplements: probiotics, vitamin C

Week Three: Deep Detox

For this final phase, we are going deep by adding a cleansing cocktail to our routine from Weeks One and Two. And if you also want to lighten your digestion, have a smoothie for breakfast and/or dinner. (See recipes)

Daily Diet Routine for Week Three:

Upon waking: eight ounces room temperature water with two tablespoons fresh lemon juice

> twenty to thirty minutes before breakfast: Liver tincture
>
> Breakfast: Turkey Sausages with Sautéed Kale
>
> Snack: Cleansing Cocktail (see recipe)
>
> Lunch: Cleansing Apple and Zucchini Salad
>
> Two hours after lunch: Liver tincture
>
> Snack: Jicama slices with almond butter
>
> Dinner: Savory Protein Smoothie (recipe, page 180)
>
> One hour before bed: One tablespoon ground flax or chia seeds in six ounces water
>
> Hydration: drink-filtered water, herbal teas, mineral broth (recipe, page xxv)
>
> Supplements: probiotics, vitamin C

CLEANSING COCKTAIL

4 ounces unsweetened cranberry juice
2 ounces apple juice with no added sweetener
2 ounces aloe vera juice
2 teaspoons spirulina
1 tablespoon ground flax or chia seeds

Mix all ingredients well in a blender. Sip slowly.

This mixture can be prepared ahead of time and stored in the fridge until ready to drink.

Note: if you use chia seeds, they will swell up after about 10 minutes, so if you don't consume it right away, the cocktail will become more like a smoothie.

What to Enjoy:

Proteins	Vegetables	Fruits	Grains / Starches	Beverages
Organic poultry: (chicken, turkey, duck, quail)	**Dark leafy greens:** Collard Kale Chard	Apples Pears Berries Citrus (no grapefruits) Peaches	Amaranth Buckwheat 100% Brown rice Millet Quinoa	Herbal Teas Freshly pressed vegetable juices
Organic eggs	**Cruciferous:** Broccoli Brussels	Nectarines	Wild rice	Unsweetened
Grass-fed beef	sprouts Cabbage	*Note: While on a detox, stay*	**Good fats** Coconut oil	nondairy milks:
Grass-fed lamb	Cauliflower **Salad greens:** Arugula	*away from high-sugar fruits such*	Palm oil (see note on page 235 on	Almond Hemp Rice
Sustainably sourced seafood:	Dandelion Watercress Romaine	*as bananas, grapes, mangoes, and*	sustainability) Organic butter or ghee	Coconut milk
Wild salmon Halibut	Radicchio **Root vegeta-**	*pineapples.*	Extra virgin olive oil	Filtered water
Sardines Scallops Shrimp Striped Bass	**bles:** Beets Celery Root Sweet Pota- toes		Sesame oil	Green teas
Beans and lentils	Kohlrabi **Others:** Artichokes Celery Cucumber Squashes (zucchini, butternut, kabocha, delicata)			

I encourage your to visit your local farmers' market to get the freshest produce and to connect with local growers and your community. In addition to wholesome protein, vegetables, and fats, don't forget to add herbs and spices to your cooking. They not only enhance flavor, but also contain wonderful antioxidants and nutrients.

• •

CAUTION WITH KALE

While drinking raw vegetable juices has many benefits during a detox, do not use goitrogenic vegetables, such as kale, broccoli, cauliflower, and collard greens. They are called *goitrogenic* because they can damage your thyroid when eaten raw or juiced. There are numerous cases of people who drank raw juices made with these vegetables daily and ended up with hypothyroidism.[5]

• •

Best herbs and spices to use:

Herb /Spice	Detox Action
Cilantro	Chelates (pulls out) mercury.
Basil	Traditionally used for parasites and as an immune stimulant.
Cumin	Helps with liver detox, stimulates digestive enzymes, and breaks apart excess mucus. (See recipe section below for a detox tea made with cumin, coriander, and fennel seeds.)
Rosemary	Antibacterial, antifungal, antiviral, and has a powerful decongesting effect on the liver.
Dill	Helps promote good digestion and is also antibacterial.
Cayenne	This fiery spice speeds up metabolism and circulation.
Turmeric	Highly effective against inflammation; purifies the blood; also great for the liver.
Ginger	Helps diminish any potential side effects that come with a cleansing program, like nausea or digestive upset due to the detoxifying effect.

More information on the healing qualities of herbs and spices can be found in chapter 1.

ADDITIONAL TIPS FOR SUCCESS

- Detox your pantry and fridge before your own detox. Toss out all things that may sabotage your success, such as candy bars, cookies, ice cream, convenience/frozen dinners, chips, etc.
- Plan and shop ahead for what you will need.
- Keep some healthy emergency snacks on hand just in case you start to get cravings.
- Totally commit yourself to do it, and to doing it well.
- Use a food journal and diary to track your progress.
- Ask your partner or a good friend or family member to help support your effort.
- Plan a very special reward for yourself when it's done.
- Get a good-quality water filter that filters out fluoride and chloride/chloramine.
- Be aware of some common side effects: headaches (especially if you are a regular coffee drinker), fatigue (your body is working hard to facilitate the detox, so rest well; energy will increase as the detox progresses), and minor skin eruptions (toxins are being pulled out from cells and may be released through pores in the skin). All these are actually good signs that the detox is working. Be patient—these side effects will usually subside after a few days.

TIPS FOR DINING OUT WHILE ON A DETOX

Believe it or not, it is actually easier to eat out than eat at home during a detox! After all, in a restaurant you can't go back to the kitchen and get seconds, vegetables always seem to taste better, and there's no mess in your kitchen to clean up!

Here are some tips to help you behave and make better choices

- Don't allow the enemy on your table. When the waiter brings the bread basket, send it away.
- Start with a leafy green salad with an olive oil vinaigrette.

This is not only nutritious, but will also fill you up.

- Try having two appetizers or an appetizer, a vegetable side dish, and a salad rather than a large entrée.
- If you are having alcohol, stick with red wine and wait until you've eaten something, so that the alcohol doesn't go straight to your head and also upset your blood sugar balance. Stop after one glass, and switch to sparkling mineral water.
- Be the inquisitive and informed diner. Ask your waiter how dishes are prepared and what ingredients are in them. Ask for substitutions when appropriate.
- If your entrée is served with refined carbs, such as pasta, white rice, or bread, ask the waiter to substitute vegetables for the starch.
- Follow the three-bite rule. If a dessert is worth it, order it, but share it and only have three polite bites.
- Enlist support and ask your dining partner(s) to help you stick to your program before you go out.
- Keep in mind that you will have many opportunities to dine out, but you can't do a successful detox all the time. So stick with it—you will feel well rewarded at the end!

A Perfect Detox Day

Morning

7:00 a.m. Rise and Shine

Do a short five minute cleansing breath exercise or meditation

Drink eight ounces warm/hot water with lemon juice

Enjoy your preferred morning exercise

Take your liver tincture

Dry skin brushing, then shower

Breakfast: Green or herbal tea

Vitamin C: 500 mg and probiotics

Midmorning snack, 10:30 a.m. (if needed): one apple with one tablespoon almond butter or Cleansing Cocktail (recipe, page 171)

Vitamin C: 500 mg

Afternoon

Lunch, 1:00 p.m.: Grilled chicken or fish over large green salad with dressing

Herbal or green tea

Vitamin C: 500 mg

Get out for a short walk and enjoy the sun and fresh air

3:00 p.m.: Liver tincture

Midafternoon snack, 3:30 p.m. (if needed): Jicama Chips with
Guacamole (page 186)

Herbal tea or mineral broth

Vitamin C: 500 mg

Evening

6:00 p.m. Light exercise such as yoga or walking

7:00 p.m. Dinner: Savory smoothie or steamed vegetables with
turkey sausage

Calming herbal tea (chamomile, nettle, passion flower)

9:00 p.m. Relax and unplug from your computers, laptops,
iPhones, iPads, Blackberries, etc.

Drink water mixed with ground flax or chia seeds (omit this if
you had a smoothie with flax seeds in it earlier)

Enjoy an Epsom salt bath with lavender oil

Evening meditation, read something calming, or listen to
soothing music

10:00 p.m. To bed, and sweet dreams!

Favorite Detox Foods

These foods are particularly beneficial during a detox, so have them frequently during and afterward to support your liver and other organs.

Artichokes contain *inulin*, a polysaccharide that helps stimulate the kidneys and immune system. Inulin works by feeding the good bacteria in the large colon while clearing harmful bowel bateria that can negatively affect the liver's filtration system. Other foods that contain inulin include: burdock root, Jerusalem artichokes (aka sunchokes), chicory, onions, and garlic.

Avocados are one of the most nutritious fruits around. They contain vitamins E and K, along with folate and B_6 plus minerals such as magnesium and potassium, both of which are important for cardiovascular health. This luscious green fruit is also endowed with *lutein*, a carotenoid that is critical to good vision and skin. As if that weren't enough, avocados are superb for detox because they provide glutathione, a powerhouse antioxidant that the liver needs to do its job right. Hooray for avocados!

Beets contain a special class of phytonutrient known as *betalains*, which help calm inflammation, provide antioxidant properties, and assist the liver in the Phase 2 detoxification pathway. This yummy root vegetable also contains *betaine*, another antioxidant that helps lower homocysteine levels. (*High homocysteine is linked to risk of heart disease.*) But wait, there's more! You can't beat beets for eye health, since they also contain *lutein and zeaxanthin*, both of which protect the integrity of the retina, thus preventing macular degeneration.

Cabbages belong to the cruciferous family of vegetables known for their sulfur-containing compounds, which support liver function. Although the three main types of cabbages (red, green, and savoy) all have health-promoting nutrients, red and purple cabbage is extremely high in *anthocyanin*, a polyphenol that has been well researched for its ability to improve blood circulation (thus helping to prevent hypertension), promote vision health, and protect the liver from oxidative damage. It is the rich red, purple, or crimson colors in vegetables and fruits that signal the presence of *anthocyanin*. Blackberries and blueberries are notable examples.

Note: Cruciferous vegetables (cabbage, kale, Brussels sprouts, broccoli, cauliflower) contain goitrogens, chemicals that inhibit thyroid hormones. Cooking greatly mitigates this problem, so enjoy this family of vegetables cooked. *The only exception is sauerkraut, which is raw and fermented and is actually very good for health.*

Bitter salad greens (arugula, endive, radicchio, dandelion, frisée) are packed with magnesium and potassium. Both minerals maintain alkalinity in the body, and help buffer the effects of stress. Dandelion, in particular, is the star of bitter greens when it comes to detox.

RECIPES FOR A REVITALIZING DETOX

Breakfast

BUBBLE AND SQUEAK WITH POACHED EGGS

YIELD: 1 serving
This is a variation of a traditional English breakfast food in which leftover vegetables are cooked with mashed potatoes until crispy and brown. The dish gets its name from the sounds made while cooking.

2 tablespoons coconut oil
¼ small cabbage, finely shredded
sea salt, to taste
1 cup cooked sweet potato, mashed
freshly ground pepper, to taste
2 poached eggs (recipe, page 91)
2 tablespoons Mighty Cilantro Pesto (recipe, page 17)

Heat a cast-iron skillet on medium-high heat. Add the oil.

Toss in the shredded cabbage and add a little salt and pepper. Cook until tender.

When the cabbage is ready, add the mashed sweet potato and mix with the cabbage to form a pancakelike shape. Heat well on one side, about 2 minutes, listening for the "bubble and squeak," then flip and cook for another 2 minutes.

Top with poached eggs and Mighty Cilantro Pesto.

AMARANTH PORRIDGE WITH COCONUT MILK AND GINGER

YIELD: 2–3 servings

1 cup amaranth, whole grains (preferably soaked overnight)
3½ cups filtered water
pinch of sea salt
½ teaspoon grated fresh ginger
¼ cup coconut milk
¼ cup almonds or walnuts, lightly chopped
¼ teaspoon ground cinnamon
1 tablespoon maple syrup

Put first four ingredients in a pot and bring water to boil. Lower heat to a simmer and cook amaranth until thickened and soft, stirring occasionally, about 20 minutes. Add more water if it becomes too thick.

Spoon into serving bowls and top with coconut milk, nuts, cinnamon, and maple syrup.

Leftover pudding makes a delicious quick snack.

PEAR AND CINNAMON SMOOTHIE

1 serving protein powder
½ pear
1 tablespoon almond or cashew
*   butter*
½ teaspoon ground cinnamon
¼ cup coconut milk or hemp milk
pinch of sea salt
6 ounces filtered water
pinch of sea salt

Put all ingredients in a blender and blend until smooth.
    Pour into a glass and sip slowly.

SWEET POTATO AND COCOA SMOOTHIE

This is one of my favorite smoothie recipes. The natural sweetness of sweet potato pairs beautifully with the rich, dark nuance of unsweetened cocoa powder.

1 serving protein powder
½ cup cooked sweet potato,
*   mashed*
1 tablespoon unsweetened cocoa
*   powder*
1 tablespoon almond butter or
*   tahini*
½ teaspoon ground cinnamon
¼ teaspoon nutmeg
½ teaspoon grated fresh ginger
¼ teaspoon cayenne (optional)
1 tablespoon ground flax seeds
pinch of sea salt
6–8 ounces filtered water

Put all ingredients in a blender and blend until smooth.
    Pour into a glass and sip slowly.

SAVORY PROTEIN SMOOTHIE
YIELD: 1 serving

1 serving protein powder
5-6 almonds or cashews or 1 tablespoon tahini
½ cup cooked butternut squash, mashed
3-4 leaves romaine or butter lettuce
2-3 fresh basil leaves, or ¼ cup cilantro leaves
¼-½ cup unsweetened coconut milk (not the "light" version: full-fat coconut milk is what nature intended) or hemp or almond milk
6 ounces filtered water
1 tablespoon ground flax seeds
pinch of sea salt

Put all ingredients in a blender and blend until smooth.

Pour into a glass and sip slowly.

• •

HOW TO CHOOSE A HIGH-QUALITY PROTEIN POWDER

There are numerous brands of protein powder out there in health food stores and it can be very confusing to select the right one. The first thing to avoid is anything made from soy protein or soy isolates. It is very important that the product be organic. Good ingredients include hemp, rice, or pea protein. Whey protein powder sourced from cows (which graze on pastures and are not subjected to any growth hormones or antibiotics) and produced at low temperatures is also good, though if you know that you have a dairy allergy, use the plant-based options instead. Also choose products with the least amount of added sweetener. (See the Shopping Guide at the end of chapter 8 for brand recommendations.)

• •

Lunch or Dinner

Serve a protein with the vegetable-only dishes, such as grilled fish or lamb.

ARTICHOKE AND CHICKEN SALAD

YIELD: 1 serving

1 globe artichoke
1 small chicken breast or thigh,
cooked
1 tablespoon extra virgin olive oil
1 teaspoon Dijon mustard
¼ cup chopped fresh parsley
1 tablespoon chopped fresh dill
sea salt and freshly ground
pepper, to taste
dipping sauce for the artichoke
leaves: mix 2 tablespoons
olive oil with 1 teaspoon
lemon juice

Trim off the stem and put artichoke in a steamer with the leaves pointing downward. Steam for approximately 30 minutes, or until leaves can be pulled out without resistance.

Remove the leaves and set them aside. Remove any thistles from the heart with a spoon and cut the heart into small cubes.

Cut the cooked chicken into small cubes, or shred by hand.

Mix olive oil with Dijon mustard in a large bowl and toss in chicken meat and cubed artichoke heart. Add chopped dill and parsley. Season to taste with freshly ground pepper and sea salt.

Arrange the leaves in a circular pattern and place the chicken salad in the middle.

AVOCADO AND CUCUMBER SOUP

YIELD: 1 serving

½ avocado
1 tablespoon lemon juice
½ cup chopped cucumber, peeled
and seeded
1 cup vegetable or chicken stock
sea salt and freshly ground
pepper, to taste
½ cup chopped cilantro
1 teaspoon extra virgin olive oil
pumpkin seeds, for garnish
(optional)

Put all the ingredients except the olive oil and pumpkin seeds in a blender and blend until smooth.

Pour into a bowl and drizzle with the olive oil. Top with pumpkin seeds if desired.

Since this soup is uncooked, it will provide you with all the raw nutrients and enzymes from the avocado, cucumber, and cilantro still intact.

ROASTED BEETS WITH GARLIC
YIELD: 1-2 servings

2 medium red beets, peeled and cut into 1-inch pieces
5-6 garlic cloves, peeled
2-3 tablespoons extra virgin olive oil
sea salt and freshly ground pepper, to taste

Preheat oven to 375°F.

Put the cut beets and garlic on a baking sheet lined with parchment.

Drizzle the olive oil over the vegetables and season with salt and pepper.

Loosely cover with another piece of parchment and roast until the beets are tender, about 20 minutes. (Cutting the beets into smaller pieces will reduce cooking time, helping to retain nutrients, especially the *betalains.*)

Serve with a salad of organic greens and dandelion.

Store leftover beets in the fridge. Great to snack on in lieu of candy bars and other junk detox saboteurs.

CABBAGE AND SHIITAKE MEDLEY
YIELD: 2 servings

2 tablespoon coconut oil or ghee or sesame oil
2 slices fresh ginger root, minced
½ medium onion, sliced
8-10 fresh shiitake mushrooms
½ small red or green cabbage, thinly sliced
sea salt and freshly ground pepper, to taste

Heat a sauté pan on medium heat and add the oil of your choice. Toss in the ginger and onion slices and cook for a minute.

Add the shiitakes along with the sliced cabbage and sauté until tender. If the mixture appears too dry, add a little water or stock (about 2 tablespoons) to moisten.

Season with salt and pepper, to taste.

ARUGULA AND SAUERKRAUT SALAD WITH CHICKEN

YIELD: 1 serving

2 cups packed arugula leaves
⅓ cup raw sauerkraut,
   purchased from a good
   organic foods market or
   homemade (recipe, page 98)
1 tablespoon juice from the
   sauerkraut
¼ cup extra virgin olive oil
sea salt and freshly ground
   pepper, to taste
1 cooked chicken breast or thigh,
   shredded
handful of cilantro or dill
   (optional)

Mix the arugula and sauerkraut with kraut juice and olive oil. Toss well.

Add salt and pepper, to taste.

Top with chicken and herb, if using.

GREEN GODDESS CLEANSING DRESSING

YIELD: approx. 1 cup

This is a dairy-free version of the classic, which usually contains mayonnaise and sour cream. Use this with a bitter green salad, as a topping for grilled meat, or with scrambled eggs for breakfast.

⅓ cup extra virgin olive oil
1 tablespoon lemon juice
½ cup packed cilantro leaves
½ cup loosely packed tarragon,
   dill, or basil
½ cup chopped green onion
½ avocado
⅓ cup filtered water
2 anchovies (optional)
sea salt and freshly ground
   pepper, to taste.

Put all ingredients into a blender and blend until smooth. Adjust flavor with salt and pepper.

BITTER GREENS WITH SWEET CREAMY TAHINI DRESSING
YIELD: 2-3 servings

2 cups packed arugula leaves
2 cups chopped dandelion
greens
1 small head radicchio, torn into
small pieces
1 head endive, chopped into
small pieces

Toss all ingredients together in a salad bowl.

Sweet Creamy Tahini Dressing
2 tablespoons raw apple cider
vinegar
⅓ cup extra virgin olive oil
1 tablespoon flax oil
1 garlic clove, crushed
2 tablespoons tahini
½ teaspoon ground cinnamon
1 teaspoon maple syrup or raw
honey
1-2 tablespoons filtered water
sea salt and freshly ground
pepper, to taste

Put all ingredients in a blender or food processor and process until well blended.

Toss with the bitter green mixture and serve immediately.

CHICKPEA, CUCUMBER, AND HERB SALAD
YIELD: 1-2 servings

1 cup cooked chickpeas
1 medium English cucumber, cut
    into small dice
1 cup loosely packed cilantro
1 cup loosely packed parsley
½ cup roughly chopped mint
    leaves
1 green onion, finely chopped
¼ cup extra virgin olive oil
1 tablespoon raw apple cider
    vinegar
1 tablespoon nutritional yeast
sea salt and pepper, to taste

Put the chickpeas, cucumber, herbs, and green onion in a bowl.

Add the rest of the ingredients and mix well.

Serve on a bed of arugula, if desired. You can also add shredded chicken to boost protein.

CLEANSING APPLE AND ZUCCHINI SALAD
YIELD: 4 servings

2 medium zucchini, shredded
½ teaspoon salt
3 apples, unpeeled, cored and
    julienned
⅓ dried cranberries
½ cup chopped walnuts or
    pecans
⅓ cup chopped parsley
sea salt and freshly ground
    pepper, to taste

Cut or grate zucchini into fine shreds and toss with the sea salt. Put zucchini in a colander and place over a bowl. Leave the mixture for about 1 hour. The salt will mellow the raw zucchini as well as draw out water.

Discard the zucchini water.

Toss all ingredients together and drizzle with dressing (recipe follows).

Dressing:
YIELD: approx. ⅔ cup
⅓ cup fresh lemon juice
½ teaspoon ground cinnamon
1 teaspoon Dijon mustard
⅓ cup extra virgin olive oil
sea salt and pepper

Put all the ingredients in a clean glass jar, screw lid on tight, and shake the jar until dressing is well mixed.

Snacks

JICAMA CHIPS WITH GUACAMOLE

YIELD: approx. 2 cups

For the guacamole:
2 medium ripe avocadoes
1 small tomato, seeded and
chopped into small dices
1/3 cup red onion, cut into small
dices
1/3 cup fresh cilantro leaves,
finely chopped
Sea salt and fresh ground black
pepper, to taste
2-3 Tablespoons fresh lime juice
1 small jalapeno pepper, seeded
and minced (optional)

Jicama chips:
1 medium jicama*, peeled, sliced
into ¼" slices

Peel and scoop out the avocado into a bowl. Use a fork to mash the avocado, then add in the rest of ingredients. Mix well. Serve a dollop of guacamole on a jicama slice, or "chip."

*Jicama, also known as the Mexican water chestnut, has a crunchy texture and tastes like a cross between a potato and an apple. It is high in fiber, vitamin C, and potassium, and low in calories.

GLORIOUS GREEN HUMMUS

YIELD: approx. 1 cup

1 cup cooked chickpeas
2 garlic cloves, crushed
2 cups fresh herb mixture: basil,
parsley, cilantro, tarragon,
mint, dill
3 tablespoons tahini
⅓ cup extra virgin olive oil
2 tablespoons lemon juice
¼-½ teaspoon cayenne
sea salt and freshly ground
pepper, to taste

Put the cooked chickpeas in a food processor with the garlic, herb mixture, and tahini. Pulse a few times until mixture is well blended.

With the food processor running, drizzle in the olive oil and lemon juice. If it is too thick, thin out with more olive oil or a little water.

Add cayenne and sea salt and pepper, to taste.

Blend again until all the seasoning ingredients are well incorporated.

STRAWBERRY COCO-CHIA PUDDING

YIELD: 3-4 servings

This rich and substantial pudding gives all the satisfaction of a sinful-tasting treat, without the guilt. (Recipe from Jennifer Caroff, Natural Chef and Health Coach, www.foodsolutions.com.)

1½ cups coconut milk
3 cups organic strawberries, trimmed
1-2 tablespoons maple syrup
½ teaspoon vanilla extract
1 teaspoon lemon or lime zest
½ cup chia seeds

Combine coconut milk, strawberries, maple syrup, vanilla, and zest in a blender and blend until smooth and creamy. Add a little more maple syrup as needed.

Put the chia seeds in a separate bowl and pour the mixture over them. Blend well.

Allow mixture to thicken in the fridge for at least 4 hours or overnight.

Serve garnished with additional strawberries.

AYURVEDIC DETOX TEA

This classic blend of spices has been used traditionally in Ayurvedic healing for centuries.

¼ teaspoon cumin seeds
¼ teaspoon coriander seeds
¼ teaspoon fennel seeds
8 ounces filtered water

Put seeds in a cup. Bring water to a boil and pour over the seeds. Allow to steep for 10 minutes, then strain.

Sip slowly and enjoy the subtle fragrance and warming quality of the tea.

HOW TO TRANSITION OFF A DETOX

Once you have accomplished your detox, you want to maintain the clean slate by continuing to be mindful of what you put in and on your body. If you do not have a dairy or corn allergy, then you can reintroduce those items slowly.

- Upon waking, drink a large glass of hot water with the juice of a lemon.
- Dry skin brush at least four times per week.
- Enjoy an Epsom salt bath several times per week or have regular saunas.
- Carve out time each day to do a short meditation or relaxation session. Just ten minutes can make a world of difference.
- Keep going gluten-free, especially if you want to maintain your current weight, continue to lose a few pounds, or sustain that good energy and good digestion!
- If you have a dairy allergy, keep going dairy-free as well. Typical signs of dairy allergies are constant nasal drip, acne or other skin problems, bloating, and abnormal bowel movements, such as constipation or diarrhea. If these symptoms cleared up or improved during the detox, that's your cue to ditch dairy, though fermented products such as kefir and yogurt may be fine. Test by eating plain, unsweetened kefir or yogurt on an empty stomach in the morning and refrain from eating or drinking anything except water for at least three hours. Pay close attention to how your tummy feels, and whether you experience any congestion.

- Follow the golden rule of optimal eating:

Eat like a King for breakfast, a Prince for lunch, and a Pauper for dinner.
—ADELE DAVIS

- Always have good-quality protein and fats at each meal and keep carbohydrates at a minimum.
- If you are a coffee drinker, cut down to no more than three cups per week and enjoy green or black teas instead. (Coffee causes acidity by draining minerals from the body.)
- Just say no to processed/fake sugars. Enjoy natural sweet-

eners, such as raw honey, maple syrup, Sucanat, palm sugar, and stevia, in moderation.

- Enjoy dried fruits in moderation. If you want something sweet, reach for a square of dark chocolate (seventy percent cacao or greater)—it has minimal sugar and is a super-sexy superfood!
- Snack on protein-rich foods, such as nut butters, hummus, and organic cold cuts.
- Concentrate on eating organic foods and support your local farmers' markets.
- Take a food-based multivitamin daily.

Case Study

Marie is one of the most loyal participants in my detox workshops, and that's because she has experienced remarkable shifts in her health ever since she started a few years ago. I can count on her signing up every spring and fall.

I remember that when she attended my twenty-one-day "Dump the Junk" detox class, she was very hesitant and anxious that she wasn't going to be able to cut out all the "avoid" foods required while cleansing, especially gluten. She was also worried that she would feel hungry all the time. However, when she came back the following week for our second session, she reported that she felt much more clear-headed and, to her surprise, didn't really miss bread. She was enjoying the protein smoothies for breakfast and found eating a big salad with chicken or fish quite satisfying. She did crave cheese, so I asked her to have a tablespoon of nut butter instead.

At the end of the twenty-one-day detox, Marie shared with the class that she was now able to climb the three flights of stairs to her apartment without pain in her knees and she was even walking up a fairly steep hill in her neighborhood for exercise. She also lost eight pounds. What is remarkable is that Marie was 60 years old when she attended her first detox workshop and now, three years later, she looks and feels ten years younger.

Now, to be honest, it wasn't smooth sailing all the way. About two months after her first detox, Marie traveled to see her daughter on the East Coast and started to eat breads and pasta again, triggering a reversal to some of her poor eating habits, which included cheese and ice cream. She consulted with me when she regained some of the weight she had lost. I coached her to get back on the gluten-free track and also suggested that we do a test for food allergies. The results showed that she was indeed allergic to gluten, dairy, and almonds. I told Marie that if she wanted to avoid further weight gain and the return of her joint pains, she needed to concentrate on calming the inflammation caused by eating what she was allergic to. I asked her to follow the steps outlined in "How to Transition Off a Detox" (page 187) faithfully and to avoid the items to which she was allergic.

Several months passed. It was time for my autumn detox class, and Marie signed up again. On this second round, she did really well again. She shed more pounds, slept much better, and had much more energy than when she first detoxed. She was totally convinced of the importance of keeping her body clean and vowed to detox twice a year, which she has done ever since.

Notes for Chapter 6

1   Peter Bennett and Stephen Barrie ND, *7–Day Detox Miracle* (New York: Three Rivers Press, 2001), 22

2   Melissa Palmer MD, *Hepatitis & Liver Disease: What You Need to Know* (New York: Avery, 2004), 8.

3   Michael Murray ND, *Dr. Murray's Total Body Tune-Up* (New York: Bantam Books, 2000), 81.

4   Ibid, 91

5   Rachel Zimmerman, "The Dark Side of Kale (and How to Eat Around It," 1/10/2014, http://commonhealth.wbur.org/2014/01/the-dark-side-of-kale-and-how-to-eat-around-it.

Chapter 7

Celebrate with Good Mood Foods

I am thankful for the mess to clean up after a party because it means I have been surrounded by friends.
—NANCIE J. CARMODY

Who doesn't like a party? After all, it's a chance to dress up, get together with a bunch of people, eat, drink, and be merry, right? Well, everybody likes a party until the next morning when they struggle to wake up in spite of a hangover, feeling like beached whales with equally big headaches and sandpaper tongues.

Whether it's an office, holiday, cocktail, or Sunday football party, junk food and alcohol seems to be the norm. Even classier soirees will still have hors d'oeuvres and dishes replete with ingredients determined to expand your waistline, exacerbate allergies, and drum up regret. So how can you attend a party, have fun with friends, savor the food and libations, but circumvent the saboteurs that will make you feel less than festive afterward?

First, let's look at some of the worst things that may show up on a party platter and dissect why you should steer clear of them, then we will look at a few strategies to employ before heading off to the bash, so that you are armed with the tools to resist what should be resisted and can enjoy your party without compromising your health.

There's a tendency to assuage oneself with phrases such as, "Oh, I'll just binge out for this party, this time only, and get back to my regular routine" or "I'll indulge a little tonight, and I'll fast tomorrow." The problem is, one binge can become the trigger whereby you toss caution to the wind, and end up being in the "party" mode for days, or even months! Some people can rein it in, while for others it's much harder. For instance, if there's an overgrowth of candida yeast present in your body, that excess mixture of alcohol, sugar, refined carbohydrates, and trans fats can feed those dastardly microbes and give them an edge against the good ones, causing further cravings that may get out of control. So, party safe and follow the guidelines in the upcoming pages.

After that, we will look at healthy and fun ways to host a party and how to celebrate clean and green with mood-boosting foods, beverages, and organically oriented décor.

· ·

CANDIDA CAUSES CRAVINGS

Candida albicans is one of the many microorganisms living in our gut. When it gets out of control, typically after antibiotic use, it can suffocate the good gut microbes and take over. Because candida and other harmful microorganisms living in our digestive tract thrive on sugar, they will cause you to crave candy, breads, pastry, fruit, and alcohol, causing urges that can rule your days and nights. Without a proper balance of good bacteria to keep things in check, acidity and inflammation will become rampant. A candida yeast overgrowth can lead to many negative symptoms, such as fatigue, allergies, headaches, psoriasis, and mood issues.

· ·

DON'T PARTY WITH SABOTEURS

Rare is the host who makes everything from scratch nowadays, and chances are, even if she or he is doing some of the cooking, there may still be more processed ingredients than organic, wholesome ones.

While we can be in complete control of what we put into our mouths at home, the peer pressure of your fellow revelers at a party can tip you into the danger zone. It's hard to say no when everyone around you is chomping down and liquoring up. Your best defense is to arm yourself with knowledge of what ingredients are in those greasy, crispy tidbits and negotiate accordingly. To help you see the real picture of what toxins may be lurking in that bowl of corn chips or selection of appetizers, let's take a look at some of the most popular items on the party table and find out why you should navigate away from them.

TOP TEN PARTY FOODS TO DITCH

Chips

Although it's really hard to resist the munchy crunchiness, chips may be one of the worst snacks ever, and they pose multiple health threats. It doesn't matter whether they're made from corn, potatoes, whole grains, rice, or anything else. First, chips are carb heavy, so they will spike up your blood sugar. Second, they are heated to very high temperatures, which releases *acrylamide,* a harmful chemical linked to cancers and nerve damage. Third, they are typically high in bad fats, since they are usually fried in vegetable oils such as canola, cottonseed, or soy. And fourth, not only does the high heat damage the oils, but ingestion will also lead to omega-6 vs. omega-3 imbalance (see page 138). As if all that were not bad enough, chips that are fat-free or low-fat are even worse when they contain Olestra.

• •

THE LOW-FAT, NO-FAT POISON

Olestra, also known as Olean, is added to fat-free or low-fat chips and crackers. When it first appeared on the market in the 1990s, products containing this ingredient came with a label that warned consumers of the possibility of "loose stools." Despite numerous health complaints linked to Olestra, the FDA removed the labeling mandate in 2003, so now buyers may get the runs and not know that it could have been caused by their bag of low-fat chips. Olestra also appears to interfere with the body's ability to absorb some crucial nutrients like beta-carotene, lycopene, and the fat-soluble vitamins (A, D, E, and K).

• •

Processed Cheeses and Cheese Spreads

There is nothing to smile about when it comes to processed cheeses. Not only are they made with many additives and dyes, but the milk is often from conventional cows raised with recombinant bovine growth hormone (rBGH) or recombinant bovine somatotropin (rBST). These synthetic hormones are given to cows to increase milk production; however, animals given the hormone are more prone to udder infections. As a result, higher amounts of antibiotics are used. Milk from cows given growth hormones contains more IGF-1 (Insulin Growth Factor-1). Although humans naturally make IGF-1, elevated levels have been linked to colon and breast cancer.

But that's not all. Processed cheeses have other unsavory ingredients, such as chemical emulsifiers, that contribute their unique individual health hazards:

- Sodium phosphate: kidney damage
- Potassium phosphate: severe allergies, dizziness, muscle cramps
- Tartrate: constipation, dry mouth and eyes, stomach pain, vomiting

There may not even be real milk in your processed cheese! Many big food producers are using MPCs (milk protein concentrates), created by putting milk through an ultra-filtration process that removes all of the liquid and smaller molecules, including the healthy minerals and vitamins that dairy should contain. What is left is a dry substance high in protein that's used as an additive in products like processed cheese, frozen dairy desserts, crackers, and energy bars. Protein molecules are damaged when subjected to extreme processing. Ingesting damaged protein will cause digestive issues and can also initiate allergies.

· ·

REAL CHEESE, PLEASE

If you are not allergic to dairy, real raw cheeses can be one of the healthiest foods to snack on. Old-fashioned ways of cheese making, using live cultures and slow fermentation processes, not only turn milk into a delicious food, but also enhance the bioavailability of nutrients such as calcium and vitamins A and D.

· ·

Commercially Produced Preserved or Cured Meats

Don't you just love that platter of deli cold cuts? All nicely laid out in concentric circles, ripe for the picking. And for meat eaters foraging at a party where there's only finger foods, those slices of salted protein can seem like a godsend. However, there's the devil to pay if you regularly consume meats that are highly processed. If you are a carnivore, please recognize that there are many points of concern, from ethical to environmental factors, that affect the quality of what ends up on your plate.

Animals raised on conventional feedlots are most often living in unnatural conditions that cause them great discomfort, resulting in suffering and disease. For example, cattle that are kept in confinement often develop respiratory problems, viruses of the digestive tract, as well as bacterial and parasitic infections. In order to control the plethora of illnesses, these animals are given antibiotics. According to a study done by John Hopkins University, eighty percent of antibiotics on the market are sold to feedlots. The overuse of antimicrobial drugs contributes to the emergence of drug-resistant organisms, which pose obvious dangers. On top of that, artificial hormones are also given to spur growth so that more profit can be made; however, the cost is an increase in diseases in both animals and humans. The use of recombinant bovine somatotropin (rBST), also known as rBGH, has been shown to increase infections in animals, and it is also linked to an increase in breast, prostate, and colorectal cancers in humans. And we haven't even covered what goes into the processing!

Sodium benzoate, nitrates, and nitrites are but some of the common preservatives added to cured meats. Let's take a brief look at each of these:

- Sodium benzoate is a very cheap preservative added to foods and household products to prevent molds and bacteria from forming. While it extends shelf life, it is a health hazard for humans because it can deprive our cells of oxygen, which can lead to cancers and neurological diseases such as Parkinson's.
- The terms *sodium nitrite* and *sodium nitrate* are used interchangeably, so many consumers don't know the difference. (It really comes down to a difference in atomic structure: sodium nitrite has two oxygen atoms and one nitrogen atom, while sodium nitrate has an additional oxygen atom.) Once in our digestive system, nitrates are converted to nitrite, which then is then converted to nitrosamines. This last compound has been found to pose risks for developing pancreatic cancer.

Traditionally home cured meats are very different from commercially processed items. When shopping for items like bacon, salami, or prosciutto, read the label or ask your butcher what goes into them. Also opt for meats that come from pasture-raised animals.

Canned Fruits and Vegetables

Canned fruits and vegetables are typically drenched in sugar (or high-fructose corn syrup) and salt, respectively. Since the products are packed in cans, there is no need to use the most flavorful fruits or vegetables, thus the excessive use of flavoring agents to help pump up the taste. Even worse, the cans are often lined with a toxic plastic chemical, bisphenol-A, which is a xenoestrogen. This coating leaches into the food and when ingested can cause an excess of man-made estrogen in our bodies. Breast and prostate cancers are spurred by too much estrogen.

Commercial Crackers, Cookies, Breads, and Other Baked Goods

Besides containing gluten, these baked goods are often made from flours that are bleached with *benzoyl peroxide* (the active ingredient in acne creams and hair dyes), *chlorine dioxide* (also used to bleach paper and textiles), or *azodicarbonamide* (found in foamed plastic and synthetic leather). *Potassium bromate* is also added to artificially strengthen the flour. Use of chlorine, peroxides, and bromates has been banned from many countries, including the European Union, because they are known carcinogens. In addition to bleaching, there is an exhausting list of preservatives found in factory-made wheat products, including tertiary butylhydroquinone, or TBHQ. It is a form of butane. Need I say more?

Look at this list of unrecognizable ingredients from a well-known baked product:

> Enriched Flour Bleached (wheat flour, niacin, ferrous sulfate, thiamin mononitrate, riboflavin, folic acid), Water, Soybean and Palm Oil, Sugar, Hydrogenated Palm Oil, Baking Powder (baking soda, sodium acid pyrophosphate, sodium aluminum phosphate). Contains 2 percent or less of: Partially Hydrogenated Soybean Oil, Mono and Diglycerides, Vital Wheat Gluten, Dextrose, Salt, Potassium Chloride, Xanthan Gum, TBHQ and Citric Acid (preservatives), Yellow 5, Color Added, Red 40.

Roasted Party Nuts

These little nuggets are coated with salt, sugar, hydrogenated fats, and preservatives. The combo of sugar, fat, and salt makes them very easy to overconsume. High roasting temperatures can damage the oils and protein in nuts and make them toxic when digested. Many also contain cottonseed oil. Cotton plants are heavily sprayed with pesticide, and since they aren't considered a food crop, there is no regulation. Cottonseed oil is also a GMO product.

Microwave Popcorn

Aside from all the processed carbs and refined salt, some microwavable popcorn contains highly unhealthy trans fats added for shelf stability. Plus, the insides of the bags are often coated with chemicals to prevent the popcorn from sticking.

• •

GMO-FREE POPCORN

Despite the fact that ninety percent of the corn produced in this country is genetically modified, it appears that the kernels used for popcorn are not GMO tainted. What a happy surprise for all you popcorn lovers! The important thing is not to micro-wave it: use real organic butter or coconut oil to coat your popcorn, and season it with sea salt. Pop your popcorn the old-fashioned way, using a pot with a lid, on top of the stove.

• •

Diet Sodas

Regular sodas are bad enough, but the diet versions contain aspartame or other artificial sweeteners, which ironically increase appetite by triggering the hunger hormone, ghrelin. Fake sugars are also linked to neurological problems and cancers.

To top it all off, diet sodas are high in phosphorous. Good bone health depends on a proper balance of calcium and phosphorous. Therefore, over-consumption of sodas can tilt the balance with too much phosphorous, and the effect can leach calcium from bones, leading to osteoporosis.

Deep-Fried Anything

Vegetable oils turn rancid under high, deep-fry temperatures, and the heat also skews the omega-6 to omega-3 balance, leading to inflammation and acidity in the body. In addition, the high temperatures used in deep frying damage the protein structures of foods, making them much harder for us to digest and assimilate.

Cocktails/Mixed Drinks

There's nothing more elegant than a cocktail in a martini glass. You look more sophisticated holding one. And that's about how many you should have: one.

Many mixed drinks, whether they come in a martini glass or not, are packed with liqueur and sugar. And depending on the drink, they may also be tainted with food coloring and preservatives.

Other bad libations are any drinks mixed with Coke or tonic. They feel "light," but before you know it you've consumed three or four, equivalent to well over six hundred calories!

UNDERSTANDING ADDITIVES

Basically, most processed foods have additives and coloring added to them.

Additives are routinely used to:
- Slow spoilage
- Prevent fats and oils from becoming rancid or developing an off flavor
- Prevent cut fruits/vegetables from turning brown
- Fortify or enrich the food with synthetic vitamins and minerals (to replace those that are lost during processing)
- Improve taste, texture, and appearance

Numerous studies have found additives and food dyes are sources of many health complaints, including headaches, nausea, weakness, difficulty breathing, allergies, hyperactivity, and hives.

COUNTING CALORIES

When you are eating the *Happy Foods* way, counting calories is basically a waste of time and brainpower, since quality comes before quantity when we eat nutrient-dense, whole, organic foods. The only time that I suggest you be mindful of how many calories you take in is when they are coming from highly processed, high-carb, high-sugar, highly rancid-fat-tainted foods. There's a popular saying that junk food calories are empty calories, but they are not really empty. They are full of crap!

The problem is, we lose track of how much we eat when we are also socializing and drinking. Here's a list of what is commonly consumed at a typical office party:

- 1 cocktail = 180 calories
- 2 glasses of wine = 200
- 1 spring roll = 165
- 10 corn chips = 140
- 3 ounces guacamole = 250
- 3 ounces cheese = 300
- 5 crackers = 80
- 2 pigs-in-a blanket (cocktail size) = 130
- One 2-ounce chocolate brownie = 350

That adds up to nearly 1,800 crappy calories!

HOW TO PREPARE YOURSELF BEFORE ATTENDING A PARTY (to Prevent Being Sabotaged by Junk Foods and Too Much Booze)

- Eat before you go! Stabilize your blood sugar with protein and fat. Have a good meal before you head off to the party, or have a healthy snack.
- Good choices are: avocado, organic cold cuts, nut butter with celery, eggs, and yogurt.
- Get mineralized: Drink a cup of mineral or bone broth (recipes, page xxv).
- Take probiotics, or eat some fermented vegetables, such as sauerkraut or kimchi.
- If you want a sweet treat, bring along your own dark chocolate and sneak in a bite, instead of eating the usual processed cookies and cakes.
- During the party, drink a glass of water for every alcoholic beverage.
- Use a wine glass or cocktail glass for your water so that it feels like you are having a drink. Sometimes it's just the need

to hold something in their hand while socializing that makes people drink more then they intend.

- Wear your tight, sexy clothes, so that vanity will keep you from eating too much: your tummy might show, or you might run the risk of popping a button.
- Carry a little stash of Celtic Sea Salt® and dab a few grains on your tongue to help refresh your taste buds and replenish electrolytes.

• •

BENEFITS OF CELTIC SEA SALT®

While table salt should never be on your dining table or in your food, Celtic Sea Salt® is one of the best sea salts you can get. Thanks to its high mineral content, it has been shown to balance blood sugar, improve heart function, dispel mucus, provide electrolytes, and create alkalinity in the body.

• •

Two Secret Ingredients to Fight Saboteurs

So, you still can't trust your own willpower, even when adequately prepared beforehand at home? Here are two super secret ingredients to help you fight off the party saboteurs:

Gymnema sylvestre, the Sugar Slayer

This plant has its origin in India, where it has long been used to treat diabetes. When the leaves are chewed, they release a peptide that immediately interferes with our taste buds' ability to taste sweetness, hence the name "sugar slayer," or *gurmar* in Hindi.

Drink a cup of gymnema tea just before you go to the party, or simply carry a few leaves with you and chew on it. It will affect your taste buds for about thirty to forty minutes.

L-glutamine, the Carb Craving Buster

Glutamine is an amino acid found in many parts of the body, including muscles and the skeleton. In the brain, it is converted to *glutamate*. Don't confuse L-glutamine with the glutamate found in MSG (monosodium glutamate), which is an artificial flavor enhancer infamous for causing the

"Chinese restaurant syndrome" and is known as an excitotoxin, meaning it kills neurons in your brain and can damage your nervous system.

According to Dr. Julia Ross, author of *The Mood Cure*, L-glutamine can quickly ward off a carb binge, and even her extremely MSG-sensitive patients have been able to take L-glutamine and not suffer any of the typical side effects.

You can get L-glutamine as a supplement. To use, simply open a capsule and put it on your tongue.

Note: Long-term use of L-glutamine supplementation may cause adverse effects for those who don't need it. So only use this when you have a sugar or carb attack and want to stop it. Also include foods with L-glutamine in your diet on a regular basis. Foods with L-glutamine include: cabbage, beef, pork, cottage cheese, egg whites, poultry, and yogurt.

REMEDY FOR THE NEXT DAY

If you messed up and overindulged, don't panic or make yourself feel worse with guilt and remorse. What's done is done; move on to taking actions that will help mitigate the damage. Here are a few rescue remedies to employ:

When you get home:
- Take an extra probiotics supplement, if you did not do so before the party.
- Load up on extra vitamin C. (Take 500 mg in divided doses.)
- Drink plenty of filtered water.
- Before going to bed, drink a large glass of water with one tablespoon ground flax seeds. (This adds extra fiber to help you detox.)

Next day:
- Eat very clean, and have plenty of green vegetables.
- Drink herbal teas such as dandelion, nettle, milk thistle, red clover, or chamomile.
- Drink mineral or bone broth to alkalinize.
- Get some sunshine to resync your circadian rhythm if you had a late night.
- Take a sauna to sweat out toxins.
- Sleep well to make all those wonderful hormones we talked about in the sleep chapter.

Now, let's really have some fun and host your very own party free of trans fats, gluten, processed sugar, artificial food dyes, and food additives like benzoyl peroxide, TBHQ, azodicarbonamide, and other life-depleting ingredients we can't pronounce! The goal is to make everyone really happy after the party, as well as during. Ready?

PARTY RIGHT

You don't have to be Martha Stewart to throw a party that will have people praising your hosting talents. All it takes is a little forethought, creativity, and planning. Make it simple, elegant, and sustainable by not using plastic plates and utensils. Steer clear of processed foods and invite the bounty of nature by choosing whole, organic, and locally sourced ingredients whenever possible. Jump into the joy of gathering people together to delight in each other's company and celebrate with gratitude.

Almost as important as the good food and libations, the choice of décor and utensils really adds to the ambiance and style of a party. Tempting though it may be to use disposable plates, cups, and such, they just add to the landfill. Although biodegradable alternatives are better, they still require resources and many such products are actually made from GMO corn. So, your best choice is to use real tableware. After all, if you put in the time and effect to cook the best foods for your party, shouldn't you use nice plates and utensils too?

Nothing sets the tone for a party better than good decoration. You don't have to spend a ton of time or money, either. Sometimes the simplest embellishments can make a huge difference.

DECORATION IDEAS FOR YOUR PARTY TABLE

- Light up with candles placed in small mason jars or paper bags.
- Make floral arrangements with foraged flowers/greens/branches.
- Decorate with found shells from the beach, pine cones, or colorful pebbles.
- Use banana leaves to line a table, or as a platter to hold appetizers (found at Asian/Latino markets).
- If you are having a sit-down meal and need placemats, use parchment or butcher paper, which you can purchase at an

art supply store. You can even decorate with hand-drawn designs.

- If you don't have enough platters or dishes, ask your friends, family, and neighbors. Ignite the spirit of sharing by pooling resources.

Garnishing Ideas

It's true that we eat with our eyes. Just the sight of something yummy can make us salivate. If you take a little extra time to dress up a dish with a few touches of flourish, it can mean the difference between adequate and sensational.

Fresh herbs

- Simple and elegant, sprigs of thyme or oregano placed on a dish can dress it up beautifully, and the scents they release add to the aroma of the food.
- Chopping parsley or cilantro and sprinkling on a plate of appetizers or a main course adds a splash of green and flavor.

Edible flowers

- Flowers are the essence of sensuality and the fullest expression of a plant. Blossoms also contain nutrients that are good for us, such as polyphenols.
- Place a few nasturtiums or pansies on a salad for both taste and esthetics.
- Top off a drink with rose petals or lavender sprigs.
- Put blossoms in ice cube trays, fill with water, and put in the freezer to form flower ice cubes.
- Add petals and herbs together to make a beverage. See recipes at the end of this chapter for Lemon Verbena Ice Tea or Rose Vanilla Tonic.

Note: Not all flowers are edible, so be careful and consult with a floral guidebook or botany expert if you are unsure about the safety of a certain plant.

Citrus slices

Lemon, lime, or orange slices go with almost anything. When in doubt about what to use to garnish a plate, default to a thin slice of lemon. But here are a few more suggestions:

- Citrus peel twists: use a lemon zester to make strands of just the peel and put them over appetizers or a salad.
- Citrus ribbons: using the side channeling groove that comes on many lemon zesters, run it from the top all the way around the citrus in a spiral to make a long ribbon of peel. You can tie this into a bow and put it on a dish.
- Cut thin slices of citrus and arrange them around the perimeter of a large serving platter, then put your ingredients in the center.

Fruits

Use fruits in season to complement and highlight the ingredients in your dishes.

- Add summer berries to salad greens or desserts, or add a few berries to a champagne cocktail.
- Sprinkle pomegranate seeds on hearty meat dishes or grilled eggplants.
- Serve sliced stone fruits with grilled chicken or vegetables.
- Add apple or pear slices to a cheese platter.

Chocolate

Who doesn't like chocolate? Make chocolate decorations with melted chocolate and a piping bag or use chocolate leaves.

CHOCOLATE LEAVES

3 ounces dark chocolate, chopped
6-8 small leaves, about 2 inches long, from your garden or potted plants (not sprayed with pesticide), rinsed and patted dry

Melt chocolate in a double boiler, or a small bowl suspended over a small pot of simmering water.

Prepare a flat plate lined with parchment. Brush melted chocolate on one side of the leaves and place, chocolate side up, on the parchment-lined plate. Put them in the fridge to set for about 30 minutes.

Carefully peel the leaves away from the chocolate. Now you have chocolate leaves! Place on a cake or dessert as decoration.

Note: If you have leftover melted chocolate, just lick it up or make hot chocolate.

PARTY IDEAS

- Gluten-Free Tea Party: Just like an old-fashioned tea party, but without gluten and processed sugar.
- Eat with the Season: Only cook and serve the produce that is in season in your local area.
- Rice Noodle Party: You cook the noodles and offer different toppings and sauces for the guests to assemble themselves.
- Gluten-Free Pizza Party: Same idea as the rice noodle party, but guests can also make their own pizza doughs and toppings.
- Sushi Rolls with selection of fillings: Cook some sushi rice and prepare fillings for everyone to roll their own.

RECIPES FOR A SMASHING BASH

Finger Foods

TANGY KALE CHIPS

These are amazingly delicious and addictive.

2 large bunches kale, stems removed, torn into large pieces
2 tablespoons tamari
1 teaspoon crushed red pepper, or cayenne
1 tablespoon lime juice

Preheat oven to 250°F.

If the kale pieces are still wet from being washed, put them in a salad spinner and dry them well. Transfer to a large bowl.

Toss with the rest of the ingredients, making sure that each piece of kale is coated.

Arrange the kale pieces in a single layer on a baking sheet lined with parchment.

Bake for about 20 minutes, flip the pieces over, and continue to bake until they are crisp, approximately 30–40 minutes total.

MUSHROOMS STUFFED WITH CHORIZO SAUSAGE

YIELD: 24 tapas

This classic Spanish tapa is a super-simple appetizer that only has two major ingredients.

24 medium cremini mushrooms, stems removed and reserved for another use*
3-4 tablespoons extra virgin olive oil
sea salt and freshly ground pepper
2-3 links cooked chorizo sausage, cut into 24 slices, about ¼ inch thick
⅓ cup chopped parsley, for garnish
* Don't waste the stems. They can be frozen until ready to use and added to a mineral broth for extra flavor and nutrients (recipe, page xxv).

Preheat oven to 375°F.

Put the stemmed mushrooms in a large bowl and drizzle them with olive oil, sea salt, and pepper.

Line a baking sheet with parchment and place the mushrooms, gills facing up, in a single layer on the parchment.

Stuff each mushroom with a slice of the chorizo sausage.

Bake until mushrooms are tender, about 15 minutes. Garnish with chopped parsley.

ENDIVE BOATS WITH SPICY SHRIMP FILLING

YIELD: 20 boats

The briny sweetness of bay shrimp is a wonderful complement to the nutty, mildly bitter flavor of endives.

2-3 heads endive

8 ounces cooked bay shrimp*
(about ¾ cup)

1 small avocado, cut into small cubes

8-10 oil-cured olives, pitted and chopped

2 tablespoons extra virgin olive oil

¼ cup chopped fresh dill or cilantro

½ small tomato, seeded and diced

1 tablespoon fresh lime juice

¼-½ teaspoon cayenne

sea salt and freshly ground pepper, to taste

*If you can't find bay shrimp, you can chop regular cooked shrimp into small pieces, or use cooked chicken instead.

Carefully peel off 20 leaves from heads of endive by cutting about ½ inch off the base. Set the leaves aside.

In a medium mixing bowl, mix the remaining ingredients. Taste for seasoning and add more cayenne if you like it hot.

Spoon the bay shrimp filling into the endive leaves and serve.

MUSHROOM PÂTÉ ON POTATO CROSTINI

YIELD: 12 crostini

For the Mushroom Pâté

2 tablespoons coconut oil

½ medium onion, cut into small dice

2 garlic cloves, minced

4 ounces cremini mushrooms, stems removed, roughly chopped

1 teaspoon dried thyme

1 teaspoon dried sage

2 teaspoons tamari

⅓ cup extra virgin olive oil

⅔ cup walnuts, soaked for 4–5 hours with ½ teaspoon fresh lemon juice, then drained

2 tablespoons fresh lemon juice

sea salt and freshly ground pepper, to taste

Heat a sauté pan on medium heat and add the coconut oil. Toss in the diced onions and sauté for about one minute, then add the garlic, mushrooms, thyme, sage, and tamari. Cook for about 6–7 minutes, stirring frequently, until mushrooms are tender.

Allow mixture to cool slightly and transfer to a food processor. Add the walnuts, olive oil, and lemon juice. Puree until smooth. Add sea salt and freshly ground pepper, to taste.

For the Crostini:

A large cast-iron skillet is ideal for making these crostini.

3–4 tablespoons coconut oil

2 medium Yukon Gold potatoes, peeled and sliced into ¼-inch rounds

sea salt, to taste

chopped parsley or chervil, for garnish

Put a skillet on medium-high heat and add 1 tablespoon coconut oil.

Swirl pan to coat well. Place the potato slices in one single layer in the pan.

Allow to brown on one side for 3–4 minutes, then flip over and brown for another 3–4 minutes. Lightly season with sea salt.

Transfer cooked slices to a paper towel.

Add more coconut oil to do the next batch and follow steps 2–4 until they are all done.

To serve:

Spread a rounded teaspoon of the mushroom pâté onto each crostini. Garnish with chopped parsley or chervil.

SAGE AND THYME VEGETARIAN PÂTÉ

⅔ *cup beluga or other lentils,*
soaked with 1 teaspoon
lemon juice for at least 5
hours or overnight
2 tablespoons olive oil
1 small onion, sliced
2 garlic cloves, minced
2 teaspoons dried thyme
2 teaspoons dried sage
sea salt and freshly ground
pepper, to taste
2 tablespoons lemon juice
⅔ *cup walnuts, soaked overnight*
with 1 teaspoon lemon juice
and drained

For crudités:
lightly blanched cauliflower or
broccoli pieces
carrot sticks, raw celery sticks,
and cucumber slices

Drain the soaked lentils and put in a pot covered with water by 2 inches. Bring to a simmer and cook until tender, about 15 minutes.

While the lentils are cooking, heat a pan with the olive oil and sauté the onion, garlic, thyme, and sage until the onion slices are translucent. Season with salt and pepper. Allow the cooked mixture to cool.

Put lentils, onion mixture, lemon juice, and walnuts in a food processor and process until smooth. Adjust seasoning as needed.

Arrange the crudités on a large platter and serve with the pâté.

SWEET POTATO CHIPS

Much more healthy than commercially made chips, these are free of any weird additives or rancid oils. Although they do take a while to bake in the oven, they are well worth the wait.

2 medium sweet potatoes, unpeeled
2 tablespoons extra virgin olive oil
sea salt

Preheat oven to 250°F and position rack in the center of the oven.

Rinse and dry the sweet potatoes and slice them as uniformly thin as possible. (Organic sweet potatoes can be enjoyed with the skin on.) If you have a mandolin, use it; otherwise, use a very sharp knife to cut very thin slices.

Toss slices in olive oil to lightly coat, then sprinkle with salt. Lay out in a single layer on parchment paper and carefully transfer the sheet directly onto the oven rack. This allows for more air circulation, and less time for the chips to crisp. Alternatively, you can put the parchment on a baking sheet, but it may take longer to bake.

Bake for about 2 hours, flipping chips after one hour. It is also a good idea to rotate the parchment to ensure even baking.

Remove when the chips are crisp and golden-brown. Some of the slices may feel a little tender in the middle, but take them out and let them rest for 10 minutes. They will crisp up after resting.

CHEDDAR AND CARAWAY CRACKERS (GLUTEN FREE)

Instead of processed crackers, which are loaded with bad fats and gluten, these are the deliciously healthy alternative.

¾ cup brown rice flour

2 tablespoons tapioca flour

2 tablespoons potato starch

⅛ teaspoon xanthan gum

2 cups hard goat cheddar, grated

2 tablespoons coconut oil

1 large egg, pasture-raised or free-range, at room temperature

1 tablespoon filtered water

2 teaspoons caraway seeds

¾ teaspoon sea salt

freshly ground pepper, to taste

Preheat oven to 350°F.

In a large bowl, combine the flours, starch, and xanthan gum. Add the cheese and stir gently to combine well.

Melt coconut oil and pour into a medium bowl. Allow the oil to cool, but add the egg, water, caraway seeds, and salt and pepper while still liquid. Mix well.

Add the liquid mixture to the dry ingredients and form a ball. Divide it in half and press each half into a disk. Wrap each disk with parchment and allow to rest in the fridge for about 35–40 minutes.

Roll dough out into ¼-inch-thick disks and cut into squares or triangles. Transfer the cut pieces to a baking sheet lined with parchment paper.

Bake for about 25–30 minutes, or until the crackers are light brown to golden brown.

GLUTEN-FREE PIZZA

YIELD: 3 crusts

1 cup chickpea flour
1 cup brown rice flour
1 cup sorghum flour
¼ cup arrowroot
1 teaspoon xanthan gum
1 teaspoon baking powder
1 teaspoon sea salt
⅓ cup extra virgin olive oil +
  extra for brushing
1¼ cups filtered water
toppings for your pizzas: tomato
  sauce, pesto, pepperoni,
  olives, cheese, etc.

Preheat oven to 325°F.

Put the dry ingredients in a bowl and mix well.

Add olive oil, then slowly add water ½ cup at a time, while mixing with your hands. Add enough water to produce pliable dough that holds together. You may need to add more water.

Divide the dough into thirds and shape each into a disc.

Lightly flour a countertop with rice flour and roll each disc into an 8-to-9-inch round.

Carefully transfer the rounds onto parchment-lined baking sheets and prebake for 10 minutes.

Remove and allow the crusts to cool. Brush with olive oil and add whatever toppings you like. Increase oven temperature to 350°F.

Bake pizzas with toppings for 20 minutes.

SUSHI RICE

YIELD: about 6 sushi rolls

Traditional sushi rice is made from white rice stripped of the outer husk, which contains most of the nutrients. Using brown rice is a healthy and tasty substitute.

For the sushi rice:
2 cups short-grain brown rice
3 cups filtered water
¼ cup brown rice vinegar
1 tablespoon palm sugar or
  Sucanat

For the filling and condiments:
1 avocado, cut into thin slices
6-8 cooked shiitake mushrooms,
  sliced
1 small cucumber, cut into thin
  strips
6 nori sheets
wasabi
pickled ginger
tamari

Additional filling options:
raw sushi-grade tuna
smoked salmon
cooked crabmeat

Rinse the rice well in a colander.

Transfer the rice to a pot. Add the water and bring to a simmer, then reduce heat to low and cover. Cook for about 40 minutes, or until the water is absorbed and rice is tender.

Whisk the sweetener and vinegar together.

Pour the cooked rice onto a tray or into a large bowl. Add the vinegar mixture to the rice and stir well to coat. Allow rice to cool.

Gather your guests and have everyone make a roll. If you have more guests, the recipe can be doubled or tripled.

REAL POTATO SALAD

A real potato salad starts with real mayonnaise made from pasture-raised eggs, not one that comes in a jar tainted with additives and soybean or canola oil.

For the DIY Mayonnaise:
YIELD: 1½ cups
1 large egg, pasture-raised or
*   free-range, at room tempera-*
*   ture*
1 egg yolk, at room temperature
1 teaspoon Dijon mustard
1 teaspoon lemon juice
¾–1 cup extra virgin olive oil
sea salt and ground white
*   pepper, to taste*

Put the eggs in a blender along with the Dijon mustard and lemon juice. Blend for a few seconds.

Turn the blender on low speed and add the olive oil in a very slow stream until the mixture is thick.

Add seasoning and blend for a few more seconds. Taste and add more seasoning as needed.

Store mayonnaise in a glass jar. Keeps for about 7 days in the fridge.

Note: Because the eggs are uncooked, be sure to get pasture-raised or free-range eggs. Do not use conventional eggs.

For the Real Potato Salad:
YIELD: 2–4 servings
4–6 Yukon Gold potatoes, cooked
*   and peeled*
1 cup frozen peas, thawed
⅓ cup capers
⅓ cup chopped fresh dill
sea salt and freshly ground
*   pepper, to taste*
½–¾ cup DIY Mayonnaise
*   (recipe above)*

Mix the potatoes, peas, capers, dill, and salt and pepper in a bowl.

Gently fold in the mayonnaise. Add salt and pepper as needed.

Serve at room temperature or chilled.

You can also add chopped apples and top with toasted nuts.

NAPA CABBAGE SLAW WITH SPICY CASHEW DRESSING

YIELD: 4-6 servings as a side dish

1 medium head Napa cabbage,
cored, cut crosswise into
¼-inch slices
1 large carrot cut into fine julienne (matchstick strips)

For the Dressing:
¾ cup raw cashews, soaked in
filtered water for at least 5
hours or overnight
1-2 small red Thai chiles, or 1
teaspoon cayenne (more if
you like it hot!)
juice from ½ lime
¼ cup brown rice vinegar
¼ sesame oil
¼ cup grapeseed oil
2 teaspoons tamari
sea salt and freshly ground
pepper, to taste

Garnish
⅓ cup toasted pumpkin seeds
2-3 green onions, thinly sliced

Put the cabbage and carrots in a large bowl.

Drain the cashews and put in a blender along with the rest of the dressing ingredients. Blend until smooth and creamy. Adjust with seasoning ingredients as needed.

Pour dressing over the cabbage and garnish with toasted pumpkin seeds and sliced green onion.

MAR Y MUNTANYA (CHICKEN AND PRAWN STEW WITH CHOCOLATE)

YIELD: 4 servings

Although this dish may seem complicated, the steps are easy to manage, and it will be the hit of any dinner party. The combo of ingredients is made irresistible with the addition of dark chocolate!

1 pound wild shrimp, with shells
3 tablespoons extra virgin olive oil
1 large onion, minced
4 chicken thighs, bone in
4 chicken drumsticks, bone in
1 cup dry white wine
2 bay leaves
freshly ground pepper, to taste
sea salt, to taste

For the mole, or paste:
5-6 garlic cloves, roughly chopped
1 bunch parsley, leaves only
20 almonds, ground in a spice grinder or processor
2 ounces bittersweet chocolate (70 percent cacao or greater)
pinch of sea salt

Peel and devein the shrimp, reserving the shells.

In a large pot, sauté the minced onion with 2 tablespoons of the olive oil on medium heat.

While the onion is sautéing, heat a cast-iron pan with the remaining olive oil and brown the chicken pieces for about 2 minutes on each side. Season with a little salt and pepper.

Put browned chicken on top of the onion.

Make a quick shrimp stock that will add depth of flavor to your dish. Simply put the shells in a pan with some olive oil and sauté for a minute to release the flavor, then add about ½ cup white wine and 2 cups water. Simmer for 20 minutes, strain, and add to the onion and chicken in the pot.

The liquid should just cover the chicken pieces halfway up. Pour in the rest of the wine and more water if necessary.

Bring to a low simmer and add the bay leaves and a few pinches of salt. Cover loosely with a lid and cook for about 45–50 minutes, until the chicken pieces are tender.

While the chicken is cooking, prepare the mole: Place the garlic and parsley in a mortar and pestle. Grind to a paste, adding the ground almonds toward the end. (You can also use a food processor here, but it's so much more sensual using a mortar and pestle!)

Stir in the chopped chocolate pieces. Set aside.

When the chicken is tender, add the shrimp and cook through, about 10 minutes.

Stir in the paste, or mole. Mix gently and be prepared for the heady fragrance that will be released into your kitchen!

Check for seasoning; add more salt and pepper if needed.

Simmer for another 5 minutes. Serve immediately.

Great served with saffron-scented rice.

BLACK BEAN MOCHA BROWNIES
YIELD: 16 brownies
This gluten-free recipe also has the surprising ingredient of black beans!

coconut oil for coating pan
⅓ cup brown rice flour
1 teaspoon baking powder
¼ teaspoon sea salt
¾ cup cooked black beans
½ cup coconut oil, softened
2 large eggs, pasture-raised or free-range
1 teaspoon finely ground coffee beans
¼ cup unsweetened cocoa powder
⅓ cup Sucanat or palm sugar
1 teaspoon vanilla extract
2 ounces dark chocolate (70 percent cacao or greater), melted

Preheat oven to 350°F. Grease a 9-by-9-inch square baking pan with coconut oil.

In a small bowl, mix the rice flour, baking powder, and salt. Set aside.

Put the beans, coconut oil, eggs, coffee, cocoa powder, sugar, vanilla, and melted chocolate in a food processor. Process until smooth.

Add the dry ingredients and pulse a few times until just incorporated.

Pour batter into the prepared pan and bake until the sides are set but the middle is still a little soft, about 20–25 minutes.

Allow to cool for 30 minutes before cutting.

AMARANTH RAISIN COOKIES

YIELD: approx. 20 cookies

These gluten-free cookies are moist with a cakelike texture.

2 cups amaranth flour
⅔ cup arrowroot
1 teaspoon baking powder
2 teaspoons vanilla extract
¼ teaspoon sea salt
3 tablespoons maple syrup
5 tablespoons coconut oil or
* butter*
3 tablespoons filtered water
⅔ cup grated carrots
⅔ cup raisins
1 teaspoon grated fresh ginger
* (optional)*

Preheat oven to 350°F. Line a baking sheet with parchment.

Put the dry ingredients in a bowl and mix well.

Melt the coconut oil in a small pot on low heat. Remove as soon as it is liquid. Allow to cool slightly, then add maple syrup and water.

Add the dry ingredients to the wet ingredients, then fold in grated carrot and raisins, and grated ginger, if using.

Scoop one well-rounded tablespoon of cookie dough onto the baking sheet. Flatten it with your palm to make a ½-inch-thick disc. Repeat with the rest of the dough.

Bake for 30–35 minutes, or until they are light-brown.

Optional: Melt some dark chocolate and dip half of each cookie in it, then put on a plate lined with parchment to set.

BITTERSWEET CHOCOLATE FONDUE WITH APPLES

YIELD: 4–6 servings

Fondues are great for a party, since they bring everyone around the fire. (Well, a very small fire, but the concept is the same.) It's worth it to invest in a fondue set—you can make both sweet and savory fondues with an endless variety of ingredients.

10 ounces bittersweet chocolate (70 percent cacao or greater)
¾ cup organic half-and-half or coconut milk
½ teaspoon vanilla extract, or ½ vanilla bean, split in half
3 cardamom pods
1 cinnamon stick
2 medium Fuji or Jonathan apples, cored and sliced into wedges

Chop the chocolate into small pieces and put in a glass or stainless-steel bowl. Add the half-and-half or coconut milk.

Suspend the bowl over a small pot filled halfway with water. Bring the water to a simmer and melt the chocolate mixture, stirring to combine. Add the vanilla and spices.

Pour the chocolate mixture into a fondue bowl and set over the heating element.

Using skewers, spear wedges of apple and dip them into the chocolate sauce. Yum!

GLUTEN-FREE APPLE PIE WITH DAIRY-FREE CREAM
YIELD: 8 servings

1 cup brown rice flour
⅔ cup almond meal
⅓ cup quinoa flour
1 teaspoon xanthan gum
2 tablespoons Sucanat or
* organic turbinado sugar*
pinch of sea salt
6 tablespoons coconut oil, at
* solid state*
6 tablespoons cold filtered water,
* or more, as needed*

Prepare a 9-inch pie pan by lightly coating with coconut oil and dusting with brown rice flour. Set aside.

Put the dry ingredients in a bowl and mix well using a fork, then transfer the flour mixture to a food processor.

Measure the coconut oil into a small bowl. Be sure that it is at a solid state; coconut oil will become liquid when the ambient temperature is too warm. Flake the coconut oil in small chunks into the flour mixture.

Pulse a few times until the mixture looks like cornmeal. While pulsing, add cold water one tablespoon at a time to form a moist dough. The dough should just hold together without being too dry or too wet. It should feel like putty and should not stick to your hands.

Lightly flour a clean countertop with brown rice flour and turn the dough onto the prepared surface. Very gently knead and shape dough into a disk about 5 inches in diameter.

Transfer dough to a large piece of waxed or parchment paper, about 12 inches x 12 inches. Lightly flour a rolling pin with brown rice flour and gently roll the dough until it is about ¼ inch thick.

Place the pie pan over the dough and flip the dough onto the pan. Using your fingers, gently press dough into the pan, trimming off excess dough around the rim.

Using a fork, pierce the dough in several places. This will prevent the dough from rising when baking.

Chill in the fridge for 30 minutes.

Meanwhile, make the apple filling.

For Apple Filling:

2 tablespoons coconut oil

¼ cup organic cane sugar or
Sucanat, or more, as needed,
depending on the sweetness
of the apples

6 medium Fuji apples, peeled,
cored, and cut into ¼-inch
slices

2 teaspoons ground cinnamon

zest of one lemon

Preheat oven to 350°F.

Heat a large skillet with the coconut oil on medium-high heat. Add the sugar. When the sugar starts to melt, toss in the apple slices.

Sprinkle with the cinnamon and stir well to coat. Taste a slice of apple for sweetness. If needed, add more sugar.

Cook for about 5–6 minutes.

Remove the apple slices to a bowl and toss with the grated lemon zest.

To Assemble the Pie

When the crust is chilled, prebake the pie crust for 25 minutes. Allow to cool.

Arrange the apple slices in a concentric pattern on the prebaked pie crust. Bake for 25 minutes more. Allow to cool before serving.

For the Dairy-Free Cream:

(The total time to make this
recipe is about 5 hours.)

1 can full-fat coconut milk, preferably Thai Kitchen Organic
Coconut Milk

1 teaspoon vanilla extract

Pour the coconut milk into a medium stainless-steel bowl. Freeze for one hour.

Using an electric mixer, beat on medium speed for 30 seconds.

Return to the freezer for 30 minutes.

Then add the vanilla extract and beat again for 30 seconds.

Return the chilled coconut milk to the freezer again and allow the mixture to completely freeze through, about 3 hours.

When you remove the frozen coconut milk from the freezer it will be solid. Leave the bowl on your kitchen counter for about 30 minutes. You will find that the coconut milk has transformed into a thick coconut cream. It will hold this shape for quite a long time.

Spoon onto the apple pie when ready to serve.

Any leftover coconut cream can be stored in the fridge.

SEASONAL FRUIT SALAD WITH EXOTIC SPICES

YIELD: 6 cups
Use whatever seasonal fruits are available with this beautiful spice blend. All the summer berries and melons are wonderful when the weather is warm. During the cooler months, pears, persimmons, pomegranates, and citrus fruits provide color and plenty of vitamin C.

6 cups fruits of choice
1 teaspoon ground cardamom
1 teaspoon ground cinnamon
½ teaspoon ground coriander
1 tablespoon Sucanat or palm
  sugar
pinch of sea salt

Place ingredients in a large bowl and mix well.

Store in the fridge until ready to serve.

Libations

(For mocktails, see recipes for Maca Mocktail, page 48, and the Sparkling Blush Refresher, page xxiv.)

MINT AND CUCUMBER WATER

YIELD: 6–8 servings

One cucumber, thinly sliced
1 small bunch mint leaves, stems
    removed
½ gallon filtered water

Put the ingredients in a pitcher and allow the cucumber and mint to infuse the water for about 30 minutes before serving. Add ice if desired.

LEMON VERBENA ICED TEA

YIELD: 6–8 servings

One small bunch lemon verbena,
    or 5–6 tea bags
½ gallon filtered water
Honey or maple syrup, to taste
5–6 slices fresh lemon

Put the lemon verbena sprigs or tea bags in a pot. Add the water and bring to a simmer.

Turn heat off and let the tea steep for 10–15 minutes. Strain, and add the sweetener of your choice.

Allow to cool, then pour into a pitcher. Add lemon slices and ice to serve.

Garnish with a sprig of fresh lemon verbena if you wish.

ROSE VANILLA TONIC
YIELD: 4-6 servings

½ cup organic rose buds, or 6-7
    rose tea bags
dried organic rose petals or
    buds, for garnish
1 vanilla bean, sliced in half
    lengthwise, or ½ teaspoon
    vanilla extract
3-4 tablespoons raw honey
4 cups filtered water
sparkling mineral water

Put the rose buds or tea bags and vanilla bean (if using) into a pot with the water. If you are using vanilla extract, add it later.

Bring to a simmer, then turn the heat off, add honey, and allow to steep for 15 minutes. Strain and press gently on the steeped roses to extract maximum flavor. Add the vanilla extract, if using.

When ready to serve, fill a glass with half of the tonic and top off with sparkling mineral water. Garnish with a rose petal or bud.

Chapter 8

Complete Kitchen Makeover

Is your kitchen in disarray? Got scary slimy things lurking behind the mayo jar on the back shelves of your fridge? Are boxes of mystery ingredients still hanging around with expiration dates long past?

If so, then it's time for a complete kitchen makeover! A clean, well-organized kitchen will not only encourage you to cook more, it will also make you feel better about life. After all, the kitchen is the hearth of your home and is the place where health and happiness can be achieved by preparing good food.

You don't need fancy equipment or shelves stocked full of stuff. You just need to have the best of the basics that reflect our organic, nontoxic, and sustainable model. Keep the most relevant dry goods in your pantry and cupboards and make the effort to shop for fresh produce at your local farmers' markets, co-ops, and organic grocery stores.

PANTRY ESSENTIALS

Gluten-Free Grains for Cooking
- amaranth
- brown rice, and other varieties of whole-kernel rice
- buckwheat
- millet
- quinoa
- wild rice

Enjoy grains in their whole forms, or purchase the milled versions for gluten-free baking.

Nuts

- almonds
- Brazil nuts
- cashews
- pecans
- pistachios
- pine nuts
- walnuts

Seeds

- flax
- hemp
- chia
- sesame
- pumpkin

Note: Purchase whole seeds and grind as needed. (If you use ground flax seeds on a regular basis, grind enough for a week and store in the freezer to protect the delicate omega oils.)

Legumes (Beans)

- adzuki beans
- lentils
- chickpeas (aka garbanzo beans)
- black beans
- navy beans
- heirloom beans
- split peas

. . . .

WHY SOAK GRAINS, SEEDS, NUTS?

It may seem like a lot of trouble, even strange, to soak grains overnight or for several days before cooking, but that is precisely what our ancestors did before processed foods.

Why go through the extra step and time? Because all seeds want to survive and germinate. Nature has endowed these tiny powerhouses of life with special chemicals to survive passage through the digestive system of a ruminant animal (those with four stomachs: cows, goats, sheep) and still be able to propagate on the other side. We human animals have only one stomach, and are poorly equipped to deal with the natural protective chemicals such as *phytic acid* and *enzyme inhibitors* contained in seeds. Phytic acid binds with calcium, magnesium, iron, copper, and zinc, making it very difficult to absorb these minerals. And enzyme inhibitors, which prevent seeds from becoming active in the digestive tract, also inhibit our own digestive enzymes.

When not soaked or sprouted, seeds, nuts, and grains leach minerals out of the body and also cause digestive problems.

. . . .

. . . .

SPROUTING

The process of sprouting, or germination, transforms the characteristics of grains and seeds by removing antinutrients (such as phytic acid and enzyme inhibitors) and increasing the content of vitamins, such as C, B complex, and carotenes. The process also makes these vital nutrients bioavailable to us.

To learn how to sprout, visit: http://www.vegetariantimes. com/blog/how-to-soak-and-sprout-nuts-seeds-grains-and-beans/

. . . .

Baking Dry Goods
- baking powder
- baking soda
- xanthan gum (helps bind gluten-free flours)
- vanilla extract/vanilla beans
- dry yeast

Common gluten-free baking flours: the milled version of gluten-free grains listed above, plus these which are also popular for baking:
- sorghum

- coconut flour
- almond and other nut flours (nuts ground fine for baking)

Sweeteners

It is no secret that our addiction to sugary foods has undermined our health. Debilitating ailments from diabetes to heart disease to cancer have all been linked to too much sugar in the diet.

In 1915, the average American consumed about fifteen to twenty pounds of sugar per year. According to the current USDA consumption reports, that average has shot up to three pounds per week. That means at least one hundred fifty pounds per year, per person! It's shocking, but not surprising, considering that highly refined sugars in the forms of sucrose (table sugar), dextrose (corn sugar), and high-fructose corn syrup are added to many processed foods such as bread, breakfast cereals, mayonnaise, peanut butter, ketchup, spaghetti sauce, and a gamut of microwaveable meals.

The Fake Sweet Demons

Aspartame converts to formaldehyde and then to formic acid, which in turn causes metabolic acidosis (just a fancy term for too much acid in the body) and is also a known carcinogen. Formaldehyde is also an embalming fluid. (Marketed as NutraSweet, Equal, and Spoonful)

Acesulfame K contains the carcinogen methylene chloride. Long-term exposure to methylene chloride can cause headaches, depression, nausea, and mental confusion. It is also toxic to the liver and kidneys. And since methylene chloride also affects the central nervous system, exposure can lead to visual, auditory, and motor disturbances. It has also been recognized as a possible human carcinogen by the International Agency for Research on Cancer. (Marketed as Sunett and Sweet One).

Saccharin (Sweet'n Low) was originally derived from coal tar. Today it is manufactured by combining anthranilic acid (used, among other things, as a corrosive agent for metal) with nitrous acid, sulfur dioxide, chlorine, and ammonia. As with the other artificial sweeteners, saccharin is carcinogenic.

Sucralose (Splenda) is made when sugar is treated with trityl chloride, acetic anhydride, hydrogen chlorine, thionyl chloride, and methanol in the presence of dimethylformamide, 4-methylmorpholine, toluene, methyl isobutyl ketone, acetic acid, benzyltriethlyammonium chloride, and sodium methoxide, making it unlike anything found in nature. If you read the fine print on the Splenda website, it states that "although sucralose has a structure like sugar and a sugar-like taste, it is not natural."

In addition to all the negative side effects of artificial sweeteners, they are also related to weight gain because they cause you to crave carbohydrates.

Healthy Sweeteners to Enjoy (in moderation)

When it comes to eating sweets, the key is *moderation*, even when using healthy sweeteners. These are natural options to try instead of the highly processed or artificial ones:

- raw honey
- Sucanat
- date sugar/syrup
- brown rice syrup
- maple syrup
- molasses
- stevia
- palm sugar

Notes on Agave and Xylitol

Although these two sweeteners have become popular lately, they each have their negative issues, and so I caution against using them, except occasionally.

Agave

Although it comes from a plant, the blue agave, most commercial agave syrup on the market is highly processed and contains about ninety percent fructose. Your liver has to process this high amount of fructose, and overuse can lead to the same health issues as with high-fructose corn syrup.

Xylitol

A highly processed sugar usually derived from birch or corn. It has been touted as a "healthy" sweetener because it doesn't raise blood sugar level and has antibacterial properties. However, when overused, it can cause diarrhea and stomach discomfort for some people. It is also highly toxic to dogs.

In addition, xylitol is produced using a form of industrial processing known as sugar hydrogenation, which requires a catalyst. In the case of xylitol, a nickel-aluminum alloy is used, which means that there are traces of metals in this sweetener. Another consideration is that GMO corn is used to produce most of the xylitol on the market.

Thickeners

Conventional ways of thickening sauces usually include adding wheat-based flours or cornstarch, both of which are not optimal for health. Wheat contains gluten and conventional cornstarch is made from GMO corn.

Try these gluten-free options. In addition to their ability to thicken liquids, they also provide some degree of nutrition and exhibit healing qualities.

Agar agar (or kanten)

Made from Irish moss (a type of seaweed). It has been used in Asia for hundreds of years.

The basic Agar Gel recipe is two teaspoons of powder to two cups liquid. Soak the agar in the liquid for about ten to fifteen min. Bring to a boil and simmer, stirring, until the agar completely dissolves, about five minutes.

Arrowroot

This thickener has several advantages over cornstarch. It has a more neutral flavor, so it's a good thickener for delicately flavored sauces. It also works at a lower temperature, and it tolerates acidic ingredients and prolonged cooking better. It is not a good thickener for dairy-based sauces, since it turns them slimy.

If you are using it to replace cornstarch, use one tablespoon arrowroot in place of two teaspoons cornstarch. To replace flour, use half as much arrowroot as flour. If the recipe calls for one tablespoon flour, substitute one and a half teaspoons arrowroot.

To keep an arrowroot-thickened sauce thick, stir until just combined. Overstirring can make it thin again.

Kudzu (or Kuzu)

This plant has been used for centuries in Asia for digestive health, to calm inflammation, and to help stabilize blood sugar and lower blood pressure.

To thicken one cup of sauce: use one tablespoon kudzu powder dissolved in one tablespoon water, added to the sauce while it is simmering. Stir until sauce is thickened, then remove immediately. Great for making puddings (recipe, Comforting Cocoa Pudding, page 157).

• •

KUDZU, THE VINE THAT ATE THE SOUTH

This plant was introduced to the United States in 1876 from Japan and was widely propagated in the 1930s as a means to control soil erosion. The problem is, the warm, humid weather of the southeastern U.S. is so conducive to kudzu that it started to grow out of control, leading to nicknames such as "mile-a-minute" or "foot-a-night." The vines grow as much as a foot per day during summer months, climbing trees, power poles, and anything else they contact. Under ideal conditions kudzu vines can grow sixty feet each year. Currently, more than six million dollars per year is spent on trying to control this tenacious vine.

• •

Seasonings

(See chapter 1 for a list of top ten spices for your kitchen.) Store seasonings in dark or opaque jars or cans and use them within three months of purchasing, since potent volatile oils dissipate with time and with exposure to air or light.

Salt

Salt is indispensable for optimal health, not to mention that it makes food taste great! But not any salt will do. Common table salt is stripped of nutrients and also contains toxic additives. In contrast, high-quality sea salt provides minerals and nutrients that are critical for cellular function. Salt deficiency can lead to negative health issues, such as goiters and other thyroid-related illnesses.

Dr. Thomas Cowan, a well-known physician and author of *The Fourfold Path to Healing*, states:

> Many illnesses are caused or exacerbated by trace-mineral deficiencies. These can be avoided by the liberal use of Celtic Sea Salt® in your cooking and the complete avoidance of all other salts, all of which contain only pure sodium chloride.[1]

· ·

WHY TABLE SALT IS TERRIBLE

According to many health experts, sodium chloride lacks the nutritive values of unrefined natural salts because it is highly processed and contains many chemical additives, such as *sodium ferrocyanide*, also known as Yellow Prussiate of Soda (YPS). Another is *ferric ferrocyanide*, an anticaking agent.

However, toxic chemicals are not the only problem posed by using table salt. Prolonged use can cause a whole gamut of health problems, because instead of providing necessary minerals for the body, it actually depletes them. And lack of minerals such as potassium and magnesium can send the body into a state of acidity, which then becomes the catalyst for many diseases, including cancer.

> The consequences of utilizing salt in a devitalized form is a poorly functioning immune system, initiation and acceleration of chronic illness, and promotion of acidity.[2]
>
> —DR. DAVID BROWNSTEIN,
> AUTHOR OF *"SALT YOUR WAY TO HEALTH"*

Compared with table salt, which only contains sodium and chloride, unrefined Celtic Sea Salt® has sulfur, magnesium, potassium, calcium, silicon, iron, and other trace minerals, in addition to sodium and chloride. Other healthy mineral salts are Redmond's and Bokek.

· ·

Condiments/Flavorings

There are condiments besides ketchup, which is laden with high-fructose corn syrup, and artificially colored mustard from a taxi-yellow squeeze bottle. Here's a selection of delicious and flavorful condiments that will complement and enhance your dishes and boost their nutritional value.

Coconut aminos: Made from coconut sap, this is a perfect condiment for those who are allergic to soy-based products.

Tamari: Wheat-free soy sauce

Miso: Made from fermented soybeans, miso contains probiotics, which is a plus. Note that to benefit from its healthful properties, it should never be heated to boiling, since this will kill off the good bacteria.

Raw sauerkraut and other lacto-fermented vegetables: These are among the best natural sources of probiotics, as well as vitamins and minerals.

Mirin: A naturally fermented wine that adds a touch of sweetness to foods. Goes well with tamari and ginger.

Fish Sauce: Another fermented liquid flavoring item. Use sparingly: a little goes a long way. Look for brands that are naturally fermented, without the addition of sugars or preservatives.

SUPERFOODS

Superfoods contain naturally concentrated amounts of vitamins and minerals that are easily absorbed. They also add flavor and texture when added to dishes, sprinkled over salads or soups, and added to smoothies.

Sea Vegetables provide easy-to-absorb nutrients, especially iodine and trace minerals found in seawater. Enjoy kelp, dulse flakes, wakame, hijiki, and nori.

Nutritional Yeast is an excellent source of B complex vitamin and amino acids. Look for nutritional yeast that is low-heat processed and grown on beets. Also contains chromium, which helps stabilize blood sugar.

Bee Pollen contains twenty-two amino acids, twenty-seven minerals, and more than five thousand enzymes. This superfood should be taken in small amounts, building up to a tablespoon or so per day. Avoid pollen that has been dried at temperatures exceeding 130°F.

(See chapter 2, page 67, for a listing of additional superfoods.)

Best Oils for Cooking

Using the right fats can have a profoundly positive effect on your physical and mental well-being. Let's start with the good fats, the benefits of using them, and some dos and don'ts.

Good Fats	Benefits	Dos and Don'ts
Coconut oil	Contains medium-chain fatty acids and lauric acid. Antimicrobial. Good for the thyroid and brain function.	Good for high-heat cooking. You can also use this on your skin.
Ghee (clarified butter)	Used for centuries in Ayurvedic healing, ghee is purified butter, which can hold high heat.	Use in moderate- to high-heat cooking.
Butter (organic and raw)	Used for thousands of years, butter is a healthy fat containing vitamins A, D, E, and K, along with *butyric acid*, which helps build beneficial gut flora.	Can be used in high-heat cooking.
Extra virgin olive oil	Contains Omega oils 3, 6, 9, along with phytonutrients that benefit the heart. Best when used unheated.	Do not use in high-heat cooking. Great used on the skin to moisturize.
Sesame oil (toasted and untoasted)	Studies show that sesame oil helps lower hypertension. Contains *lignans*, a class of antioxidants.	Use the untoasted oil for medium-heat cooking and the toasted version as a condiment oil.
Lard	When sourced from pigs that are raised in their natural environment, lard provides vitamins A and D as well as minerals.	Very stable fat, which can be used for high-heat cooking.

| Duck/chicken fat | When sourced from free-range animals, the fat will contain vitamins A and D, plus minerals. | Very stable fat, which can be used for high-heat cooking. |

Look for oils that are organic and unrefined—and choose a variety of them, so that you get an array of those wonderful essential fatty acids for optimal health.

Here are the smoke points for various oils:

Oil	Smoke Point
Coconut	350°F/175°C
Ghee (clarified butter)	450°F/230°C
Butter	350°F/175°C
Extra Virgin Olive Oil	325°-375°F/165°-180°C
Sesame	350°-410°F/175°-210°C
Lard	370°F/185°C
Duck/Chicken	375°F/190°C

• •

PROBLEM WITH PALM OIL

Although palm oil is considered by many nutritional profes-sionals to be a healthy oil to use, it is environmentally problem-atic: the global demand for palm oil is causing deforestation and destruction of animal habitats. If you chose to use palm oil, please purchase from companies that are engaging in sustain-able harvesting.

• •

The Bad Fats

Bad Fats	Why	More Information
Hydrogenated oils (Crisco, margarine)	Degrades the structure of our cellular membrane, interrupting metabolic process. Causes weight gain and promotes heart disease.	For more information: www.naturalnews. com/ 024694_oil_food_oils. html
Canola oil	Made from the rapeseed plant, all of which is genetically modified, even those labeled organic.	For the health hazards of GM foods: http://www.seedsofdeception.com
Vegetable/seed oils (corn, cottonseed, safflower, soy, sunflower, peanut)	High content of omega-6 in vegetable oils causes inflammation.	Use very sparingly.

Note: Never use flax oil for cooking, because this very delicate oil will be damaged by heat.

· ·

VEGETABLE OILS: VILLAIN OF INFLAMMATION

First, to clear up any confusion over the term, "vegetable oils" refers to oils that are pressed from the seeds or kernels of plants, not from vegetables.

Second, recall our earlier discussion about PUFAs (polyunsaturated fatty acids) in chapter 5, regarding omega-6 and omega-3. Both of these essential fatty acids (EFAs) are needed for proper cellular function; however, too much omega-6 leads to systemic inflammation. And that's where the problem comes in when we consume excess amounts of vegetable oils, because the main EFA contained in them is omega-6.

· ·

EATING WITH THE SEASONS

Eating local and seasonal foods attunes us to the rhythm of the universe and inspires us to look forward to the passage of time as we anticipate the crops of each season.

Best Autumn Foods and Why

Every year, as the weather cools with the coming of September, I look forward to the warm and radiant hues of orange and crimson found in pumpkins, persimmons, apples, and oranges. Autumn signals the time of reaping mature crops and celebration of the harvest moon.

Apples	When eaten raw, apples provide vitamin C and quercitin and boost immunity. They also contain pectin, which helps regulate cholesterol and blood sugar balance.
Artichokes	Powerhouse detoxification properties for the liver. Also has *inulin,* which helps promote good bacteria in the gut.
Hard squashes	Loaded with minerals and beta-carotenes and a great source of complex carbohydrates and fiber. Hard squashes include: pumpkins, butternut, kabocha, and kuri.
Mushrooms	Well researched for their amazing ability to boost the immune system and prevent cancers. All edible mushrooms provide health benefits. ***Note:*** *Never eat mushrooms raw, because their cellular structures are very difficult to digest without cooking and they contain irritating and toxic compounds, which are mitigated when cooked.*
Chestnuts	Relatively low in calories compared to other nuts. Good protein content along with magnesium, potassium, and folate. Good fiber too! (one hundred grams provides approximately eight grams of fiber.)
Pomegranates	High antioxidant value. Very high content of *punicalagins,* a potent antioxidant.
Persimmons	Actually a berry, not a fruit, containing a gamut of antioxidants with impressive names like *gallocatechin, lutein,* and *lycopene.* Good for your eyes and for fighting off free radicals.

Best Winter Foods and Why

As we begin the process of hibernation in winter, roots and tubers provide us with nutrients drawn deep from the ground. Vegetables such as parsnips, rutabagas, and beets give us building and warming carbohydrates *without* gluten and are packed with minerals and vitamins.

Hard squashes	Loaded with minerals and beta-carotenes. Hard squashes include: pumpkins, butternut, kabocha, and kuri.
Parsnips	A root vegetable related to the carrot and fennel. It is low in calories, yet provides protein and fiber along with minerals such as copper, potassium, and magnesium. Parsnips also have vitamins C, K, and folates. A delicious alternative to potatoes, especially for those who are avoiding edibles from the nightshade family.
Sweet potatoes	Unlike other starchy roots, sweet potatoes can actually balance blood sugar. Very high in beta-carotene, vitamin C, and manganese, as well as fiber.
Turnips	A member of the cruciferous family, which also includes broccoli, cauliflower, and cabbage. Turnips contain *indole-3-carbinol*, which fights cancer, and also has *sulforaphane* to promote liver health.
Brussels sprouts	A member of the cruciferous family of vegetables, this sulfur-containing "mini cabbage" is great for cancer prevention due to its high *glucosinolate* content.
Celery root	Celery root has excellent calming, analgesic, antiseptic, anti-allergic, and other therapeutic properties.
Navel oranges	A wonderful source of vitamin C. Perfect for keeping sniffles away as the weather turns cold. Enjoy the fruit in its whole form rather then juicing.

Best Spring Foods and Why

As the winter frost melts and the first songbirds begin to sound their musical twitterings, young shoots begin to push up from the soil and their green vibrancy awaken us from the slumber of winter.

Spring is the perfect time to do a liver cleanse (see chapter 6), so enjoy dark leafy greens and the bittersweet flavors of dandelion, mustard greens, and nettles.

Avocados	Good monounsaturated fats, no cholesterol. Avocados have folate and other B vitamins, vitamin C, minerals, and fiber. Considered an aphrodisiac by the Aztecs, it is known as the love fruit of California!
Spring garlic (*also known as young garlic or green garlic*)	The appearance of spring garlic signals the start of spring. It is the immature harvest before the garlic bulb develops. A very seasonal and delicate treat, containing manganese, vitamin C and B$_6$, and, when eaten raw, *allicin* (the same compound found in mature garlic).
Nettles	Don't let the stingers deter you from enjoying the amazing benefits of nettles! Vitamin C, calcium, choline, magnesium, and chlorophyll are but a few of its merits. Drinking nettle tea will help combat spring allergies too.
Fresh garden peas	These starchy little green pearls are packed with vitamin C, K, and B$_1$, along with magnesium, zinc and copper, fiber, and amino acids.
Grapefruit	Contains *lycopene* and is very high in vitamin C.
Radishes	Contains potassium, folate, and fiber. There are many different types to enjoy. Great for the liver, gallbladder, and weight loss.
Spring salad greens	Contains minerals, fiber, and folate. Tender spring garden greens such as arugula, dandelion, and mustard greens are the best source. Their mildly bittersweet flavors tone the liver and kidneys.
Edible blossoms	Delight in the profusions of blooms! Try nasturtiums, rose petals, pansies, and squash blossoms. Edible flowers are not only beautiful to behold, but their vibrant colors reflect the presence of antioxidants such as *carotenes* and *zeaxanthin*.

Best Summer Foods and Why

As Helios rides his chariot across the sky, the long, hot days of summer call for foods that hold an abundance of water to quench thirst and bring vitamins and minerals for growth and renewal. So enjoy these foods as we stay up late and luxuriate in the warm, languid nights.

Berries	Antioxidant packed, lots of vitamin C, and low in sugars. Enjoy strawberries, blackberries, blueberries, boysenberries, and many other varieties.
Melons	Many types of melons contain *citrulline*, which helps boost nitric oxide, a chemical that helps circulation.
Cucumbers	Cucumbers are known to contain *lariciresinol*, *pinoresinol*, and *secoisolariciresinol*–three lignans that research shows have a connection with reduced risk of cardiovascular disease as well as several types of cancer, including breast, uterine, ovarian, and prostate cancers.
Garlic	Well known for its benefits for heart health, garlic also contains selenium, a trace mineral that helps against the toxic effects of mercury and cadmium. Selenium also helps fight free radical damage.
Summer squashes	These tender, warm-weather versions of hard winter squashes are harvested before the rind develops to retain their delicate, edible skins. With such names as pattypan, yellow crookneck, and zucchini, how can you resist? Along with vitamin C, summer squashes contain *zeaxanthin and lutein,* which are important for eye health.
Tomatillos	Packed with vitamin C, potassium, and fiber. A wonderful alternative to tomatoes.
Okra	Stabilizes blood sugar. Okra's mucilaginous quality binds to and feeds good bacteria in your digestive tract, which promotes healthy digestion and immunity.

KITCHEN Rx

When it comes to medicinal foods, you'll be amazed at the healing powers of ingredients that you have right in your own kitchen. (Well, that is, if you have stocked your kitchen according to the recommendations in *Happy Foods*).

Here are a few of my favorite kitchen remedies:

Condition	Ingredient/s	How to Use
Sore throat or bad breath	Sea salt	Dissolve 1 teaspoon in 4 ounces of filtered water and gargle. Do not swallow.
Upset tummy, nausea, seasickness	Ginger root	Put a thin slice in your mouth and chew. You can also make a cup of ginger tea.
Insomnia	Chamomile or warm milk with ¼ teaspoon nutmeg (if avoiding dairy, try almond milk or coconut milk)	Chamomile: steep chamomile in hot water for 6–8 minutes, then sip slowly. Milk: heat to a gentle boil, then add nutmeg.
Indigestion	Ginger or fennel tea	Ginger: 2–3 slices of fresh ginger steeped in hot water for 6–8 minutes. Sip slowly. Fennel: 1 teaspoon fennel seeds steeped in hot water for 8–10 minutes. Sip slowly.
Hangover	Kudzu powder	1 tablespoon dissolved in 3 ounces water or broth with a little grated fresh ginger.

. . . .

KUDZU: GOOD FOR ALCOHOLIC RATS

For generations, kudzu has been used in China for the treatment of headaches, dysentery, high blood pressure, and muscle aches. More recently, in the early 2000s, studies conducted on rats that were made addicted to alcohol showed that supplementing with kudzu helped curb their cravings for booze.

It is believed that *isoflavones* and other nutrients in kudzu help balance blood sugar and lessen the effects of alcohol by inhibiting certain enzymes.

A study done in 2005 by Dr. Scott Lukas of McLean Hospital in Boston showed that human subjects given kudzu capsules for a week drank almost fifty percent less alcohol than a control group.

. . . .

OF POTS AND PANS

There is an endless selection of pots and pans made from many types of materials and in countless different styles, so it can be rather overwhelming to decide on which to purchase. I recommend sticking with the basic, nontoxic, low-reactive materials listed below.

Cast Iron

Slow to heat up, but once at temperature, it provides even heating and facilitates browning of foods for better texture and flavor. Cast-iron pans can also withstand very high heat, making them oven safe.

Since iron is a reactive metal, cast-iron pans will react with high-acid foods, so refrain from using lemon juice, vinegar, or tomato sauces in these pans, since they will draw out excess iron and cause your food to turn brown or even black.

Although cast-iron pans require a little extra care, the effort is well worth it. Over time, you will have a beautiful nonstick surface that is not toxic.

Maintenance: wash only with hot water and a hard brush, and do not soak because it will cause the pan to oxidize, or rust. After washing, put the pan over a low flame to dry out completely, then coat with a thin layer of oil to protect the surface.

Copper

Copper is the best at conducting heat and provides very even cooking. Copper pans work best when they are lined with stainless steel, since copper reacts with acidic foods. These lined copper pans are good for high-heat, fast-cooking techniques such as sautéing/stir fry.

Stainless Steel

Resistant to corrosion, scratches, and dents. Stainless steel also does not react with alkaline or acidic foods. However, it is a poor conductor of heat, so most stainless-steel pans have a copper or aluminum core.

Enamel

Cookware coated with enamel provides a good, nontoxic, nonstick cooking surface and does not react with acidic ingredients. Care should be taken not to scratch the surface with wired brushes.

Say No to Nonstick!

Nonstick pans release carcinogenic compounds into the environment when heated. They are toxic to manufacture as well.

The nonstick cookware coating contains a chemical called *perfluorooctanoic acid* (PFOA), which has been linked to cancer and birth defects in animal studies. When nonstick pans are heating to high temperatures, they release toxic chemicals, which are poisonous for pet birds and can also cause flulike symptoms in people.

To find out more, go to the website of the Environmental Working Group (EWG), one of the best resources for information about toxicity: http://www.ewg.org/research/healthy-home-tips/tip-6-skip-non-stick-avoid-dangers-teflon

BASIC COOKWARE

Casserole dish: Wonderful for using in the oven and making one-dish meals.

Dutch oven: Perfect for using on top of the stove or in the oven. Keeps moisture in and ideal for making braised meat dishes.

Sauté pans: Different sizes are available; ten-inch and twelve-inch are the most useful.

Griddle: Not just for making pancakes, a griddle is very versatile, especially when made from cast-iron. Good for cooking burgers, steaks, grilling vegetables, etc.

Wok: Can also double as a steamer or for smoking foods. Perfect for quick stir-frying, for vibrant vegetables.

Pots: Good to have different sizes. A big stockpot is a must for making mineral broth/bone broth.

Roasting pan: Get one with a rack, super for roasting chicken and meats.

Baking sheets: Just get the basic ones (no nonstick, please) and line with parchment.

Griddle: Perfect for pancakes and crepes, and can also be used to cook a burger. (Cast-iron is your best choice.)

Steamer: Steaming is a wonderful way to preserve nutrients and to heat things up, instead of using a microwave. Made from bamboo, aluminum, or stainless steel.

Slow cooker: A busy person's best friend. Although foods cooked in slow cooker don't have the texture and flavors of high-heat cooking, it is a wonderful tool to ensure that you come home to a home-cooked meal made from scratch. Great for overnight cooking.

Baking pans: Designed for use in the oven, these come in many varieties and materials, including cake pans, springform pans, pie pans, baking sheets, and loaf pans. Many are made from aluminum, which can leach out into foods. Line baking sheets with unbleached parchment paper to buffer direct contact with food.

And then there's silicone. The little "e" makes a big difference! Silicon is natural; silicone is synthetic. Many items of bakeware and other kitchen products are made from silicone. While manufacturers claim that silicone products are safe and do not release harmful gases under high heat, the safety factor is still inconclusive.

KNIVES

Knives are the most essential tools in the kitchen. There are many varieties out there and a good set of knives can be quite costly. However, you really only need a few essential ones for everyday cooking, plus a sharpening steel.

Chef's knife: A good-quality chef's knife should be well balanced, with the weight of the blade equal to the weight of the handle. Blades range from eight to twelve inches. Always handle the knife and feel how it fits in your hand before purchasing.

Paring knife: After the chef's knife, this is the second most used cutting implement in the kitchen. Use for paring and trimming vegetables and fruits. As with the chef's knife, handle for comfort before purchasing. The blade can range from two to four inches.

Boning knife: This knife is used for separating raw meat from the bone. The blade is shorter than a chef's knife and narrower and more rigid to allow easier maneuvering around the bones and muscles.

Slicer: They have a long, thin, narrow blade in order to make smooth slices in a single stroke. Slicers for meats are typically fifteen to eighteen inches long. Slicers used for breads or tomatoes are often serrated or scalloped.

Sharpening steel: This tool is indispensable for keeping your knives sharp. While they can be made from different materials such as ceramic and diamond-impregnated steel, hard steel is best because the metal is magnetic, which helps the blade retain proper alignment and collect metal shavings.

OTHER KITCHEN TOOLS

In addition to the core kitchen equipment, such as knives, pots, and pans, here's a list of basic tools that will make your life easier in the kitchen.

- Food processor
- Coffee grinder (to grind seeds and spices)
- Blender
- Wire whisks
- Cooking thermometer
- Tongs
- Can opener
- Spatulas
- Measuring cups and spoons
- Citrus squeezer
- Microplane grater
- Scale
- Mixing bowls
- Wooded or bamboo chopping board
- Colanders
- Wooden or bamboo utility spoons

STORAGE: THE GREEN WAY TO KEEP FOODS FRESH AND CLEAN

The first principle of storage: Whatever you use should not release toxins into the foods you are storing. Therefore, the safest containers are glass or ceramic-lined. So, out with the plastic, please! Plastic ziplock bags and plastic containers can leach chemicals into your food, especially when in contact with foods that have fats in them.

- Store in glass containers, such as mason jars or Pyrex. Ceramic-lined containers are also good.
- Use linen/cotton bags for vegetables and herbs so that they can "breathe" and last longer. To keep the produce fresh, do not wash until ready to use.
- Tip: Instead of putting fresh herbs in the fridge, put them in a small glass or mason jar with water and leave them on your kitchen counter. That way, you'll remember to use them, and they're decorative. You can use them to brew herbal teas.
- Paper bags and butcher paper are other good materials to use for storage.
- Paper is particularly good for ingredients that need to "breathe," such as mushrooms.

Here are a few guidelines for avoiding plastic:
- When using an electric mixer, choose glass or Pyrex instead of plastic because bits of plastic can chip and end up in your food and then your tummy.
- Use wooden or bamboo cutting boards, but care for them properly by washing with hot water and soap. Allow them to dry well to prevent bacterial buildup. Consider using a dedicated cutting board for animal proteins and one for vegetables.
- Cover food in the microwave with a paper towel instead of plastic wrap. (You really should not be using a microwave oven, though, because the radiation they emit is a known health hazard. In addition, studies have shown that foods lose their nutritional value when heated in microwave ovens.)[3]

• •

BYOB

That would be: "bring your own bag" to the grocery store, farmers' market, or any store, for that matter. Plastic and other shopping bags are a major blight on the environment. Most of the time we only use a bag once, for carrying something from the store to our car and then home. We are destroying our environment for a momentary convenience. It has been estimated that we use one billion plastic bags per year in the U.S. Look at the devastating statistics associated with this use:

Twelve million barrels of oil are required to make one billion bags.

Each year, four billion discarded plastic bags end up in the environment. Tied end to end, that's enough to circle the globe sixty-three times.

Over one million birds and mammals are killed each year by ingesting these bags.

• •

OUR MOST PRECIOUS RESOURCE: WATER

We take the most precious of all resources completely for granted, yet it is *the* most life-sustaining substance on earth. We can go without food for about three weeks, but without water, we won't survive beyond three days.

Many of us have the luxury of just turning on the tap and watching water come cascading out. We don't think much about it or what's in the water, yet it should be foremost in our minds. The quality can mean the difference between vibrant health and hydration or a slow accumulation of toxins from contaminants such as fluoride, chloride, and heavy metals.

Our bodies are composed of at least sixty percent water and it is the primary component of our bodily fluids, including blood, lymph, digestive juices, sweat, urine, and tears. In addition, water is essential to circulation, digestion, absorption of nutrients from foods, and elimination of waste. Water also carries the electrolytes and mineral salts that help spark the electrical currents in the body. In short, water *is* life!

Unfortunately, most tap water in the U.S. today is treated with chemicals including chlorine, chloramine, fluoride, and phosphates, among others. According to the EWG (Environmental Working Group), our drinking water is contaminated with a highly volatile cocktail of pharmaceutical drugs, industrial chemicals, and xenoestrogens.

Xenoestrogens are molecular compounds similar to our own natural estrogen. That means that these man-made estrogen mimickers can land on the same receptor sites as estrogen and cause "estrogen dominance," or an overload of estrogen, which leads to hormonal imbalance and estrogen-driven cancers.

Jane Houlihan, EWG vice president for research, says: "Environmental Working Group (EWG)'s studies show that tap water across the U.S. is contaminated with many industrial chemicals, and now we know that millions of Americans are also drinking low-level mixtures of pharmaceuticals with every glass of water."

What's in Your Water?

Use the Environmental Working Group's National Drinking Water Database to find out: http://www.ewg.org/tapwater/

Types of Water

Distilled

Distilled water is actually just tap water that has been boiled until the minerals are steamed out. In addition, it may also be highly filtered to remove all minerals. It is great for ironing and may be appropriate for some detoxification programs, but not for regular, daily use. (We need minerals to stay hydrated.)

Spring or Mineral Water

Walk into any grocery store and you will see shelves full of "spring" water. This is the "natural" water found in underground springs, near the earth's surface. The water in different parts of the country provides different amounts of mineral content.

However, most spring/mineral waters come in plastic bottles, which are a major source of contaminants and have been shown to cause cancers. Not to mention their devastating effects on the environment.

True mineral water is spring water that is found deeper in the earth in underground pools. Even though the water is naturally bubbly, carbon dioxide is added to make it carbonated. Mineral water may contain undesirable contamination.

Filtered

There are many ways of filtering water to remove toxins such as heavy metals, chemicals, and bacteria. There are a variety of units that can filter out the main water source for the entire house, or you can just buy a filtering device that fits over an individual faucet.

WHAT TO TOSS OUT

Now that you know what foods and utensils to stock for your kitchen, let's discuss items that you should get rid of. If you've read through *Happy Foods,* then you should have a pretty good idea. But just in case you have doubts, here's a list for you to make the process easier. Think of it as both an external and internal detox. By getting rid of unhealthy foods that you should not eat, you are not only cleaning up your kitchen, you are also preventing excess toxins from entering your body.

- Gluten-containing foods: breads, pasta, flours, cookies, crackers, etc.
- Processed sugars: white sugar, sugar substitutes, corn syrups
- Man-made flavor enhancers: MSG (monosodium glutamate), MAG (monoammodium glutamate), hydrolyzed vegetable protein
- Vegetable oils: canola, soy, peanut, cottonseed
- Nonorganic processed snacks in boxes: cereals, crackers, cookies, etc.
- Canned goods: fruits, vegetables, soups
- Nonstick or aluminum pans
- Plastic containers
- Toxic cleaning agents (see below for healthy options)
- Table salt

Note: Read the labels carefully. If there's anything you can't pronounce, it's probably not good for you or your family. Basically, the mantra for processed foods is: "When in doubt, toss it out."

TRULY CLEAN CLEANERS

There are many health risks associated with conventional cleaners, and the man-made chemicals in these products have been linked to allergies, asthma, cancer, hormone disruption, neurotoxicity, and other negative health issues. Considering that we need to use cleaning agents all the time, it should be obvious that using green, nontoxic cleaners will create a much healthier and more harmonious environment, not only for our homes, but also for the earth.

- Replace oven cleaners by making a paste with water and baking soda.
- Instead of using corrosive drain cleaners, use baking soda and vinegar, or a mechanical snake. (You can get one at any

hardware store.)

- To sanitize your sponge, put it in the dishwasher along with your dirty dishes.
- Clean your kitchen counters or kitchen floor with a mixture of vinegar and water (¼ cup vinegar:1 quart water), and add a few drops of natural essential oils such as tea tree oil or lavender. The vinegar and water mixture is also great for cleaning windows, especially when you use newspapers to wipe them dry.
- Choose a nontoxic dish soap.
- Refrain from using "antibacterial" soaps. Wash your hands often with regular soap and water if you are concerned about germs.
- Use compostable garbage bags, and participate in composting if it is available as part of your garbage collection service.

SHOPPING GUIDE

Amazake: www.grainaissance.com

Amber lightbulbs: https://www.lowbluelights.com/index.asp

Blackout curtains: www.moondreamwebstore.comwww.moondreamweb-store.com

Block out blue lights from your computer: https://justgetflux.com/

Celtic Sea Salt and natural gourmet foods: www.selinanaturally.com

Coconut butter: www.nikkiscoconutbutter.com or www.nutiva.com

Coffee substitute: www.dandyblend.com; www.teeccino.com

Dawn simulator alarm clock: http://northernlighttechnologies.com/sad-light-store/sunrise-clock

Dry skin brushing: http://www.mindbodygreen.com/0-12675/a-step-by-step-guide-to-dry-skin-brushing.html

Fish sauce: www.redboatfishsauce.com

Gluten-free breads: http://udisglutenfree.com/product-category/breads-rolls-buns/

Gluten-free grains: www.bobsredmill.com

Herbs and spices: www.mountainroseherbs.com

How to perform a dry skin brushing: http://dryskinbrush.blogspot.com/

Liver tincture: www.gaiaherbs.com or www.localharvest.org

Raw sauerkraut brands: Check in with your neighborhood organic grocery stores for brands that are local to your area.

Reducing EMF/EMR (electromagnetic frequency/electromagnetic radiation): http://electromagnetichealth.org

Stevia powder: www.mountainroseherbs.com

Superfoods: www.radiantlifecatalog.com

Water filters: www.radiantlifecatalog.com; www.heartspring.net

Whey protein powder: www.radiantlifecatalog.com

WEBSITES

Eat Wild: www.eatwild.org

Ecology Center: www.ecologycenter.org

Environmental Working Group: www.ewg.org

Local Harvest: www.localharvest.org

Weston A. Price Foundation: www.westonaprice.org

BOOKS

The Fourfold Path to Healing, by Thomas Cowan MD (New Trends Publishing)

Grain Brain, by David Perlmutter MD (Little, Brown and Company)

Nourishing Traditions, by Sally Fallon (New Trends Publishing)

Salt Your Way to Health, by David Brownstein MD (Medical Alternatives Press)

Sugar Blues, by William Dufty (Mass Market Paperback)

Super Natural Home, by Beth Greer (Rodale Press)

Wheat Belly, by William Davis MD (Rodale Press)

The Yoga of Eating, by Charles Eisenstein (New Trends Publishing)

OTHER RESOURCES

To locate a farmers' market near you: http://search.ams.usda.gov/farmers-markets/

Join the Slow Food movement: www.slowfoodusa.org

List of safe seafood: http://www.seafoodwatch.org/

Genetically modified organism watch list: http://www.foodandwaterwatch.org/food/genetically-engineered-foods/

Notes for Chapter 8

1   Thomas S. Cowan MD, The Four Fold Path to Healing (NewTrends Publishing: Washington, DC, 2004).

2   David Brownstein, MD, Salt Your Way to Health (Medical Alternatives Press: West Bloomfield, 2006), p. 36.

3   Joseph Mercola MD, "Why Did the Russians Ban an Appliance Found in 99% of American Homes?" May 18, 2010, http://articles.mercola.com/sites/articles/archive/2010/05/18/microwave-hazards.aspx.

About the Author

After graduating from the California Culinary Academy, **KAREN DIGGS** flew off to Hong Kong. There, she worked as a chef for the Mandarin Oriental Hotel, and also helped open two eateries in the magnificent city of 7 million people.

In 2004, while washing dishes in her kitchen, Karen had an epiphany, "Wow, maybe it's good to combine cooking with nutrition?!" After all, didn't the Father of Western Medicine Hippocrates once say "Let food be thy medicine and medicine be thy food."

So, Karen went back to school and in 2006 obtained her certification as a Nutrition Consultant from Bauman College. Now, Karen merges her deep and innate culinary skills with her knowledge of holistic nutrition to help individuals achieve optimal health through detoxification and weight loss workshops, therapeutic cooking classes, and private nutrition consultations.